BRAVE HUMANISM

BRAVE HUMANISM

BLACK WOMEN REWRITING THE HUMAN IN THE AGE OF JANE CROW

Mollie Godfrey

THE OHIO STATE UNIVERSITY PRESS
COLUMBUS

Copyright © 2025 by The Ohio State University.
All rights reserved.

Library of Congress Cataloging-in-Publication Data
Names: Godfrey, Mollie, 1979– author.
Title: Brave humanism : Black women rewriting the human in the age of Jane Crow / Mollie Godfrey.
Description: Columbus : The Ohio State University Press, 2025. | Includes bibliographical references and index. | Summary: "Examines how an early twentieth-century generation of Black women writers were committed to reclaiming and redefining the human on their own terms. For Pauline Hopkins, Nella Larsen, Zora Neale Hurston, Ann Petry, Gwendolyn Brooks, and Lorraine Hansberry, narrative forms offered intellectual space to challenge the white supremacist and patriarchal logics of Western humanism that underwrote de jure segregation"—Provided by publisher.
Identifiers: LCCN 2024055008 | ISBN 9780814215296 (hardback) | ISBN 9780814284117 (ebook)
Subjects: LCSH: American literature—Women authors—History and criticism. | American literature—African American authors—History and criticism. | American literature—20th century—History and criticism. | African American women—Intellectual life—20th century. | Humanism in literature. | LCGFT: Literary criticism.
Classification: LCC PS153.B53 G63 2025 | DDC 810.9/928708996073—dc23/eng/20250118
LC record available at https://lccn.loc.gov/2024055008

Other identifiers: ISBN 9780814259429 (paperback)

Cover design by N. Putens
Text composition by Stuart Rodriguez
Type set in Minion Pro

For Sylvia

CONTENTS

Acknowledgments		ix
INTRODUCTION	The Brave Humanism of Black Women Writers	1
CHAPTER 1	Of One Blood: Blood Brotherhood in the Black Woman's Era	28
CHAPTER 2	No Sanctuary: Plagiarism, Primitivism, and the Politics of Recognition	55
CHAPTER 3	Folk in the Flesh: Insides, Outsides, and the Object of Anthropology	85
CHAPTER 4	Networks of Care: Sentiment, Sociology, and the Protest Fiction Debate	111
CHAPTER 5	Renaissance Women: Vision and Vulnerability in the Black Chicago Renaissance	141
CODA	Bravery and the Backlash: Lorraine Hansberry at the Forum	172
Bibliography		183
Index		211

ACKNOWLEDGMENTS

This project has been a journey, one I could not have made without the support of so many wonderful mentors, interlocutors, and friends along the way. I want to start by thanking my original readers on this project, Jacqueline Goldsby, Kenneth Warren, Deborah Nelson, and Michael Flug. Your guidance and wisdom have been instrumental in shaping this work. I also want to thank the many friends and colleagues who have helped me think through this project from its earliest stages and have supported me in countless other ways. My gratitude and appreciation go to Melissa Barton, Jeremy Rosen, Joshua Kotin, Nathan Wolff, Lubna Najar, Amy Gentry, Heather Keenleyside, Rachel Watson, Moacir P. de Sá Pereira, Christopher M. Brown, Allyson Hobbs, Christopher Freeburg, and Tom Perrin, as well as Eden Osucha, Therí Pickens, Ruth Lexton, Charles Nero, Bradley Proctor, Melissa Daniels-Rauterkus, Janet Neary, Cedric R. Tolliver, John C. Charles, Jonathan W. Gray, Deborah E. Whaley, Kinohi Nishikawa, Eurie Dahn, Martha J. Cutter, Koritha Mitchell, Alex Gil, Vershawn Young, and McKinley Melton. Your insights and camaraderie have been invaluable. I also want to thank my wonderful colleagues at James Madison University for reading drafts and providing much-needed moral support along the way, especially Allison Fagan, Erica Cavanagh, Sofia Samatar, Besi Muhonja, Lauren Alleyne, Joanne Gabbin, Seán McCarthy, Douglas Harrison, Brooks Hefner, David Babcock, Matthew Rebhorn, John Ott, Michael Gubser,

Case Watkins, Kristin Wylie, Taimi Castle, Gianluca De Fazio, Cara Meixner, Melissa Alemán, Siân White, Heidi Pennington, Mary Thompson, Melinda Adams, Becca Howes-Mischel, Holly Yanacek, Danielle Price, Becky Childs, Dabney Bankert, Bethany Nowviskie, David Owusu-Ansah, and Delores Phillips. I could not ask for a more supportive intellectual community than the one you have shared with me.

A special thanks to my editor, Ana Jimenez-Moreno, and the fantastic staff at The Ohio State University Press for their professionalism and care for this project, and to the anonymous manuscript readers whose feedback pushed the project in all the right directions. Earlier versions of chapters 1 and 2 also appeared as "Of One Blood: Humanism, Race, and Gender in Post-Reconstruction Law and Literature," *CLA Journal* 59, no. 1 (September 2015): 47–74, and as "Rewriting White, Rewriting Black: Authentic Humanity and Authentic Blackness in Nella Larsen's 'Sanctuary,'" *MELUS* 38, no. 4 (Winter 2013): 122–45. They are reprinted here with revisions by permission of the College Language Association and Oxford University Press, and I am grateful to the editors of these journals and their readers for their guidance and suggestions along the way. I am also appreciative of my gracious colleagues in the Modern Language Association, American Studies Association, College Language Association, MELUS, C19, Futures of American Studies, and the Society for the Study of Midwestern Literature.

My heartfelt thanks also go to the archivists and librarians at the Vivian G. Harsh Research Collection; the Schomburg Center for Research in Black Culture; the Bancroft Library; the Spelman College Archives; the Howard Gotlieb Archival Research Center; the Rare Book and Manuscript Library at the University of Illinois at Urbana-Champaign; the Beinecke Rare Book and Manuscript Library; the Smithsonian National Museum of African American History and Culture; the Department of Special Collections at Princeton University Library; the Amistad Research Center; the Stuart A. Rose Manuscript, Archives, and Rare Book Library; and the Library of Congress. I would especially like to thank the incredible people in JMU's Interlibrary Loan office—April Beckler, Mikki Butcher, and Paula Green—for helping me track down so many of the sources upon which this project depends. Much of my archival research would also not have been possible without the support of my department's administrative assistant, Rose Gray, or without financial support from the NEH Summer Stipend program, JMU Department of English, JMU College of Arts and Letters, and the Edna T. Shaeffer Humanist Award, as well as additional support from the Society for the Study of Midwestern Literature and the Pauline Elizabeth Hopkins Society.

My deepest appreciation goes to my family, my extended family, and my wonderful partner, James Bywater, who has been my first and last reader, cheerleader, and pillar of strength at every stage of this project. I am especially grateful to the women in my family who have inspired me from an early age: my aunt Aviva Rohde, my grandmother Sylvia Sherwood, and my mother, Laurie Godfrey. Nothing I do would be possible if they hadn't shown the way.

INTRODUCTION

The Brave Humanism of Black Women Writers

In 1970 Margaret Walker published an essay called "The Humanistic Tradition of Afro-American Literature," in which she troubled the commonplace idea that humanism belongs to the West. Turning on its head the traditional humanist assumption "that the black author must transcend race in order to write universally," Walker argued that it was white Americans who had a "complete lack of understanding and sense of common humanity."[1] For many white Americans, she argued, "humanity was beyond [their] comprehension" because America's "segregationist philosophy" had led to their complete "failure to understand other human beings."[2] In contrast to what passed for humanism, but was really just "the old racism," Walker advocated for "a new humanism" grounded in the insights of Black literature, which came "not from Greece or Rome," nor from the "European Renaissance" and "European man," but from the "constant search for freedom, peace, and human dignity" that required the Black writer "to speak loudly against social injustice."[3] Far from believing that we must "transcend" our historical circumstances to be human or to be free, she argued that "the new humanism" recognizes that "we *are* the historical process."[4] Walker would elsewhere connect this Black humanistic

---

1. Hemenway, *Zora Neale Hurston*, 307; and Walker, "Humanistic Tradition," 127.
2. Walker, "Humanistic Tradition," 127.
3. Walker, "Humanistic Tradition," 130, 122, 125.
4. Walker, "Humanistic Tradition," 130, emphasis added.

vision with her advocacy for Black studies and Black feminism, arguing not only that the "Humanities . . . obviously begins in Africa with black humanity" but that Black women are an important part of "that humanistic tradition."[5] "Female, Black, and Free," she proclaimed, "this is what I always want to be."[6]

Walker was in many respects a titan of twentieth-century African American literature—a member of the South Side Writers Group in Chicago, a writer for the Federal Writers' Project, and the first Black writer to win the Yale Younger Poets prize for her collection *For My People* (1942). After teaching for almost two decades at Jackson State College, she completed her first novel, *Jubilee* (1966), the very first in a now booming genre of neo–slave narratives.[7] In 1968 she founded at Jackson State the Institute for the Study of the History, Life, and Culture of Black People, one of the first Black studies centers of its kind in the nation.[8] She also organized a bicentennial festival in honor of Phillis Wheatley in 1973, bringing together twenty-three Black women writers to celebrate their literary forebear. The festival was, she later said, the "spark that lit a prairie fire—only a few years later, those women would be the very ones to proclaim a new renaissance in belles lettres, and black women's writing would go on to rise to unprecedented heights."[9] And yet Walker's humanism, Black activism, and feminism—and the connections between them—have been largely forgotten or obscured by better-known figures. Popular and critical attention to *Jubilee* was usurped by the success of Alex Haley's *Roots* in 1976, and when Walker accused Haley of plagiarizing portions of her earlier novel, she was characterized as "a crazy old jealous woman" and criticized "for having the nerve to hurt this black man," even though similar accusations by white male authors were legally vindicated.[10] As Walker's literary reputation went into decline (bolstered also by the reaction to her critical take on another Black male literary giant, Richard Wright), her foundational role in the Black

---

5. Walker, "Humanities with a Black Focus," 100; and Walker, "On Being Female, Black, and Free," 11.

6. Walker, "On Being Female, Black, and Free," 11.

7. See Rushdy, "Neo-Slave Narrative," 87. Subsequent neo–slave narratives include Ernest Gaines's *The Autobiography of Miss Jane Pittman* (1971), Gayl Jones's *Corregidora* (1975), Alex Haley's *Roots* (1976), Octavia Butler's *Kindred* (1979), and—perhaps best known in the genre—Toni Morrison's *Beloved* (1987), among others.

8. See Brown, *Song of My Life*, 67. The first Black studies department was founded the same year at San Francisco State College.

9. Walker, "Phillis Wheatley," 36. Writer Alice Walker wrote her well-known essay "In Search of Our Mothers' Gardens" as a talk for the festival; it was published as an essay in *Ms.* magazine the following year and later republished as the title essay of Walker's collection *In Search of Our Mothers' Gardens: Womanist Prose* (1983).

10. Walker, quoted in Nobile, "Uncovering Roots," 37. See, for example, Dugdale, "Roots of the Problem." See also Parry, "Politics of Plagiarism."

Women's Literary Renaissance was overshadowed by the institutional success of such writers as Alice Walker and Toni Morrison.[11] Similarly, in books on the rise of Black studies and Black studies programs, institutes, and departments, her name is never mentioned.[12] In the end, as poet Nikki Giovanni once put it, Margaret Walker had become "the most famous person nobody knows."[13]

As Walker's work and its legacy suggest, there is a long record of Black feminist humanism in the history of Black women's writing, and an equally long record of that work being sidelined or silenced. As early as the 1890s, Black female writers and activists such as Frances E. W. Harper, Anna Julia Cooper, and more were calling on one another to be united in "the grand and holy purpose of uplifting the human race," demanding "a total transformation of the social order" to serve the human community's least privileged members.[14] They believed that "because women were disadvantaged in the patriarchal power structure," they were better positioned to "value and promote social justice."[15] As subsequent scholars have noted, there is a direct lineage from Anna Julia Cooper's 1892 claim that "only the BLACK WOMAN can say 'when and where I enter . . . then and there the whole *Negro race enters with me*'" to the 1970s Black feminist slogan "Until Black Women Are Free, None of Us Will Be Free," and to the Black Lives Matter (BLM) movement's 2010s slogan "All Lives *Can't* Matter, Until Black Lives Matter," which BLM co-founder Alicia Garza explains includes "the lives of Black queer and transfolk, disabled folks, Black-undocumented folks, folks with records, women and all Black lives along the gender spectrum."[16] As Brittney Cooper notes, the fact that such political commentary "written in the second decade of the twenty-first century" sounds so "eerily similar to commentary from Anna Julia Cooper

---

11. See, for example, Fabre, "Margaret Walker's Richard Wright." On the impact of the Wright biography on Walker's reputation, see Graham, *Where My Soul Lives*, xxxi.

12. Aside from one mention of her poetry, Walker's name does not appear in Ibram X. Kendi's *The Black Campus Movement*, Martha Biondi's *The Black Revolution on Campus*, or Abdul Alkalimat's *The History of Black Studies*. One exception is Joyce A. Joyce's *Black Studies as Human Studies*, which argues that "the tradition of African-American letters . . . serves as a precursor for the intellectual and community service duality of . . . Black Studies" and includes a chapter on Walker's literary work (4, 87–98).

13. Giovanni, in a promotion for Judith McCray's California Newsreel documentary, *For My People: The Life and Writing of Margaret Walker*, quoted in Graham, preface to *Fields Watered with Blood*, xi.

14. Harper, "Woman's Political Future," 46; and Carby, *Reconstructing Womanhood*, 70.

15. Palmer-Mehta, "'We Are All Bound Up Together,'" 200.

16. Cooper, *Voice from the South*, 31, emphasis in original; Taylor, "Until Black Women Are Free"; Love Has No Labels, "Fight for Freedom," emphasis in original; and Garza, "Herstory." See also the closing line of Crenshaw's "Demarginalizing the Intersection," which states that "the goal" is to "facilitate the inclusion of marginalized groups for whom it can be said: 'When they enter, we all enter'" (167).

writing in the nineteenth century," not to mention to the words of "Pauli Murray, Toni Cade Bambara, and bell hooks writing in the twentieth," suggests "that not enough has changed."[17] It also suggests that Black women's voices have too long gone unheard.

Brave Humanism: Black Women Rewriting the Human in the Age of Jane Crow aims to unpack Black women writers' long-silenced reimagining of the human in the years that preceded the academic emergence of Black feminist theory. Since the postcolonial, poststructuralist, and feminist revolutions of the 1960s and '70s, it has become commonplace to critique humanism for its false universalism, anthropocentrism, and ahistoricism. *Brave Humanism* argues, however, that long before these well-known critiques of Western humanism emerged in the post–civil rights era, and long before the embrace of humanistic language became visible again in the slogans of the Black Lives Matter movement, a similar set of critiques and embraces were being made by an earlier generation of Black women, the very people most excluded by the logic of Western humanism and most committed to reclaiming and redefining the human on different terms. For the writers under study here—Pauline Hopkins, Nella Larsen, Zora Neale Hurston, Ann Petry, Gwendolyn Brooks, and Lorraine Hansberry—the capacity of narrative forms to place human identities in particular sociohistorical contexts offered a direct challenge to the white supremacist and patriarchal logics that underwrote de jure segregation, beginning with the *Plessy v. Ferguson* decision of 1896 and ending with the Civil Rights Act of 1964. Scholars are now shifting the lexicon for the de jure segregation era from Jim Crow to Jane Crow, civil rights activist Pauli Murray's term to describe the early to mid-twentieth-century "framework of 'male supremacy'" she recognized as living alongside the legal system of "white supremacy."[18] *Brave Humanism* shows that the Black women writers who were enmeshed in these frameworks were also engaged in imaginative projects of critique and creation: they exposed the white supremacist and patriarchal logic of Western humanism as it evolved over the decades to support Jane Crow, and they worked toward their own visions of humanity and human freedom—visions that would come to inspire later generations.

In turning to the decades that separate Anna Julia Cooper from later Black feminists, this book unpacks the historically undervalued efforts of Jane Crow–era Black women writers to dismantle the exclusionary frameworks through which their own creative efforts were often judged. Reading these writers' creative work in the context of the shifting production and reception

---

17. Cooper, *Beyond Respectability*, 143.

18. Murray, "Why Negro Girls Stay Single," 5. See also Hardison, *Writing through Jane Crow*, 1–2; Thaggert, *Riding Jane Crow*, 22–23; and Cooper, *Beyond Respectability*, 88.

pressures of the segregation era, I argue that the frameworks by which Black women's writing was judged were themselves fictions, propped up by dominant narratives about race, gender, and the human. Much like the colorblind racism of the post–civil rights era, the putatively humanist frameworks of the segregation era were attractive to white America precisely because they held out the superficial promise of racial equality while forever precluding its arrival, which these frameworks did by questioning Black people's alignment with white-defined Western humanist "norms." Over the course of the Jane Crow era, these shifting frameworks violently shaped the critical assumptions with which Black women writers were forced to engage, from Pauline Hopkins's confrontation with legal and biological accounts of race and gender in the 1890s to Nella Larsen's entanglement with modernist claims about artistic originality and authenticity in the 1920s; from Zora Neale Hurston's rewriting of anthropological depictions of the folk in the 1930s to Ann Petry's rejoinder to sentimental and sociological accounts of race and gender in the 1940s; and from Gwendolyn Brooks's resistance to Cold War–era investments in the "universal man" in the 1950s to Lorraine Hansberry's refusal of liberal caricatures of Black radicalism in the 1960s. Though the Black women writers under study here had varied responses to these shifting but always exclusionary humanist frameworks, their work is united in insisting that an emancipatory conception of the human must be theorized through—rather than in opposition to—the lived experience of Black women.

By recovering Jane Crow–era Black women writers' undervalued intellectual work of critique and creation, this book also intervenes in critical conversations about the relationship between Black creative and intellectual work and our ideas about human agency and collectivity. Indeed, while many scholars look to Black literature for signs of agency, self-determination, and resistance, others see within these humanistic investments the ongoing operation of violence, exclusion, and subjection. Some scholars have turned to Black feminist postcolonial writers for a way past this analytic impasse. I chart a prehistory of that critical turn, focusing on how Black women writing before the 1960s and '70s used their creative work to expose their exclusion from Western humanism while also retheorizing the human in and through their own image. Their work both supports recent efforts to reclaim antiracist and antisexist formulations of the human as a foundation for Black people's liberation and reinvigorates our understanding of the political stakes of segregation-era Black women's writing. In recovering this hidden intellectual genealogy, this book offers a more nuanced history of Black women's engagement with the idea of the human and places a longer history of Black women's writing at the heart of humanist and posthumanist study.

Taking its title from *All the Women Are White, All the Blacks Are Men, But Some of Us Are Brave* (1982)—the volume that inaugurated the field of Black women's studies—*Brave Humanism* explores the contours of Black women's rearticulations of the human over the course of the ninety years that separate Anna Julia Cooper's 1892 declaration from that 1982 anthology. In doing this, my goal is to honor both my book's indebtedness to this foundational Black feminist text and the bravery of the earlier Black female voices under study here. *But Some of Us Are Brave* highlighted the courage necessary not only to make Black women's experience visible, but also to stake a claim for the value and necessity of Black women's intellectual work—rooted in their lived experience—in a context traditionally occupied by white male discourse and invested in "discrediting" Black women's "intellectual power."[19] As the anthology's editors, Akasha Hull and Barbara Smith, emphasized: "Merely to use the term 'Black women's studies' . . . in a white-male world is an act of political courage."[20] *Brave Humanism* similarly aims to highlight the bravery of Jane Crow–era Black women writers—specifically their bravery to speak from a position outside the dominant discourse, to challenge that discourse from their position as Black women and, in doing so, to lay the groundwork for the fields of Black women's studies and Black feminist theory that followed them.

But Some of Us Are Brave was put together by several former members of the Combahee River Collective (CRC, 1974–80), whose 1977 statement—included as a centerpiece of the 1982 volume—is often credited as an important articulation of intersectional Black feminism, even though the specific term *intersectionality* was coined by Kimberlé Crenshaw twelve years later to describe the interlocking effect of sexism, racism, and other forms of oppression on Black women's lives.[21] Because Black feminist theory challenges any politics that treats white or male experiences as universal, it is often lumped together with other post-1960s critiques of so-called humanism. However, the CRC was clear that they understood Black feminism *to be a humanism*. Their statement begins with "the shared belief that Black women are *inherently* valuable, that our liberation is a necessity not as an adjunct to somebody else's but because of our need as human persons for autonomy."[22] With this nod to Enlightenment discourse on the "inherent" rights of "Man," the CRC read themselves into the narrative of human rights despite knowing that this narrative was not "coded" to embrace them; they "desire[d] it but with a

---

19. Hull and Smith, "Politics of Black Women's Studies," xviii.
20. Hull and Smith, "Politics of Black Women's Studies," xvii.
21. See Crenshaw, "Demarginalizing the Intersection," 149; Nash, *Black Feminism Reimagined*, 7; and Taylor, introduction to *How We Get Free*, 4.
22. Combahee River Collective, "Black Feminist Statement," 15, emphasis added.

difference."²³ In so doing, they insisted that concepts of human rights and liberty must be theorized through the experience of the least free, rather than the experience of the most free. As they explained, "Our freedom would necessitate the destruction of all the systems of oppression."²⁴ Furthermore, because they believed that their "right to build and define political theory and practice based upon" their own experience was essential to Black women's liberation, they also believed that the goal of human liberation required "coalition building and solidarity" rather than exclusionary concepts of sameness.²⁵ Inspired by the call of other US women of color to get "into the habit of listening to each other," CRC co-founder Barbara Smith concluded her subsequent anthology, *Home Girls* (1983), with Bernice Johnson Reagon's essay on coalition-building, explaining later that she "wanted people to leave the book" with "the idea of working together across differences."²⁶ This emphasis on theorizing out of the experience of the least free and building coalitions across differences sharply distinguishes Black feminist humanism from Western Enlightenment–based models.

In developing these differences from Western humanism, the CRC drew on an alternative genealogy of thinkers who are often excluded from traditional considerations of humanist thought. Indeed, while Black feminist theorists often spoke about how Black women were "turning to each other," they were also explicit that their ideas were drawn from the work of prior Black women activists and intellectuals.²⁷ As the CRC explained:

> There have always been Black women activists—some known, like Sojourner Truth, Harriet Tubman, Frances E. W. Harper, Ida B. Wells Barnett, and Mary Church Terrell, and thousands upon thousands unknown—who had a shared awareness of how their sexual identity combined with their racial identity to make their whole life situation and the focus of their political struggles unique. Contemporary Black feminism is the outgrowth of countless generations of . . . work by our mothers and sisters.²⁸

In the same vein, Patricia Hill Collins describes Black feminism as "a process of self-conscious struggle that empowers women and men to actualize a

---

23. Morsink, *Inherent Human Rights*, 18–24; and Muñoz, *Disidentifications*, 12, 15.
24. Combahee River Collective, "Black Feminist Statement," 18.
25. Smith, "Barbara Smith," 61, 63.
26. Bambara, foreword to *This Bridge Called My Back*, vii; and Smith, "Barbara Smith," 64. See also Reagon, "Coalition Politics."
27. Bambara, preface to *The Black Woman*, 4.
28. Combahee River Collective, "Black Feminist Statement," 14.

humanist vision of community," which she identifies as a throughline across "the ideas of Anna Julia Cooper, Pauli Murray, bell hooks, Alice Walker, Fannie Lou Hamer, and other Black women intellectuals too numerous to mention."[29] All of these women, Hill Collins argues, "have advanced the view that Black women's struggles are part of a wider struggle for human dignity and empowerment," to the extent that the "primary guiding principle of Black feminism is a recurring humanist vision."[30] But she insists that this humanist vision grew not out of Western humanism but out of "an Afrocentric historical context."[31]

Of course, Black feminism was quickly distorted by conservatives—and some allies—who accused Black feminist concepts of being "insular and divisive," rather than inclusive.[32] In the culture wars that followed, conservative critics frequently described the inclusion of Black women's literature in college courses as contrary to the supposedly universal values of "literary excellence," "innate human virtues," and "eternal truths" found in the work of "traditional authors."[33] Nevertheless, and although the backlash continues, Black feminist intellectuals have continued to insist on their more capacious understanding of human collectivity. The explicit articulations of Black feminist theory that emerged in the 1970s and '80s, along with the promotion of Black women to positions of power in publishing, criticism, and academia, were responsible for a critical shift in seeing Black women creative writers as serious participants in intellectual discourse, a shift that authors such as Audre Lorde, Alice Walker, Toni Morrison, and many others helped to bring about. These writers were instrumental, Courtney Thorsson shows, in transforming American writing and cultural institutions by doing the work of "demarginalizing" Black women's lives.[34] In just a few short years, "these women made Black feminist writing central to magazines and trade publishing, and they laid the foundation for Black feminism in the academy."[35] As a result, the women of this generation—and Morrison in particular—are often treated as exceptional in bringing Black feminism to a wide audience and shifting American letters away from its privileging of white subjects and the white gaze.[36]

---

29. Hill Collins, *Black Feminist Thought*, 1st ed., 39.
30. Hill Collins, *Black Feminist Thought*, 1st ed., 37.
31. Hill Collins, *Black Feminist Thought*, 1st ed., 40n7.
32. Cooper, afterword to *But Some of Us Are Brave*, 381.
33. Brooks, "From Western Lit to Westerns as Lit," 36. See also Clausen, "It Is Not Elitist"; and Gerald Graff's response to both in *Beyond the Culture Wars*, 16–25.
34. See Thorsson, *The Sisterhood*, 8; and Crenshaw, "Demarginalizing the Intersection," 167.
35. Thorsson, *The Sisterhood*, 5.
36. See Carroll, "Meaning, Without the White Gaze"; and Greenfield-Sanders, *Toni Morrison*.

However, the institutional success of writers like Toni Morrison and Alice Walker has obscured the genealogy of prior Black women writers whose work contributed to the development of Black feminist theory and its reimagining of humanist discourse, a lineage evidenced in foundational essays such as Alice Walker's "In Search of Our Mothers' Gardens" (1974) and Paule Marshall's "From the Poets in the Kitchen" (1983), both of which celebrated the seen and unseen creative work of prior generations of Black women. In honoring the work of prior Black women writers, Black feminist theorists were also recognizing the fact that Black feminist intellectual thought happens not just in traditional theoretical modes but in alternative genres and spaces. Indeed, Barbara Smith's path toward Black feminism began with Black women's literature. Studying for her doctorate in the early 1970s, Smith knew that she wanted to write about Black women writers but did not know "any major Black women writers to include," and had no help from her professors.[37] Meanwhile, Alice Walker had just completed a term as writer-in-residence at Jackson State from 1968 to 1969, where she had audited a course taught by Margaret Walker and learned for "the first time" about a range of Black women writers, though "none of their work was studied in the course," perhaps because "much of it was out of print."[38] In 1972 Alice Walker was teaching in Boston, where she offered a course dedicated to Black women's literature, believed to be the first of its kind. Smith found out about the course and asked if she could audit it, studying there for the first time the work of Phillis Wheatley, Frances Harper, Nella Larsen, Jessie Fauset, Zora Neale Hurston, Dorothy West, Ann Petry, Gwendolyn Brooks, Margaret Walker, and Paule Marshall.[39] By 1973 Smith was teaching her own course on Black women's literature, featuring many of the same writers, and had gotten involved in a Black feminist organization that she would say became "the springboard for . . . Combahee."[40]

But Some of Us Are Brave features Alice Walker and Barbara Smith's syllabi in the book's final section on "Doing the Work," a collection of syllabi that represents both resources for future teachers and scholars and a record of the field's intellectual genealogy. Like more recent scholarly critics of Western humanism, early Black feminist theorists were calling for the displacement of the West's definitional hold on the human and humanism. But the included syllabi show that they were not drawing on traditional academic discourse

---

37. Smith, "Barbara Smith," 40.
38. Walker, "Zora Neale Hurston," xi–xii.
39. See Walker, "African-American Literature." Hopkins does not feature on Alice Walker's syllabus even though *Contending Forces* was brought back into print in 1969 and 1971. Hopkins's serial novels, including *Of One Blood*, were brought back into print in 1988.
40. Smith, "Barbara Smith," 41. See also Smith, "Black Women Writers."

to do so; they were drawing on the narrative world-building of earlier Black women writers such as Hopkins, Larsen, Hurston, Petry, Walker, Brooks, and their peers. *Brave Humanism* resists the long history of silencing the intellectual work of Black women by recovering these writers' contributions to the Black feminist reimagining of the human.

Humanism and Posthumanism

What is often called humanism—which I will refer to as Western humanism, or sometimes liberal or exclusionary humanism—is, most scholars agree, "a wonderfully vague concept," one of those words that has shifted over time in its usage in Western thought and "whose range of possible uses runs from the pedantically exact to the cosmically vague."[41] If Western humanism can be said to have a core idea, Kate Soper concludes, it is that it "appeals (positively) to the notion of a core humanity," or as Rob Gaylard puts it, to the notion that "human beings possess a value and dignity in themselves, as human beings."[42] While the centering of human experience can be traced to Greek philosophy, and the emphasis on the individual is traceable to the Renaissance, Western humanism's characteristic "emphasis on man's rational faculty, and the idea that human beings possess agency," is typically traced to the Enlightenment.[43] Cultural critic Stuart Hall explains:

> The Enlightenment subject was based on a conception of the human person as a fully centred, unified individual, endowed with the capacities of reason, consciousness and action, whose "centre" consisted of an inner core which first emerged when the subject was born, and unfolded with it, while remaining essentially the same—continuous or "identical" with itself—throughout the individual's existence.[44]

"Usually described as male," the Enlightenment subject became the centerpiece of the "natural rights of man" discourse in the US Declaration of Independence (1776).[45] And while this declaration was written with only white men in mind, its language circulated in international abolitionist discourse of

---
41. Badmington, *Posthumanism*, 2; and Davies, *Humanism*, 3.
42. Soper, *Humanism and Anti-Humanism*, 11; and Gaylard, "Welcome to the World," 266.
43. Gaylard, "Welcome to the World," 266.
44. Hall, "Question of Cultural Identity," 275.
45. Hall, "Question of Cultural Identity," 275; and Antieau, "Natural Rights and the Founding Fathers," 46–51.

the nineteenth century and eventually formed the basis of the United Nations' 1948 Universal Declaration of Human Rights.[46] For proponents of Western humanism, therefore, acts of oppression such as slavery, disenfranchisement, and criminalization committed under Western humanism's watch represent resolvable gaps in an otherwise progressive ideology.

Since the 1960s, however, Western humanism is more typically viewed "not as progressive but as reactionary."[47] Where Western humanism was once seen "as the philosophical champion of human freedom and dignity," a new generation of posthumanist scholars see it as an "ideological smokescreen for . . . the marginalization and oppression of the multitudes of human beings in whose name it pretends to speak."[48] Posthumanist scholars primarily take issue with what Zakiyyah Jackson describes as Western humanism's "normative construction of 'the human' as rational, self-directed, and autonomous."[49] They oppose what Cary Wolfe describes as Western humanism's "fantasies of disembodiment and autonomy," especially as they relate to the idea that "'the human' is achieved by escaping or repressing not just its animal origins" but "the bonds of materiality and embodiment altogether."[50] Posthumanists working in the fields of environmental studies, animal studies, and cyborg studies also take issue with the ways in which Western humanism's anthropocentrism has been used to justify Man's claim to dominance over the natural, animal, and technological world.[51] Furthermore, Kristen Lillvis writes, "the liberal humanist subject's supposed 'freedom from dependence on the wills of others' and unqualified possession of 'his person and capacities'" reveals "the limitations of this definition of the human for women, people of color, and the poor."[52] As Gaylard summarizes, "the idea that there is a 'core' or shared humanity which is common to humankind . . . lays itself open to the criticism that it is in fact culturally specific" and that "Enlightenment man" simply "took his norms and values as universal."[53] For critics of Western humanism, humanist ideology does not allow exclusion, domination, and violence by mistake; it allows those things by design.

In posthumanist circles, scholars tend to trace this series of critiques to post–World War II Western philosophers such as Foucault, Derrida,

---

46. See Parten, "'Science of Human Rights'"; and Morsink, *Inherent Human Rights*, 19–20.
47. Badmington, *Posthumanism*, 2.
48. Davies, *Humanism*, 5.
49. Jackson, *Becoming Human*, 13.
50. Wolfe, *What Is Posthumanism?*, xv.
51. See Jackson, "Animal," 671, 673–74.
52. Lillvis, *Posthuman Blackness*, 5.
53. Gaylard, "Welcome to the World," 266.

and Althusser.[54] However, Black studies scholars insist that such critiques of Western humanism can be traced to earlier decolonial thinkers such as Frantz Fanon and Aimé Césaire.[55] Drawing on Fanon's and Césaire's analyses of Western humanism's foundational anti-Blackness, some Black studies scholars, identifying as Afropessimists, argue that the concept of "the human" is irreparably based on the dehumanization of Black people, or their "social death."[56] Others, meanwhile, worry that posthumanists and Afropessimists alike act as if "Western humanism is the only game in town."[57] As Alexander Weheliye argues, to "reinscribe the humanist subject (Man) as the personification of the human by insisting that this is the category to be overcome" is to fail to consider "cultural and political formations outside the world of Man that might offer alternative versions of humanity."[58] In fact, these scholars remind us, Fanon and Césaire refused to let the West delimit our understanding of what it means to be human, calling instead for "a new man" and a "true humanism—a humanism made to the measure of the world."[59] Following Sylvia Wynter and Christina Sharpe, these theorists insist on "unsettling the coloniality of being" by valuing the work Black people do "in the wake" of slavery and its afterlives, supplementing Afropessimism and social death with what Fred Moten calls "Black optimism" or Kevin Quashie calls "the aesthetics of aliveness."[60] For these scholars, there exists an alternative genealogy of "black humanist discourses" that "should not be read . . . as a mere uncritical reiteration . . . of [Western] humanist discourses."[61]

This book builds on the work of these more recent scholars, while also drawing new attention to voices and genres of Black intellectual thought typically elided in scholarly conversations about posthumanism and Black humanism. Typically, these conversations tend to focus either on Black male writers

---

54. On Foucault and other European thinkers, see Davies, *Humanism*, 47–48; Wolfe, *What Is Posthumanism?*, xi–xii; and Badmington, *Posthumanism*, 4–10.

55. On European thinkers being predated by Fanon and Césaire, see Reid-Pharr, *Archives of Flesh*, 7; Gaylard, "Welcome to the World," 266; and Jackson, "Animal," 670. On African humanism, which unlike Western humanism "identifies its 'core values' as 'communalism' and 'interdependence,'" see Dolamo, "Botho/Ubuntu," 215; and Gaylard, "Welcome to the World," 270.

56. On Afropessimism and "social death," see Wilderson, *Red, White & Black*, 21; and Patterson, *Slavery and Social Death*, 38. See also Hartman, *Scenes of Subjection*, 62; and Morrison, *Playing in the Dark*, 38.

57. Reid-Pharr, *Archives of Flesh*, 8. See also Weheliye, *Habeas Viscus*, 1–2; and Colbert, *Black Movements*, 25.

58. Weheliye, *Habeas Viscus*, 9–10.

59. Fanon, *Wretched of the Earth*, 239; and Césaire, *Discourse on Colonialism*, 73.

60. Wynter, "Unsettling the Coloniality of Being/Power/Truth/Freedom," 257; Sharpe, *In the Wake*, 19; Moten, "Black Op," 1745; and Quashie, *Black Aliveness*, 10. See also the work of Afrofuturists who "identify with possibilities" outside or beyond "enlightenment notions" (Samatar, "Toward a Planetary History," 182).

61. Weheliye, "'Feenin,'" 26.

or on Black decolonial and feminist scholars writing in traditional academic discourse.[62] However, Robert Reid-Pharr has shown that a fuller genealogy of Black thinking about the human requires looking beyond academic genres "for methods of inquiry, ways of naming human being, that are not bounded by the very forms of philosophy and sociology from which black and female subjectivity are always already excluded."[63] Taking up this call, I connect conversations about Black humanist discourse to creative genres of writing that open up a more capacious inquiry into Black female thought. In this, I am also in conversation with those scholars who take "seriously that black literary and visual culture theorizes and philosophizes."[64] Drawing on Audre Lorde's "Poetry Is Not a Luxury" (1977), these scholars see Black female creative texts' power to "imagine a black world."[65] For Lorde, creative work enabled Black women to refuse the mind-over-matter rationality of Enlightenment man in favor of a revolutionary imagination grounded in the embodied experience of "feeling": "The white fathers told us: I think therefore I am. The Black mother within each of us—the poet—whispers in our dreams: I feel therefore I can be free. Poetry coins the language to express and charter this revolutionary demand."[66] Like Lorde, scholars such as Kristen Lillvis, Zakiyyah Jackson, and Kevin Quashie insist on the radical possibilities of Black women's imaginative thought.[67] Nevertheless, their studies focus almost exclusively on the creative work of post-1960s Black female writers, with an emphasis on well-known Black feminist writers such as Audre Lorde, Toni Morrison, and Lucille Clifton, or Afrofuturist artists like Octavia Butler, Nalo Hopkinson, and Janelle Monae. As a result, they locate radical Black female imaginative thought on the human in the post-1960s period.

By contrast, *Brave Humanism* traces the origins of this Black feminist thinking about the human prior to the Black feminist and decolonial critiques of the 1960s and '70s, in the very creative work that would inspire later Black feminists. In so doing, I trouble conventional accounts of pre-1960s Black women's literature's relationship to Western humanism. For example, in her 1980 account of Black women's literary history, Barbara Christian

---

62. See, for example, Allen, *African American Humanism*; Pratt, *Strangers Book*; Ferguson, *Aberrations in Black*; Reid-Pharr, *Once You Go Black*; and Scott, *Extravagant Abjection*. See also Weheliye, "'Feenin'" and *Habeas Viscus*, which give serious consideration primarily to the work of Hortense Spillers and Sylvia Wynter, both post-1960s theorists writing in the genre of academic discourse.
63. Reid-Pharr, *Archives of Flesh*, 10.
64. Jackson, *Becoming Human*, 35.
65. Quashie, *Black Aliveness*, 13.
66. Lorde, "Poetry Is Not a Luxury," 38.
67. See Lillvis, *Posthuman Blackness*; Jackson, *Becoming Human*; and Quashie, *Black Aliveness*.

characterized early Black women novelists as being too caught up in an effort "to prove" themselves on terms "derived from the prevailing definition[s]" and "Western values" of white America.[68] Christian argued that it was "black contemporary women writers" who were "challenging the very definition of woman" and were "beginning to project their own definitions of themselves as a means of transforming the content of their own communities' views on the nature of woman and therefore on the nature of life."[69] Ann duCille, writing in 2017, similarly claimed that it was only "in the seventies and eighties, spearheaded by [Toni] Morrison and Alice Walker," that Black women began to write novels that "invented new grammars," "subverted traditional structures," and were "blackened, feminized," and "unbound."[70] This book argues, instead, that we can trace such efforts to challenge "traditional structures" and "the very definition of woman"—and, with them, the very definition of human—to the work of earlier Black women writers, including Hopkins, Larsen, Hurston, Petry, and Brooks.

Traditional accounts of pre-1960s Black engagements with humanism often focus on "the politics of recognition," whereby Black subjects are positioned as asking white subjects to recognize their worthiness of being included within the category of "Man"—or as Richard Wright sardonically put it in his 1937 manifesto, "Blueprint for Negro Writing," as "begging the question of the Negroes' humanity."[71] One paradigmatic example of this gesture is the 1787 seal commissioned by the British Society for the Abolition of the Slave Trade, which featured an enslaved man in chains kneeling in prayer position with a banner reading "Am I Not a Man and a Brother?"[72] The seal promoted a male-centered model of "common humanity," much like the "rights of man" language that had appeared eleven years earlier in the US Declaration of Independence. By depicting enslaved people as supplicant and docile, the image also offered white people the power to "recognize" Black humanity, marking white people as keepers of the definition of "Man," and marking Black people's inclusion in that definition as dependent on white benevolence and Black submissiveness.[73] The humanist iconography produced by Black activists, meanwhile, took a different tone. As Steve Estes points out, "Frederick Douglass and Sojourner Truth did not beg for their freedom; ... they demanded it."[74] Likewise, the well-known "A Man Was Lynched Yesterday"

---

68. Christian, *Black Women Novelists*, 252.
69. Christian, *Black Women Novelists*, 252.
70. DuCille, "Of Race, Gender, and the Novel," 381.
71. Taylor, "Politics of Recognition," 25; and Wright, "Blueprint for Negro Writing," 99.
72. Whittier, "Our Countrymen in Chains."
73. See Toppins, "Beyond the Bauhaus."
74. Estes, *I Am a Man!*, 2.

flag mounted outside the National Association for the Advancement of Colored People (NAACP) headquarters in New York, flown in protest every time a Black man was murdered by a lynch mob throughout the 1920s and 1930s, refused the mode of supplication.[75] And the "I AM A MAN" placards carried by protesters in the 1968 Memphis Sanitation Strike did not articulate Black manhood as a question but as "a fact."[76] And yet, with the notable exception of Sojourner Truth's, most of these slogans aligned themselves with the gendered discourse of the "natural rights of man."

By contrast, the iconography of the post–civil rights movement era is typically seen as more overtly inclusive of marginalized members of the Black community. For example, in 1988 Black gay artist Glenn Ligon reproduced the "I AM A MAN" poster in a series of paintings, one of which drew attention to marks in the margins of the poster and thereby suggested a redirection of our attention to those in the margins of the civil rights movement.[77] Similarly, in 1995 Derek Charles Livingston was photographed at the Million Man March holding a sign that read: "I AM A BLACK, / GAY MAN / I AM A BLACK / MAN / I AM A MAN."[78] In 2013 a fast food strike updated the sanitation strike slogan to include "I AM A WOMAN!"[79] And in 2018 organizers invited workers to fill in the blank on signs reading "I AM ___," explaining: "We're carrying your signs . . . declaring, I AM A MAN. I am a woman. I am non-binary. I am tired of waiting. I am a fast-food worker. I am your neighbor. Yo soy un hombre. I am a patriot. I am worth every penny."[80] While intentionally aligned with Black humanist assertions of the segregation era, these post–civil rights slogans also showcase their perceived difference from those earlier ones, articulated through their refusal of sameness-oriented and male-centered understandings of humanity. The evolution of this iconography seems to align with conventional accounts of Black people's liberatory engagements with the human, moving from begging for inclusion in the Western category of "Man," to asserting Black inclusion in that category, to demanding that Western "Man" be replaced by frameworks grounded in intersectionality.

And yet the linear narrative this iconography tells downplays the challenges and ruptures that have existed along the way—the "Am I Not a Woman and a Sister?" slogan that appeared in abolitionist poetry, pamphlets, medallions, and as an engraving in George Bourne's *Slavery Illustrated in Its Effects upon Woman* (1837) (see figure 1); Sojourner Truth's 1851 speech declaring (not

---

75. *Flag, Announcing Lynching*. See Toppins, "Beyond the Bauhaus."
76. Withers, *"I Am a Man"*; and Toppins, "Beyond the Bauhaus."
77. See Ligon, *Condition Report*; and Borges de Campos, "Marks in the Margins."
78. Terry, *I Am a Man*.
79. Resnikoff, "Historic Fast Food Strike."
80. Blair, quoted in O'Connor, "Lost in Citation," 4686.

FIGURE 1. *Am I Not a Woman and a Sister?* by Black engraver Patrick Henry Reason, as it appears in George Bourne's *Slavery Illustrated in Its Effects upon Woman* (1837). From the New York Public Library Digital Collections.

asking, as white abolitionist Frances Gage later claimed) "I Am a Woman's Rights"; Ida B. Wells-Barnett's documentation of the lynching of Black women in the *New York Times*; and the photograph of a Black woman at a Memphis march just a few weeks after the sanitation strike, holding an "I AM A MAN" sign with the letters "WO" penciled in before "MAN" (see figure 2).[81] That linear narrative also disregards key moments of disruption in the literary record, including Hopkins's troubling of the race and gender dynamics of "blood brotherhood," Larsen's refusal of sexually and racially constrained human "sanctuaries," Hurston's challenge to white- and male-oriented discourses of scientific objectivity, Petry's interest in developing interracial and intraracial networks of care, Brooks's reimagining of the Renaissance Man as a poor Black woman, and Hansberry's emphasis on Black women's place as leaders in radical coalition-based politics. Conventional narratives that depict pre-1960s Black writers, intellectuals, and activists as concerned only with

---

81. See Bourne, *Slavery Illustrated*, i; Gage, "Sojourner Truth"; Robinson, "Women's Rights Convention," 160; Wells-Barnett, "Woman Lynched"; and Levy, *I AM A (WO)MAN*.

FIGURE 2. Builder Levy, *I AM A (WO)MAN*, Martin Luther King Memorial March for Union Justice and to End Racism, Memphis, Tennessee, April 8, 1968. Collection of the Smithsonian National Museum of African American History and Culture, gift of Arnika Dawkins and the Arnika Dawkins Gallery. © Builder Levy. "WO" can be seen penciled in faintly before "MAN."

earning inclusion within hierarchical and Western humanist frameworks miss the ways that many activists, organizers, and writers—Black women in particular—were always invested in challenging these systems, not just seeking access but rather insisting that their entry required, in Crenshaw's later words, a "restructuring and remaking" of the world.[82]

---

82. Crenshaw, "Demarginalizing the Intersection," 167. See also Smith's critique of the slogan, "This Ain't Yo Mama's Civil Rights Movement" as "dismissive of the unsung black women who held down the movement and who made the options" young activists "took for granted in [their lives] possible" ("Race, Gender, and Generations," 6–7).

Brave Humanism and the Fictions of Segregation

In turning its attention to those Black female writers who refused Western humanist structures long before Morrison and Walker, *Brave Humanism* builds on the work of scholars paying increasing attention to the unsung work of Black women in pre-1970s Black liberation movements.[83] In contrast to top-down, patriarchal understandings of history-making, such scholars are actively recovering the work of Black women activists and intellectuals—especially women of the Black women's club movement of the 1890s such as Frances E. W. Harper, Ida B. Wells-Barnett, Anna Julia Cooper, and Mary Church Terrell, as well as women of the civil rights movement such as Pauli Murray, Frances Beal, and Shirley Chisholm, all of whom offered varying critiques of Western humanism based on their experiences as Black women. And yet, despite the important recovery of these Black female intellectuals' contributions to the development of Black feminist thought, comparatively little attention has been paid to the intersectional intellectual work of Black women in the intervening years—the years between the Black women's club movement of the late nineteenth century and the civil rights movement of the mid-twentieth century, coinciding roughly with the *Plessy v. Ferguson* decision of 1896 and the Civil Rights Act of 1964. This book begins the work of filling this gap.

The Jane Crow period is especially worthy of attention because the twisted logic of segregation meant that public discourse around Black humanity, far from being alleviated by emancipation, was intensified.[84] In the antebellum period, slavery was often justified by classifying Black people as "a subordinate and inferior class of beings" excluded from the "people of the United States."[85] The Thirteenth, Fourteenth, and Fifteenth Amendments seemed to promise the inclusion of Black people—or, at least, Black men—under the umbrella of the Declaration's "natural rights of man." But with the collapse of reconstruction and the codification of segregation into law in 1896, there was a sharp recentering of "man" as white, with the "terms of social equality" forever delayed by the unlikely prospect of white recognition of Black "social equality."[86] In W. E. B. Du Bois's words, white people had found an excuse

---

83. See, for example, Paula Giddings's *When and Where I Enter*, Hazel Carby's *Race Men*, Gabrielle Foreman's Colored Conventions Project, Erica Edwards's *Charisma and the Fictions of Black Leadership*, and Brittney Cooper's *Beyond Respectability*.

84. On this point, see Saidiya Hartman's *Scenes of Subjection*, Douglas Blackmon's *Slavery by Another Name*, and Chandan Reddy's *Freedom with Violence*.

85. Dred Scott v. Sandford, 60 U.S. 393 (1856).

86. Plessy v. Ferguson, 163 U.S. 537 (1896).

to "shift the burden of the [so-called] Negro problem to the Negro's shoulders and stand aside as critical and rather pessimistic spectators."[87] As Ida B. Wells-Barnett's antilynching work showed, Black people were also being increasingly criminalized, disenfranchised, and violently oppressed, with this violence "justified" by classifying Black people as "monster[s]" and "a race of outlaws" who were failing to live up to the standards of civilization.[88] As Saidiya Hartman explains, Black people were no longer "chattel," but the recognition of their potential "humanity and individuality" acted not to liberate but rather "to tether, bind, and oppress."[89]

In this context, Black cultural production became an important opportunity to produce counternarratives to segregation discourse, and it came under enormous pressure to do so.[90] As Imani Perry writes, since "racial narratives are fundamental to the practice of racial inequality," it is no surprise that "the practice of deliberately 'shifting narratives' was important . . . in making progress in the pursuit [of] racial justice."[91] Black narratives, along with other forms of Black cultural production, were especially privileged by Black intellectuals during segregation, as Black people were systematically denied access to other forms of economic and political power and action.[92] Daylanne English argues that Black writers turned to the novel because novels "quite often center on an individual's negotiation of period-specific material and social conditions."[93] As Black writers encountered a nation still somehow "refusing to consider them as individuals at all," they turned "particularly and pragmatically to the novel, a form in the business of 'reproducing modern individuals,' as a literary-political strategy in a national time when neither modernity nor individuality was allocated equally."[94]

For Black women writers, doubly excluded from other spaces of political activity, creative work was an especially important space for developing and expressing their political and intellectual thought. But their contributions have been marginalized or silenced, both in their lifetimes and in the subsequent periodization of Black literary production. Sandra Govan points out that Black women writers such as Pauline Hopkins, Jessie Fauset, Dorothy West, and Alice Browning all served as Black "cultural conservators" during

---

87. Du Bois, *Souls of Black Folk*, 49.
88. Wells-Barnett, *Red Record*, 273.
89. Hartman, *Scenes of Subjection*, 5.
90. See Jarrett, *Representing the Race*, 6; and Warren, *What Was*, 9–11.
91. Perry, *More Beautiful and More Terrible*, 9–10.
92. See Warren, "Back to Black," 371–72; and Jarrett, *Representing the Race*, 7–11.
93. English, *Each Hour Redeem*, 51.
94. English, *Each Hour Redeem*, 51. See also Armstrong, *How Novels Think*, 10.

the Jane Crow era, working as editors and literary editors for such important Black periodicals as *Colored American Magazine* (1900–1904), *The Crisis* (1910–), *Challenge* and *New Challenge* (1934–37), and *Negro Story* (1944–46).[95] Era Bell Thompson, Shirley Graham Du Bois, and Esther Cooper Jackson also served in major editorial roles at *Negro Digest* (1942–51), *Ebony* (1945–), and *Freedomways* (1961–85).[96] And yet, as Gene Andrew Jarrett argues, "Men were almost always anointed the de facto deans of past African American literary movements or renaissances . . . underwriting their acquisition of critical and commercial authority and encoding male or masculine privilege in literary theories and practices."[97] Not only did Black men actively displace many of these women as editors—Hopkins pushed out of *Colored American Magazine* by Booker T. Washington, Fauset's position as literary "midwife" of the Harlem Renaissance usurped by Alain Locke, West forced to close down *New Challenge* rather than lose it to Richard Wright—they also frequently diminished the work of their female peers as "prim and dainty," "facile" and "quaint," and "for all its needlepoint competence" lacking in "social significance."[98] As these Black male deans declared "the problem of the Twentieth Century" to be "the problem of the color-line," gender was increasingly treated as secondary to, if not a distraction from, the issue of race.[99] And because the Black literary manifestos that have been used subsequently to define the breaks and continuities in Black literary production are almost entirely authored by men, current narratives of Black literary production are largely dictated by the concerns of Black male writers.

---

95. Govan, "Black Women as Cultural Conservators," 1. Hopkins served as editor from 1900 to 1904; Fauset from 1919 to 1926; West from 1934 to 1937; and Browning from 1944 to 1946.

96. Thompson served as editor at *Negro Digest* and then *Ebony* from 1947 until her retirement in the 1980s; Shirley Graham Du Bois and Esther Cooper Jackson co-founded *Freedomways* with colleagues in 1961 and Jackson served as editor until the magazine ceased publishing in 1985.

97. Jarrett, *Deans and Truants*, 24. See also Hull, *Color, Sex, and Poetry*, 30; and Smith, "Toward a Black Feminist Criticism," 157–59.

98. Hughes, *Big Sea*, 218, on Fauset, Charles Johnson, and Alain Locke as "the three people who midwifed the so-called New Negro literature into being"; McKay, *Long Way from Home*, 112, on Fauset and her novels; Wright, "Between Laughter and Tears," 25, on Hurston's *Their Eyes*; and Locke, "Critical Retrospect," 7, on Petry's *Country Place*.

99. Du Bois, *Souls of Black Folk*, 1. Hale notes that Cooper had made a claim strikingly similar to Du Bois's eleven years earlier, although unlike Du Bois, she also insisted that the Black woman's voice on the issue needed to be heard (see Hale, *Making Whiteness*, 33; and Cooper, *Voice form the South*, i–ii). On male writers treating gender as secondary, see Johnson, preface to revised edition, *The Book of American Negro Poetry*, 6; and Locke, "Fire." See also Jenkins, *Private Lives, Proper Relations*, 26–28.

Recent Black feminist literary scholarship has used Black female writers' responses to the politics of Jane Crow to trouble "the masculinist mid-twentieth-century narrative of black literary production that has remained the primary focus of contemporary scholarship."[100] Ayesha Hardison's *Writing through Jane Crow* (2014), for example, insists on the formative influence of Jane Crow–era Black women's writing and intellectual work on the politics of later generations, even if that influence has been obscured by traditional literary and intellectual histories. Candice Jenkins's *Private Lives, Proper Relations* (2007) and Koritha Mitchell's *From Slave Cabins to the White House* (2020) similarly document—though from somewhat different angles—mainstream ideological pressures on and resulting distortions of the work of Black women writers. Likewise, Emily Lordi has shown that "post-soul" artists' and critics' characterizations of the 1960s "soul" period as "racially essentialist," "masculinist," and "heterosexist," problematically exclude Audre Lorde, Aretha Franklin, and Nina Simone.[101] When we treat female artists as "representative" of their periods rather than as marginal or exceptional, Lordi argues, we can see that those periods are not as "rigidly defined."[102] Katherine McKittrick also insists that Black women's meaning-making efforts "to assert humanness" and "more humanly workable" spaces have always existed.[103] As Mitchell argues, these efforts have simply "been obscured by dominant discourses and practices"; it "remains for scholars and readers to adopt interpretive frameworks" that enable us to appreciate that meaning-making work.[104] Together, these scholars suggest that the shape of Black literary history might change if we stop seeing Black women as ancillary to male-driven movements. Instead, we must reclaim the marginalized spaces from which Black women wrote as ideal positions from which to theorize the human and periodize Black literary production.[105]

Following in the footsteps of these interventions, I argue that the centering of Black male intellectual work has made it difficult to see the intellectual, field-shifting interventions of Black women's writing on the human, even when that writing is relatively widely read, precisely because their interventions don't conform to Western humanist and male-centered expectations of

---

100. Hardison, *Writing through Jane Crow*, 10.
101. Lordi, "Souls Intact," 66.
102. Lordi, "Souls Intact," 66. See also Evie Shockley on the influence of the masculinist Black Arts Movement on the "way we understand African American works written prior to the Movement" (*Renegade Poetics*, 8).
103. McKittrick, *Demonic Grounds*, xxiv.
104. Mitchell, *From Slave Cabins*, 21, 18.
105. On the value of theorizing from the margins, see hooks, "Choosing the Margin."

the literature and politics of the segregation era. Like Mitchell, who looks at "what an affirmation-versus-protest approach has obscured," I look at what has been obscured by Western humanist assumptions about human sameness and racial difference.[106] Kenneth Warren shows that during the segregation era, Black writers were under significant pressure from both the white literary establishment and Black literary deans to conform to a binary framework in which "claiming to be *different from* and claiming to be *the same as* the dominant society could appear to have equal critical force."[107] However, rather than consenting to the idea that they must choose one or the other of these options, the authors under study here resist the false opposition of difference and sameness as it recurs in the dominant universalist discourses of their day. I explore the failure of the binary framework of sameness and difference to make sense of Black women's intellectual work, which includes Hopkins's critique of legal constructions of merit and the national family; Larsen's refusal of the paradoxical constraints of aesthetic authenticity; Hurston's troubling of the dominating gaze of anthropology; Petry's unsettling of normative models of justice; Brooks's radical reformulation of the Renaissance Man; and Hansberry's dramatic articulation of coalition politics. Building on Brittney Cooper's idea that Black female intellectuals have traditionally used their embodiment as the "zero point of their theorizing," this book examines the ways in which these Black women writers contested dominant and oppressive narratives about the human, while radically retheorizing the concept from their material experience on the margins.[108] Not only were they critiquing the colonial and patriarchal logics of Western humanism, but they were also creating something new.

Although much Black feminist literary scholarship concerns itself with the recovery of understudied texts, this book purposely concentrates on narrative fictions written by the most canonical Black female writers of their respective moments because examining canonical works offers us access to "cultural criticism's most durable assumptions."[109] I examine these authors' most critically polarizing works, chosen because the reception of these texts as controversial or incoherent exposes the fault lines in our collective thinking about race, gender, and the human. Because Black novels were widely read by white readers, my primary attention to Black women's novels and narrative fiction also helps focus our attention on an intellectual space where the pressures of the white literary establishment—and, in turn, Black writers' imaginative refusals

---

106. Mitchell, *From Slave Cabins*, 26.
107. Warren, *What Was*, 80, emphasis in original.
108. Cooper, *Beyond Respectability*, 9.
109. Mitchell, *From Slave Cabins*, 26.

of those pressures—were at their height. In addition to tracing the critical legacy of each work under study, I read each work against the dominant universalist narratives of their unique historical moments—turning to contemporaneous authors, unpublished letters, manuscript edits and marginalia, book reviews, and lesser-known works from the period to explore each historical moment, and tracing in subsequent criticism how those dominant narratives have shaped the periodization of each author's work. In this approach, I am following both duCille's call to explore not just "how these texts should be read," but how and why "critical communities constantly 'rewrite' them," and Soyica Diggs Colbert's call to look for "the figure[s]" of Black women writers "buried in the archive" who will help us tell new "histor[ies] of" Black women's "ideas."[110]

In reconsidering the politics and periodization of segregation-era Black literature through the lens of Black women's writing, this book builds on foundational scholarship on Black women's writing such as Hazel Carby's *Reconstructing Womanhood* (1987), Ann duCille's *The Coupling Convention* (1993), Cheryl Wall's *Women of the Harlem Renaissance* (1995), and Deborah McDowell's *"The Changing Same"* (1995). But where much of this early scholarship aligns with McDowell in seeing "the 'Woman's Era' of the 1890s," "the Harlem Renaissance of the 1920s and 1930s," and finally "the 1970s and 1980s" as the "defining moments" in Black women's literary history, this book puts Black women's writing of these three better-documented moments in conversation with that of the 1940s and '50s, one of the most understudied periods of Black literary history.[111] By drawing together these several generations of Black women's writing, I respond to Mary Helen Washington's call to "piece together those 'broken and sporadic' continuities that constitute black women's literary tradition," asking not only how Hopkins, Larsen, Hurston, Petry, and Brooks used their imaginative work to contest the Western humanist logics of segregation, but also how their work connects across the shifting paradigms of the Jane Crow era and into the intersectional feminisms of the 1970s and '80s.[112]

In selecting the specific works under study here, I have aimed not for an exhaustive study of Black women's narrative reimagining of the human but for a suggestive one, suggestive of the different humanistic innovations of Black

---

110. DuCille, *Coupling Convention*, 9; and Colbert, *Radical Vision*, 11.
111. McDowell, *"Changing Same,"* xv. See Tracy, introduction to *Writers of the Black Chicago Renaissance*, 1; and Bone and Courage, *Muse in Bronzeville*, 1–2.
112. Washington, *Invented Lives*, xx.

women writers working across different periods, politics, and pressures.[113] To better explore the range of these innovations, I have also chosen writers who not only represent different moments in Jane Crow writing but who also worked across a range of narrative subgenres, including serial fiction, short stories, folklore, novels, children's writing, poetic vignettes, and drama. Because the writers studied here exemplify such important historical, generic, marketplace, and sometimes political differences, they offer us the opportunity to observe the diverse shape that Black women's intersectional humanism has taken over time. My goal, in other words, is not to collapse the differences between these authors, nor to suggest that these are the only authors or artists worthy of study in this context, but to explore the rich, various, and capacious forms that Black women's brave humanism takes across the many decades of the Jane Crow era, as they critiqued and creatively reimagined the humanist frameworks of their respective historical moments.

Chapter 1, "Of One Blood: Blood Brotherhood in the Black Woman's Era," examines Pauline Hopkins's opposition to the merit-based, male-centered notions of citizenship that emerged in the aftermath of the 1896 *Plessy v. Ferguson* decision. Hopkins's periodical fiction and essays for the *Colored American Magazine* show that segregationists were as likely to justify the subordination of Black people via naturalized notions of racial difference as via the notions of "civilization," "universal" human values, and legal "sameness." By placing her serial novel, *Of One Blood: Or, The Hidden Self* (1902–3) in the context of her magazine writing on Pan-African and Black women's history, chapter 1 shows that Hopkins's work makes race and gender visible in exclusionary constructions of the "human race" and "blood brotherhood." Taken together, I argue, Hopkins's writing challenges white supremacist efforts to oppose universality to particularity, while signaling her effort to make Black women's voices central in formulating alternative models of Black liberation. The reception of her work also sets the stage for subsequent chapters, as it exposes the common critical tendency, both then and now, to dismiss the creative thought of women as incoherent, rather than recognizing it as revolutionary.

In chapter 2, "No Sanctuary: Plagiarism, Primitivism, and the Politics of Recognition," I explore Nella Larsen's experimental response to the racially

---

113. Other fiction writers worthy of further study include Frances E. W. Harper, Alice Dunbar-Nelson, Jessie Redmon Fauset, Dorothy West, Alice Browning, Paule Marshall, and Margaret Walker, the latter of whom Patricia Hill Collins describes as offering "one of the clearest discussions of Black humanism" (Hill Collins, *Black Feminist Thought*, 1st ed., 40n7). Curiously, Hill Collins's discussions of Walker's and Black feminism's Afrocentric humanism were cut from her book's second edition, ostensibly because she believed the term *Afrocentrism*—although perhaps also the term *humanism*—had become "too value laden to be useful" (Hill Collins, *Black Feminist Thought*, 2nd ed., 48; 2nd ed., xiii).

and sexually charged concern with cultural recognition that plagued Black writers of the Harlem Renaissance. Where white modernists were free to borrow from other cultures, leave behind the constraints of middle-class life, and freely express their sexualities, Black writers were hemmed in by two sets of contradictory principles: first, that their writing must not be "imitative" but rather recognizable as "authentically" Black; and second that their writing must appeal to the "universal" standards of white critics, which meant that it couldn't be too "particular." Through an analysis of Larsen's story "Sanctuary" (1930), her novels *Quicksand* (1928) and *Passing* (1929), letters, and reviews, this chapter shows that Larsen consciously Signified on the aesthetic techniques of modernism to disrupt the racial and sexual biases embedded in its most deeply held assumptions about imitation and authenticity. Like Hopkins, however, Larsen's literary experiments have been widely misunderstood. "Sanctuary," which retold a white-authored story in a Black context, was dismissed in its own time as an imitation of white writing that was inauthentically Black—the very double standard that her work aimed to deconstruct.

Turning to the folk sensibility of Zora Neale Hurston's Popular Front–era fiction, chapter 3, "Folk in the Flesh: Insides, Outsides, and the Object of Anthropology," argues that her explorations of the pleasures and pains experienced by human flesh radically refuse the presumptive association of culture with a modern bourgeois present and the folk with a nostalgic and naturalized past. Examining Hurston's folk narratives alongside other contemporaneous conceptions of the folk, this chapter shows that Hurston represents folk cultures not as naturalized constants, as was then common, but as fluid and hybrid social structures that both reinforce and resist racist, sexist, and bourgeois ideologies. Considered through this lens, Hurston's famous construction of "insides" and "outsides" in *Their Eyes Were Watching God* (1937) reads not as a reference to the insider/outsider status of the anthropological observer but rather as opening the imaginative possibility of embodied—or enfleshed—experiences not yet mediated by the structures of racism, sexism, and capitalism. For Hurston, material experiences of pleasure and pain become narrative opportunities to imagine ways of constructing human experience beyond the limitations of existing cultural norms. Although *Their Eyes Were Watching God* is often characterized as torn between modern bourgeois and nostalgic folk fantasies, this chapter shows that the novel is better understood as critiquing these problematic cultural constructions to begin the work of imagining Black feminist futurity.

In chapter 4, "Networks of Care: Beyond Sentiment, Sociology, and the Protest Fiction Debate," I look to the protest fiction debate's conflation of "mankind" with "manhood" and consider Ann Petry's fiction as refusing the terms of that debate. Whereas Richard Wright was troubled by what he saw as the feminized sentimentality of earlier Black writing and turned instead to what he described as the "hard" truths of sociology, Ann Petry's novels question the liberatory value of this sociological turn. Her novels reject the normative racial and gender politics of mid-twentieth-century sociology, while also demanding renewed attention to the racial and gender politics of sentiment. Rather than refusing sentiment, as so many of her Black male peers did, Petry formulates an alternative model of interracial and intraracial empathy—one based not on prevailing models of white female sentimentality but on a Black feminist network of care. Nevertheless, the reception of Petry's fiction—increasingly dismissed by reviewers and critics as it moved away from the "hard" social realist model set by Wright and toward feminine-coded genres such as "melodrama" and children's literature—indicates an all-too-common critical failure to confer value on the theoretical and political work of women.

Chapter 5, "Renaissance Women: Vision and Vulnerability in the Black Chicago Renaissance," turns to what has been described as the push and pull between realist and experimental modes in the Black Chicago Renaissance and accounts for this aesthetic variation not as a retreat from radicalism to liberalism, as is often claimed, but as a consistent and conscious refusal of white authority over the form and content of Black writing. Gwendolyn Brooks's aesthetic and political innovations across a range of works—from *A Street in Bronzeville* (1945) to *Maud Martha* (1953) and beyond—not only challenged the expectations of her original white publisher but also challenge ongoing critical attempts to periodize the Black Chicago Renaissance. Taken together, her work's inward turn toward making space for Black female vision and vulnerability, coupled with an outward turn toward the promise of a global worldview—constitute a powerful rejection of America's assimilationist and exceptionalist Cold War liberalism. In centering a working-class Black woman in each of these turns, Brooks explores the creative ways that midcentury Black women made space for their vision and vulnerability in the world.

Finally, in a coda on "Bravery and the Backlash: Lorraine Hansberry at the Forum," I look at playwright Lorraine Hansberry's participation in a 1964 forum called "The Black Revolution and the White Backlash," sponsored by John Oliver Killens's Association of Artists for Freedom. If the forum was something of a failed attempt to get white Americans to listen to Black perspectives on the global fight for human liberation, it was nevertheless an important declaration of Black artists' bravery to speak from a position and point of view that they knew many white Americans did not want to see or hear—to assert their right and power to speak for the human community. Hansberry's participation in the forum is especially significant both because her work looks forward to the Combahee River Collective's insistence on Black women's right to imagine worlds in which they would be free, and because it is grounded in the work of the Black women writers who came before her—women who never consented to be represented by narrative structures that would erase their humanity, and who devoted their imaginative and intellectual lives to their own brave rearticulations of human experience, solidarity, and possibility.

As demonstrated by the syllabi on Black women's literature collected in the final pages of *But Some of Us Are Brave,* the authors and works under study here have been beloved by Black feminist intellectuals for decades. In turning our attention to these relatively canonical works, my claim is not that their work has been overlooked but rather that the theoretical interventions of their work—their intersectional interventions into discourses on the human—have been underestimated and obscured. My goal is not merely to increase the attention that we give these authors and these texts but to change the quality of that attention by taking seriously their intellectual contributions to the discourses of Black feminist theory and Black humanism. Their efforts to rewrite the human show us, as Brittney Cooper put it in a recent overview of the field, that "what we build is far more important than what we destroy."[114] The work of these writers allows us to see across different periods of Black literature a shared investment in feminist and antiracist creation dedicated to the goal of human liberation—a shared investment that defines brave humanism.

---

114. Cooper, "Love No Limit," 19.

CHAPTER 1

Of One Blood

Blood Brotherhood in the Black Woman's Era

In 1996 the Black British publishing house X Press released a new edition of Pauline Hopkins's *Of One Blood: Or, The Hidden Self,* which had originally been published serially in the *Colored American Magazine* from 1902 to 1903 during Hopkins's reign as the magazine's editor.[1] X Press launched in 1992, specializing in "gritty pulp fiction" about the contemporary "lives of young black Britons."[2] In 1994 it started a line of Black classics, echoing the aims of many US-based Black presses of the 1960s to reclaim forgotten Black histories.[3] The reprinting of Hopkins's novel was part of that series. As one of Hopkins's serial novels, *Of One Blood* was less well-known than either her first novel, *Contending Forces* (1900), or Frances E. W. Harper's *Iola Leroy* (1892), both of which were originally published as stand-alone works. But unlike

---

1. *Of One Blood* was first brought back into print in 1988 in *The Magazine Novels of Pauline Hopkins,* published as part of the Schomburg Library of Nineteenth-Century Black Women Writers series.

2. Ireland, "Material Factors," 159.

3. See Ireland, "Material Factors," 157–69; Forbes, "X Press Publications"; and Monteith, "Review of *The Norton Anthology,*" 149. X Press's predecessors included Broadside Press, founded in Detroit, Michigan, in 1965; Third World Press, founded in Chicago, Illinois, in 1967; Black Classic Press, founded in Baltimore, Maryland, in 1978; and Africa World Press, based in New Jersey and founded in 1983. In the UK, prior Black presses included New Beacon Books, founded in 1966; Allison & Busby, founded in 1967; and Bogle-L'Ouverture Publications, founded in 1969.

either of those earlier novels, *Of One Blood* featured a midplot sojourn to an African kingdom that no doubt appealed to X Press's post-1960s Pan-African ethos. Retitled *One Blood,* the X Press edition's cover featured the head and naked torso of a Black man holding a Ghanaian fertility statue. This new linguistic and visual framing suggests the press's effort to align the "one blood" of the title with its own Black Power–inspired mission. According to the back cover, Hopkins's novel begins with a protagonist who "doesn't give a damn about being black and cares less for African history" but who, through his experience in a secret Ethiopian kingdom, "discovers his true blackness and the painful truth about blood, race and the 'other half' of his history which has never been told."[4]

In 2004 *Of One Blood* was reprinted again by the Givens Foundation for African American Literature in partnership with Washington Square Press. Aimed at a multicultural American audience, this publishing partnership hoped that their reprints of Black classics would enable "a new generation of readers" to "discover these books, gain a deeper understanding of our multi-faceted American history, and an increased ability to appreciate the texture of the lives that lie ahead of us."[5] Their cover depicts an abstract Black figure positioned between two Egyptian columns, a nod to the novel's exploration of the West's indebtedness to the civilizations of Africa. Their back cover also notes the protagonist's discovery of the "painful truth about blood, race, and the half of his history that was never told."[6] But instead of linking the "truth about blood" to the main character's discovery of "his true blackness," as the X Press edition did, the Givens edition declares that the "one blood" of the novel's title "refers to the biological kinship of all human beings" and was part of Hopkins's pioneering effort to "demystify biological definitions of race."[7]

Though united in their effort to recover, celebrate, and learn from Black history, these reprintings of Hopkins's novel represent two seemingly opposed ways of pursuing that goal—one, by affirming global Black solidarity by emphasizing Black people's shared Blackness (or "one blood"); the other, by refusing persistent racist investments in the notion of Black inferiority by emphasizing Black and non-Black people's common humanity (or, again, "one blood"). These seemingly contradictory readings of the "one blood" in the novel's title have also dominated the novel's critical reception. Susan Gillman argues that, in the novel's title, "paradoxically opposed, are the novel's promises of both

---

4. See Hopkins, *One Blood,* back cover.
5. Givens, epilogue to *Of One Blood,* 196.
6. See Hopkins, *Of One Blood,* back cover.
7. See Hopkins, *Of One Blood,* back cover, quoting McDowell, introduction to *Of One Blood,* xii.

racial distinctiveness, for the Ethiopian 'race,' and racial unity, for 'all races.'"[8] For Deborah McDowell, this paradox extends to the novel itself, which "has consistently baffled critics": "If we are all 'of one blood,' critics ask, how can the novel logically conclude, as it does, with a recuperation of distinct bloodlines, one the source of an 'originary' African identity?"[9] Many critics have chosen to live with this apparent "contradiction," while others have felt it necessary to choose one meaning of the title over the other.[10] Some claim that the point of the novel is to urge "the return to the purity of 'Negro blood'" and an "untainted African heritage," while others argue that the novel's message is that "equality . . . can only be realized when we concede that we are all *of one blood*, one race, one people."[11] These polarized readings of the novel's politics also extend to scholarly accounts of Hopkins's work as a whole, which includes short journalistic works fostering Pan-African pride as well as "uplift" novels that seem, in Saidiya Hartman's words, to depict "the prospects of citizenship" as "inseparable from the assimilation of whiteness."[12]

This chapter argues that recent popular and scholarly efforts to fit Hopkins's novel and oeuvre into neat separatist or universalist categories have proven problematic precisely because they read the novel's universalism through the lens of Western humanism—a framework in which the universal is represented in opposition to Black racial particularity, thus acting as a thin veil for white racial particularity. This chapter, instead, takes seriously the ways in which Black women's imaginative work of the segregation era troubles the very definition and deployment of "universal" humanity—strategically refusing the racist logic encoded in the definition of Western man. Seen through this lens, this chapter shows, Hopkins's use of the double meaning of "one blood"—as *one race* and as *one human race*—is not contradictory at all, but challenges Western perceptions of Black particularity as nonhuman and human universalism as white. By way of the ambiguity of "one blood," Hopkins's novel shows that segregationist and imperialist political systems were as likely to embrace naturalized notions of racial difference as they were to

---

8. Gillman, "Pauline Hopkins and the Occult," 63.

9. McDowell, introduction to *Of One Blood*, xv.

10. Schrager, "Pauline Hopkins and William James," 200. On embracing the contradiction, see Harris, "Not Black and/or White," 380; and Sundquist, *To Wake the Nations*, 569. On giving primacy to one meaning over others, see Kassanoff, "'Fate Has Linked Us Together,'" 168–69; Otten, "Pauline Hopkins and the Hidden Self," 230; and Stevenson, "Of One Blood, of One Race," 442–43.

11. Kassanoff, "'Fate Has Linked Us Together,'" 168–69; and Stevenson, "Of One Blood, of One Race," 442–43, emphasis in original.

12. Hartman, *Scenes of Subjection*, 153. See Carby, introduction to *Magazine Novels*, xliii, xlv; and Cassidy, "Contending Contexts," 661–62.

justify the subordination of Black cultures and peoples via a public commitment to "civilization," "universal" humanity, and political equality. The novel thereby makes visible the logic of white supremacy that hides beneath Western accounts of racial difference and human sameness alike. *Of One Blood* is not a romantic but contradictory appeal for race pride *or* human equality, but an internally consistent argument that any functional notion of human "brotherhood" must include its Black "brothers."

Of course, as the term *brotherhood* suggests, post-Reconstruction notions of shared humanity depended on not only racial but also gendered exclusions. Since, as Hartman explains, "the implied citizen of the Constitution and subject of 'we the people' was the white male," the "presumed whiteness and maleness of the citizen transposed the particular into the universal, thus enabling white men to enjoy the privileges of abstraction and a noncorporeal universality."[13] When the end of slavery necessitated an expanded understanding of citizenship, it became "of particular importance in the congressional debate on equality" to insist that "the extent to which the equality of rights" would be "extended to freedmen depended upon the transformation of former slaves into responsible and reasonable men."[14] In other words, Black people's "equality" depended on their adoption of traits that were explicitly described as race- and gender-neutral but were implicitly associated with white masculinity. Following Hanna Wallinger's suggestion that Hopkins's "negotiations of gender were never detached from her negotiations of race," this chapter investigates *Of One Blood*'s interrogation of this intersection: the subordination of Black people by "raceless" appeals to human sameness and the subordination of Black women by both "raceless" and "genderless" appeals.[15] *Of One Blood* reflects Hopkins's disagreements with the merit-based model of racial uplift found in the rhetoric of Booker T. Washington and the *Plessy v. Ferguson* decision, as well as her support for the efforts of the National Association of Colored Women's Clubs (NACWC) to make Black women's voices central in formulating alternative models of Black liberation. The critical confusion surrounding *Of One Blood* points to a larger lack of clarity about how the notions of difference and commonality were deployed in post-Reconstruction politics, and about the role that Black women and Black women's literature played in rearticulating their relationship.

---

13. Hartman, *Scenes of Subjection*, 153–54.
14. Hartman, *Scenes of Subjection*, 175.
15. Wallinger, *Pauline E. Hopkins*, 49.

Plessy v. Ferguson and the National Family

In May of 1893, a little less than a year after Homer Plessy sat in a "whites only" train car in violation of Louisiana's Separate Car Act, a handful of Black female leaders were invited to speak at the World's Congress of Representative Women (WCRW) at the Chicago World's Fair. Speaking on behalf of what Sarah J. W. Early called a "grand sisterhood" of Black women, poet and novelist Frances E. W. Harper used the opportunity to deliver her speech on "Woman's Political Future."[16] Renewing claims she had been making as early as 1866, Harper's speech advocated for what Hazel Carby describes as "a total transformation of the social order," with women united, in Harper's words, in "the grand and holy purpose of uplifting the human race."[17] Harper's speech also announced that they were standing on "the threshold of woman's era," with these words codifying the turn of the twentieth century as the "Black Woman's Era."[18] Just two years later, the Boston-based Woman's Era Club brought hundreds of Black women together for the First National Conference of Colored Women of America. There, host Josephine St. Pierre Ruffin echoed Harper in declaring that "our woman's movement is [a] woman's movement in that it is led and directed by women for the good of women and men, for the benefit of *all* humanity, which is more than any one branch or section of it."[19] The conference led to the formation of the National Association of Colored Women (NACW) in 1896, which Paula Giddings describes as "a watershed in the history of Black women," bringing pioneering figures such as Harper and Harriet Tubman together with new voices such as Mary Church Terrell, Ida B. Wells-Barnett, and Alice Dunbar-Nelson.[20] Hopkins, who had attended the group's first meeting in 1895, was one of these new voices. Serving from 1900 to 1904 as a writer and editor for the groundbreaking Black periodical *Colored American Magazine,* Hopkins used her position to run a "Woman's Department" column, report regularly on the activities of the NACW, write essays on Black female and male contributions to human history, and publish her own novels in serial form, including *Of One Blood.*

Like its title, the plot of *Of One Blood* appears, at first glance, convoluted. Reuel Briggs is a seemingly white Harvard medical student with a penchant

---

16. Early, "Organized Efforts," 720. See also VanderHaagen, "'Grand Sisterhood,'" 1–2.
17. Carby, *Reconstructing Womanhood,* 70; and Harper, "Woman's Political Future," 46.
18. Harper, "Woman's Political Future," 43. See, for example, Gates, "In Her Own Write," xxii.
19. Ruffin, "Address," 14, emphasis in original.
20. Giddings, *When and Where I Enter,* 95. See also Bacon, "'One Great Bundle of Humanity,'" 42.

for mysticism. His education is financed by a wealthy friend named Aubrey Livingston, also seemingly white. Early on in the novel, Reuel draws on his mystical knowledge to raise a woman from the dead, but she loses her memory in the process. Reuel and Aubrey recognize the woman as a very light-skinned Black woman named Dianthe Lusk, but they decide to conceal her identity from her so that Reuel can pass her off as white and marry her. It turns out, though, that Reuel is also Black, passing as white, and Aubrey uses this knowledge to force Reuel to accept a job on a two-year expedition to Ethiopia. While Reuel is off in Ethiopia with their white friend Charlie Vance and their Black servant Jim Titus, Aubrey murders his own white fiancée, Molly Vance, and forces Dianthe to marry him rather than Reuel. Dianthe then discovers that both Reuel and Aubrey are her brothers—all three of them children of Aubrey's father and an enslaved woman named Mira—and that Aubrey was switched at birth with the former plantation's legal heir. Dianthe tries to poison Aubrey, but he forces her to drink the poison instead. Meanwhile, in Ethiopia, Reuel discovers that he is the long-lost king of the hidden city of Telassar, home of the descendants of the ancient city of Meroe. He returns too late to save Dianthe but takes revenge on Aubrey and then returns to Ethiopia, where he marries an Ethiopian queen named Candace and awaits "the advance of mighty nations penetrating the dark, mysterious forests of his native land."[21]

Within this complicated plot, "of one blood" refers not only to the novel's seemingly opposed claims about distinct African bloodlines and shared human kinship, but also to Dianthe's incestuous relationships with Reuel and Aubrey. Scholars typically understand the novel's obsession with blood in terms of the nineteenth-century debate about the common (monogenetic) or distinct (polygenetic) origin of the races. Abolitionists and later Black rights activists often invoked the biblical idea of common humanity, arguing as Frances E. W. Harper did in 1866 that "we are all bound up together in one great bundle of humanity," a sentiment she linked in later speeches to the "Christian idea of human brotherhood."[22] The so-called science of polygenesis was developed by defenders of slavery at the height of the abolitionist movement and revived by Frederick L. Hoffman's *Race Traits and Tendencies* in 1896.[23] Hopkins was deeply engaged in refuting this racist pseudoscience, drawing heavily on Black author Martin Delany's earlier *Principia of Ethnology* (1879) in her own *Primer of Facts Pertaining to the Early Greatness of the*

---

21. Hopkins, *Of One Blood*, 193.
22. Harper, "We Are All Bound Up Together," 217; and Harper, "Great Problem to Be Solved," 220.
23. See Hoffman, *Race Traits and Tendencies*, v–viii.

African Race (1905), and quoting Harper's humanistic speeches in her writing for the *Colored American Magazine*.[24] *Of One Blood*'s narrator also invokes the biblical idea of monogenesis near the novel's end, saying: "'Of one blood have I made all nations of men to dwell upon the whole face of the earth,' is as true today as when given to the inspired writers to be recorded. No man can draw the dividing line between the two races, for they are both of one blood!"[25] But viewing the novel through the lens of monogenesis alone not only obscures the novel's investment in the positive value of Reuel's royal African "blood" but also renders the novel's incest plot illegible.

In fact, the novel's double or even triple meaning of "blood" is no contradiction but a clever challenge to the nation's strategic deployments of both racial difference (of which polygenesis is one example) and human sameness (of which monogenesis is one example) to justify the nation's abuse of its Black family members. As Daylanne English points out:

> Although in recent years scholars of Hopkins's fiction have focused almost exclusively on biological discourses of the body, race, and sexuality . . . perhaps no African American novelist at the time was more preoccupied with racial identity as constructed by the law than she was. Three of [her] four novels culminate in trials, with their plots turning so regularly on legal decisions that the processes of law, detection, and punishment actually threaten to submerge the discourses of blood, race, and genealogy.[26]

Of One Blood is the only one of these four novels that does not culminate in a trial or concern legal decisions, but English's attention to the legal dimensions of Hopkins's other novels illuminates Hopkins's use of the language of "blood" to resonate both with the racist pseudoscience of the nineteenth century and with post-Reconstruction legal discourse about national kinship.[27] The implicit aim of the 1896 *Plessy v. Ferguson* decision was to find a way to maintain a white supremacist vision of the nation despite constitutional amendments that outlawed that vision. *Plessy* brought about that aim by excluding Black people from the national family under the guise of their supposed inclusion, which it achieved in three key steps: by denying the role the law played

---

24. See Delany, *Principia of Ethnology,* 9–10, 19–22, 47–53, 83–91; Hopkins, *Primer of Facts*; and Hopkins, "Famous Women: Educators," 213.
25. Hopkins, *Of One Blood*, 178.
26. English, *Each Hour Redeem*, 67.
27. For a helpful discussion of the ways in which the term *pseudoscience* "obscures the emergence of scientific fields out of nonscientific contexts" and "the processes by which these fields are legitimated as science," see Rusert, "Delany's Comet," 803.

in producing racial inequities; by naturalizing the association of racial difference with racial inferiority; and by naturalizing the association of humanity, social equality, and merit with whiteness. If the court was able to naturalize the association of Blackness with inferiority and whiteness with humanity by hiding the law's role in constructing those identities, the value of extralegal discourses such as novels lay precisely in their ability to reveal what the *Plessy* decision hid. For Hopkins and her contemporaries, novels revealed human lives to be historically and legally situated, thereby disrupting the naturalized notions of Black inferiority and white humanity upon which the logic of segregation depended.

Before the Fourteenth Amendment, Black people's exclusion from the national family did not have to be hidden because it was seen as the natural extension of their presumed exclusion from the human family. For example, in the *Dred Scott* decision of 1857, Chief Justice Roger Brooke Taney argued that those of African ancestry were "a subordinate and inferior class of beings" and were therefore not part of the "people of the United States."[28] While Taney admitted that the Declaration of Independence "would seem to embrace the whole human family," he argued that this only proved that people of African descent "were not intended to be included" in that "family," and that they were not "endowed" with the "unalienable rights" of "life, liberty, and the pursuit of happiness."[29] Given the *Dred Scott* decision's conception of the national family and the human family as overlapping categories, the Fourteenth Amendment's extension of the rights of citizenship to formerly enslaved people meant that the nation was being called to widen its understanding of the national family and the human family alike.

Plessy resisted this more inclusive understanding of the national family by hiding legal constructions of racial inferiority beneath a professed commitment to the "equality of the two races before the law."[30] According to the court, even if "the object of the [Fourteenth] [A]mendment was undoubtedly to enforce the absolute equality of the two races before the law," it could not "in the nature of things" have been "intended to abolish distinctions based upon color, or to enforce social, as distinguished from political, equality, or a commingling of the two races upon terms unsatisfactory to either."[31] By claiming that racial discrimination was a "social" (i.e., private) issue rather than a "political" (i.e., public) one, *Plessy* enabled the nation to publicly endorse the equal humanity of Black citizens while simultaneously endorsing naturalized

---

28. Dred Scott v. Sandford, 60 U.S. 393 (1856).
29. Dred Scott v. Sandford, 60 U.S. 393 (1856).
30. Plessy v. Ferguson, 163 U.S. 537 (1896).
31. Plessy v. Ferguson, 163 U.S. 537 (1896).

perceptions of racial inferiority among private individuals. In the opinion of the court, "Legislation is powerless to eradicate racial instincts, or to abolish distinctions based upon physical differences, and the attempt to do so can only result in accentuating the difficulties of the present situation. . . . If one race be inferior to the other socially, the Constitution of the United States cannot put them upon the same plane."[32] In reality, of course, states also used legalized perceptions of "social" inequality to prohibit Black access to a range of legal rights. By claiming that the law was responsible for "political" recognition but not "social" recognition, *Plessy* hid the role the law played in protecting and producing inequality. *Plessy* hid its legal exclusion of Black Americans from the national family behind a public commitment to their inclusion.

Because the state refused to be held responsible for the very "social" perceptions of racial inferiority that it legalized, it also held Black citizens individually responsible for these perceptions. For example, when the plaintiff argued that "the enforced separation of the two races stamps the colored race with a badge of inferiority" and thereby contradicts the Thirteenth Amendment's protection against "burdens or disabilities that constitute badges of slavery or servitude," the court recast this critique of the law as a critique of Black people: "If this be so, it is not by reason of anything found in the act, but solely because the colored race chooses to put that construction upon it."[33] Were the legal situation reversed, the court argued, "the white race, at least, would not acquiesce in this assumption."[34] With this claim, the court implied not only that perceptions of Black inferiority were independent of Black legal status, but also that any request for public involvement in the matter constituted a tacit admission of that inferiority. The court's ruling thereby suggested that Black Americans were individually responsible for their failure to meet white people "upon terms of social equality," and that their resistance to segregation laws was further proof of their social inferiority because it indicated their inability to achieve social equality without the state's help.[35] *Plessy*'s denial of the law's responsibility created an environment in which both Black submission and Black resistance to Jim Crow laws could be perceived as proof of racial inequality.

Another reason that *Plessy*'s discourse of social equality was so effective at maintaining white supremacy was that it gave the power to "recognize" Black social equality to white Americans. A similar example of this logic is found in Booker T. Washington's 1895 "Atlanta Exposition Address," in which

---

32. Plessy v. Ferguson, 163 U.S. 537 (1896).
33. Plessy v. Ferguson, 163 U.S. 537 (1896).
34. Plessy v. Ferguson, 163 U.S. 537 (1896).
35. Plessy v. Ferguson, 163 U.S. 537 (1896).

Washington argued, as the *Plessy* decision would one year later, that racial equality must be earned: "It is important and right that all privileges of the law be ours, but it is vastly more important that we be prepared for the exercises of these privileges."[36] When recounting that speech six years later in his autobiography, *Up from Slavery* (1901), Washington justified his patience in this matter by asserting his faith in the humanity of those white people responsible for bestowing these privileges: "The Atlanta officials . . . felt it to be a pleasure, as well as a duty, to reward what they considered merit in the Negro race. Say what we will, there is something in human nature which we cannot blot out, which makes one man, in the end, recognize and reward merit in another, regardless of colour or race."[37] Washington's assertion of a common "human nature" that will "recognize and reward merit in another" coincides with *Plessy*'s assertion that "if the two races are to meet upon terms of social equality, it must be the result of natural affinities, a mutual appreciation of each other's merits, and a voluntary consent of individuals."[38] Both arguments gave white people sole authority to judge Black merit while implying that since white people will "naturally" reward merit where it is due, their failure to do so must mean that Black people were not yet deserving of that reward.

Washington's accommodation of this white supremacist logic was fiercely critiqued by his Black peers in the North, especially by Hopkins, who served in major editorial roles at the *Colored American Magazine* from 1900 to 1904, and W. E. B. Du Bois and Ida B. Wells-Barnett, both founding members of the Niagara Movement in 1905 and the National Association for the Advancement of Colored People (NAACP) in 1909. As Du Bois argued, "the distinct impression left by Mr. Washington's propaganda is . . . that the South is justified in its present attitude toward the Negro because of the Negro's degradation" and that his "future rise depends primarily on his own efforts."[39] Wells-Barnett further insisted that such efforts would never be rewarded so long as white people retained the power of measuring Black merit, writing: "[Washington] sets up the dogma that when the race becomes taxpayers, producers of something the white man wants, landowners, business, etc., the Anglo-Saxon will forget all about color and respect that race's manhood."[40] In fact, she argued, when Southern papers discussed "the separate street car law . . . it was not the servant or working class of Negroes, who know their places, with whom the white people objected to riding, but the educated, property-owning Negro who

---

36. Washington, *Up from Slavery*, 223–24.
37. Washington, *Up from Slavery*, 235.
38. Plessy v. Ferguson, 163 U.S. 537 (1896).
39. Du Bois, *Souls of Black Folk*, 49.
40. Wells-Barnett, "Booker T. Washington and His Critics," 520.

thought himself the white man's equal."⁴¹ She understood that segregationists were using the putatively colorblind notion of merit to maintain Black subordination—preventing rather than aiding Black Americans' attainment of the "full recognition of [their] political rights."⁴² As Du Bois and Wells-Barnett knew, the notions of common humanity and colorblind merit to which Washington appealed acted as a mask for white value systems and positions of power.

In contrast to Washington's view of segregation as a step "up from slavery," Hopkins, Wells-Barnett, and Du Bois argued that the transformation of political inequality into social inequality maintained many of the dehumanizing structures of slavery by another name, and that it was Black intellectuals' responsibility to make this known.⁴³ As Hopkins put it in her preface to her first novel, *Contending Forces,* "The difference between then and now, if any there be, is so slight as to be scarcely worth mentioning. The atrocity of the acts committed one hundred years ago are [sic] duplicated today, when slavery is supposed to no longer exist."⁴⁴ Even worse, as Black novelist Charles Chesnutt argued in "The Courts and the Negro" (1908), while "the opinion in Plessy vs. Ferguson is, to my mind, as epoch-making as the Dred Scott decision . . . it applies to a class of rights which do not make to the heart and conscience of the nation the same direct appeal as was made by slavery, and has not been nor is likely to produce any such revulsion of feeling."⁴⁵ Black intellectuals therefore felt it necessary to demonstrate what the *Plessy* decision had denied, that Jim Crow laws constituted a "badge of slavery or servitude," and the novel became one of the most prominent outlets for that work.⁴⁶ Because the novel enabled writers to interrogate the "individual's negotiation of period-specific material and social conditions," its value lay both in its ability to represent Black people as "modern individuals" rather than as objects of abjection and in its ability to insist on the power that legal and sociohistorical circumstances played in their lives—a power that the *Plessy* decision denied.⁴⁷

The perceived political value of the novel and literature more broadly is also evident in the speeches and essays that were circulating in the Black women's clubs and national conventions with which Hopkins was associated. As early as 1892, the year that Homer Plessy violated Louisiana's Separate Car Act, Black women's rights activist Anna Julia Cooper dedicated a chapter of

---

41. Wells-Barnett, "Booker T. Washington and His Critics," 520.
42. Washington, *Up from Slavery,* 235.
43. For more on Du Bois's efforts, see Blackmon, *Slavery by Another Name,* 245, 270–77.
44. Hopkins, preface to *Contending Forces,* 15.
45. Chesnutt, "Courts and the Negro," 902.
46. Plessy v. Ferguson, 163 U.S. 537 (1896).
47. English, *Each Hour Redeem,* 51. See also Armstrong, *How Novels Think,* 10.

her book, *A Voice from the South*, to the topic of literature, arguing that literature written by Black people could represent both the universal humanity of Black people and the "adverse winds of circumstances" that they endured, both of which *Plessy* was designed to obscure.[48] Likewise, in Victoria Earle Matthews's 1895 speech, "The Value of Race Literature," delivered at the first Congress of Colored Women in Boston, Matthews argued that it was through the literary exposition of "the unnaturally suppressed inner lives which our people have been compelled to lead" that their literature would "stand out pre-eminent . . . in the broader field of universal literature."[49] Whereas *Plessy* and Washington argued that Black Americans would earn social equality once they had proven their equal value, Cooper and Matthews argued that their equal value would only be recognized once they had exposed the unnatural, suppressive, compulsory, and inherently unequal forces shaping Black life. Hopkins drew on Matthews's argument in her preface to *Contending Forces*, taking up the call "to raise the stigma of degradation from my race" by turning to "the simple, homely tale, unassumingly told, which cements the bond of brotherhood among all classes and all complexions."[50] Unlike Washington, who downplayed the value of the arts for Black people and aligned the notion of "brotherhood" with "the guidance that the strong can give the weak," Hopkins and her Black female peers argued that literature could help cement a vision of human commonality that places on equal rather than unequal footing "all classes and complexions" of human experience.[51] Moreover, unlike the leaders of the American Negro Academy, a Black organization formed in 1897 "for the promotion of Letters, Science, and Art" that limited its membership to "*men* of African descent," Hopkins and her female peers believed that the literature of "the open-eyed but hitherto voiceless Black Woman of America" made up an "essential" part of that chorus.[52]

Of One Blood must be understood as a Black woman's attempt to articulate this inclusive model of human "brotherhood," beginning with the ways

---

48. Cooper, *Voice from the South*, 223.

49. Matthews, "Value of Race Literature," 173. A few years later, Frances E. W. Harper, author of one of the very first novels authored by a Black woman (*Iola Leroy*, 1892) and inspirational force behind the NACW, also gave a speech on "Racial Literature" at the NACW's second convention. See National Association of Colored Women, Minutes of the Second Convention, Daniel Murray Pamphlet Collection.

50. Hopkins, preface to *Contending Forces*, 13.

51. Washington, "Democracy and Education," 371; and Hopkins, preface to *Contending Forces*, 13.

52. Moss, *American Negro Academy*, 1, 38, quoted in Washington, *Invented Lives*, xviii, emphasis in original; and Cooper, *Voice from the South*, 2. See also McHenry, *Forgotten Readers*, 191–203.

in which the novel's embrace of both racial particularity and shared humanity works to challenge *Plessy*'s implicit conflation of whiteness with humanity, while also challenging *Plessy*'s implicit conflation of racial difference with racial inferiority. Hopkins's interest in both racial particularity and shared humanity also explains some of the presumed contradictions in her larger body of work, such as why she wrote novels about light-skinned heroines as well as articles promoting Black and Pan-African pride.[53] *Of One Blood* draws these genres together. It is a passing novel that refutes the perceived universality and superiority of white "blood" and culture by insisting on the particular value of Black identity and history. It shows that, in a world built on white supremacy, it is only via the embrace of Black people's particularities that a functional concept of shared humanity can be formed.[54] As she put it in her article on "The Dark Races of the Twentieth Century" (1905), these are "men who will teach the Anglo-Saxon that 'all men were created equal' and that '*all men*' are not *white* men."[55] Furthermore, as she made clear in her novels and articles dedicated to documenting the particularities of Black female experience, "*all men*" were not all *men*.

Incest and the "Hidden Self"

In *Of One Blood*, *Plessy* appears in the novel's representation of the anti-Black logic of the "hidden self." Although most critics compare Reuel's "hidden" African self to Du Bois's "double consciousness"—"an American, a Negro, two souls, two thoughts, two unreconciled strivings; two warring ideals in one dark body"—Reuel is equally well-described by the second definition that Du Bois gives: the "sense of always looking at one's self through the eyes of others, of measuring one's soul by the tape of a world that looks on in amused contempt and pity."[56] Reuel looks at himself through such eyes. When asked

---

53. See, for example, Hopkins, "Famous Men of the Negro Race"; Hopkins, "Famous Women of the Negro Race"; Hopkins, "Dark Races of the Twentieth Century"; and Hopkins, *Primer of Facts*.

54. Even in articles devoted to defining the distinctness of "the Negro," "Dark," or "African Race," Hopkins declares Black biographies and histories to be evidence of the "brotherhood of man" and the "unity of mankind" (Hopkins, "Famous Men of the Negro Race," 358; Hopkins, *Primer of Facts*, 336; and Hopkins, "Dark Races of the Twentieth Century," 331).

55. Hopkins, "Dark Races of the Twentieth Century," 330, emphasis in original.

56. Du Bois, "Strivings of the Negro People" (1897); reprinted as "Of Our Spiritual Strivings" in *Souls of Black Folk*, 5. "The hidden self" phrase is borrowed from an 1890 William James essay on dissociative disorder that also influenced Du Bois's theory of "double consciousness." See Gillman, "Pauline Hopkins and the Occult," 70–76; McDowell, introduction to *Of One Blood*, xiv; and Schrager, "Pauline Hopkins and William James."

in the first pages of the novel why he never speaks about the "Negro problem," he replies that he has a "horror of discussing the woes of unfortunates, tramps, stray dogs and cats and Negroes—probably because I am an unfortunate myself."[57] Reuel not only keeps his race hidden by calling himself an "unfortunate" rather than Black but also affirms a perspective that sees Black people as "unfortunate" and nothing else. The "hidden self," then, is a repression of Blackness that Reuel enacts not just by passing or hiding his Black identity, but by fully adopting the perspective of anti-Black "contempt and pity" upon which *Plessy* covertly insisted.[58]

Reuel's "contempt and pity" toward Blackness is reflected both in his act of passing and in his imperialist and patriarchal attitude toward Africa.[59] Aubrey tries to tempt Reuel into the trip to Ethiopia with the idea of the "good it will do to the Negro race," but Reuel is more interested in fulfilling his "dreams of wealth and ambition" by "unearthing gems and gold" that he could "carry home to lay at a little woman's feet."[60] "Seen through Reuel's eyes," argues Hanna Wallinger, "the expedition's first view of Africa combines the average Anglo Saxon-American fascination with exotic surroundings and an awareness of . . . its 'uncivilized' status."[61] However, Reuel's perspective importantly changes once he discovers the truth of his family's ancestry and Aubrey's deception. He berates himself for abandoning Dianthe to Aubrey in order "to search for gold" and feels a "flush of shame" for having hidden "his origin" merely to overcome the social and economic "difficulties of caste prejudice."[62] He comes to recognize that, in occupying the role of the white patriarchal imperialist, he has secured his individual success at the cost of maintaining power structures that exploit Black Americans and Africans: "He felt keenly now the fact that he had played the coward's part."[63]

Importantly, Reuel's revaluation of his "hidden self" is not merely an affirmation of his Black "blood" but an articulation of humanity and human civilization that includes rather than excludes Black people and Black history. Reuel insists in the first pages of the novel that "the wonders of a material world cannot approach those of the undiscovered country within ourselves—the hidden self lying quiescent in every human soul."[64] Critics often read "the

---

57. Hopkins, *Of One Blood*, 9.
58. Du Bois, *Souls of Black Folk*, 5.
59. See Gaines, "Black Americans' Racial Uplift Ideology," 445; Harris, "Not Black and/or White," 387–88; and Japtok, "Pauline Hopkins's *Of One Blood*," 404–5, 412–13.
60. Hopkins, *Of One Blood*, 59, 138, 60, 83.
61. Wallinger, *Pauline E. Hopkins*, 213.
62. Hopkins, *Of One Blood*, 148, 129.
63. Hopkins, *Of One Blood*, 129.
64. Hopkins, *Of One Blood*, 7.

undiscovered country within ourselves" as a reference to Ethiopia, the "hidden self" that Reuel has repressed by passing as white, but Reuel insists that this "hidden self" lies "in *every* human soul."[65] As Charlie discovers in Ethiopia, the knowledge of his "white" ancestors—"Romans, Greeks, Hebrews, Germans and Anglo-Saxons"—was "pioneered" by "Babylon and Egypt" and "Ethiopia."[66] This means that Black civilization lies hidden—or contemptuously repressed—at the heart of Western civilization as much as Black "blood" lies hidden within Reuel and Aubrey's white bodies.

If blood-based and culture-based accounts of Blackness are being conflated here by Reuel's, Aubrey's, and Charlie's different connections to Ethiopia, this is because Hopkins's novel purposefully rehistoricizes both biological and sociocultural accounts of racial difference. For example, Charlie finally acknowledges his "hidden self" only after he is forced to encounter the sociohistorical construction of his whiteness. To begin with, he cannot believe that Africans can produce wealth and civilization because of his stereotypical understanding of Blackness: "'Great Scott!' cried Charlie, 'you don't mean to tell me that all this was done by *ni**ers?*'"[67] Thereafter, his response is to say "nothing. He had suffered so many shocks from the shattering of cherished idols since entering the country of mysteries that the power of expression had left him."[68] These discoveries force Charlie to re-evaluate his presumptions about Black inferiority and white supremacy. When he later discovers that the lost Ethiopian city of Telassar possesses a trove of priceless jewels, but that he is unexpectedly powerless to take them, he also begins to re-evaluate his relationship to Jim Titus, a Black servant described in the novel as "a Negro of the old régime who felt that the Anglo-Saxon was appointed by God to rule over the African."[69] As Charlie says to Jim, "Here we've been romping around for almost six months after this very treasure, and now we've got it we can't hold it. . . . I for one, give in beaten. Left, I should say so; badly left, when I counted Africa a played-out hole in the ground."[70] For Charlie, white racism and imperialism had been naturalized by his experience of Black economic exploitation and dependence; to think otherwise, Charlie believes, would be "lunatic."[71]

---

65. Hopkins, *Of One Blood*, 7, emphasis added. See Japtok, "Pauline Hopkins's *Of One Blood*," 407; Kassanoff, "'Fate Has Linked Us Together,'" 169; Otten, "Pauline Hopkins and the Hidden Self," 244; Schrager, "Pauline Hopkins and William James," 198; and Sundquist, *To Wake the Nations*, 573.
66. Hopkins, *Of One Blood*, 98.
67. Hopkins, *Of One Blood*, 99, emphasis in original, redaction added.
68. Hopkins, *Of One Blood*, 101.
69. Hopkins, *Of One Blood*, 78.
70. Hopkins, *Of One Blood*, 159.
71. Hopkins, *Of One Blood*, 154.

However, once Charlie is stripped of the tools of conquest and domination to which he has become accustomed, his discovery of Ethiopian wealth can no longer be absorbed into this naturalized framework of European domination:

> [Charlie] spoke in jest, but the tears were in his eyes, and as he clasped Jim's toil-hardened black hand, he told himself that [the prime minister of Telessar's] words were true. Where was the color line now? Jim was a brother; the nearness of their desolation in this uncanny land, left nothing but a feeling of brotherhood. He felt then the truth of the words, "Of one blood have I made all races of men."[72]

This "uncanny" removal of Black economic dependency teaches Charlie that his naturalized understanding of "the color line" is dependent on historically specific circumstances. Without Charlie's social and economic dominance, the previously naturalized inequality between Charlie and Jim disappears: "The nearness of their desolation in this uncanny land . . . left nothing but a feeling of brotherhood."[73] In this way, the novel converts contemptuously repressed Black blood like Reuel's and contemptuously repressed Black cultures like Telassar's into visible Black histories: it makes the "hidden self" unhidden.

The difference between these two states, of being hidden or unhidden, also explains the difference between the two meanings of blood brotherhood as a site of equality or as a site of incest. It is clear that the slippage between the two models of "brotherhood" is intentional since, when the incest is revealed, the revelation comes in the form of the novel's title: "Did each of Mira's children have this mark?" Dianthe asks. Aunt Hannah replies, "Yes, honey; all of one blood!"[74] Here, the idea that they are "all of one blood" is "too horrible"; as Susan Gillman argues, it is "a horror."[75] Less than a page later, the narrator chimes in with a more hopeful vision of the phrase, which Gillman describes as "a promise," claiming that "no man can draw the dividing line between the two races, for they are both of one blood!"[76] And yet, these two models of blood brotherhood do not contradict one another, as critics often assume.[77] Rather, for Hopkins, incest is what happens when brothers and sisters don't act like brothers and sisters, in this case, because they don't recognize each other *as* brothers and sisters. It is not their failure to recognize each other as

---

72. Hopkins, *Of One Blood*, 159.
73. Hopkins, *Of One Blood*, 159.
74. Hopkins, *Of One Blood*, 177.
75. Hopkins, *Of One Blood*, 178; and Gillman, "Pauline Hopkins and the Occult," 63.
76. Gillman, "Pauline Hopkins and the Occult," 63; and Hopkins, *Of One Blood*, 178.
77. See, for example, Kassanoff, "'Fate Has Linked Us Together,'" 170–71.

racially distinct that is the problem, but their failure to recognize each other as family. The recognition of their "brotherhood," in Hopkins's terms, is the *solution* to the incest problem, a recognition that the novel shows is, in turn, based on the recognition of "Black" histories. If the invisibility of Black history is used to justify the abuse of Black members of the American family, then making Black history visible is necessary to reform that family.

Reading Hopkins's treatment of incest as a critique of the nation makes sense when we consider that Hopkins uses families as metaphors for the nation in all of her other fiction.[78] As Claudia Tate has argued, nineteenth-century African American domestic fiction often functioned as an allegory for Black political desires.[79] For example, in "Talma Gordon" (1900), Hopkins uses the murder of Captain Gordon to suggest the impending doom of "this old Republic."[80] Just like the Republic, Gordon bears responsibility for the destruction of his family because his imperialism and racism have betrayed the "law of heredity that makes us all one common family."[81] By contrast, the doctor's interracial marriage to Talma Gordon promises to be a "re-formation of this old Republic" more in tune with that larger "law."[82] "Talma Gordon" shows that a politically just conception of the national family must follow from the "God-implanted instinct that made Adam . . . accept Eve as bone of his bone," even as it also insists that the nation's current familial structure prevents rather than protects equal rights.[83] Likewise, the invisibility of Black history in *Of One Blood* reflects *Plessy*'s naturalization of legally produced perceptions of racial inferiority. Both render invisible the historical and legal forces that promote naturalized perceptions of Black inferiority and prevent the achievement of Black equal rights. *Of One Blood* argues that so long as Black histories are kept invisible, Black people will not be treated as the members of the national family that *Plessy* publicly proclaimed them to be.

Although Hopkins uses the language of brotherhood as a model for the national family, her critique of Aubrey's family also indicates her awareness of how this language could be misused. Exploitative and exclusive uses of familial language in nineteenth-century American thought are numerous, not only in the *Dred Scott* decision but also in Abraham Lincoln's 1858 metaphor of the

---

78. On the use of familial metaphors in *Contending Forces* (1900), see Sawaya, *Modern Women, Modern Work*, 46–47. On *Winona* (1902–3), see English, *Each Hour Redeem*, 74–76. *Hagar's Daughter* (1901–2) also uses familial mother-daughter language in its title to describe the kinship between antebellum and postbellum America.
79. See Tate, *Domestic Allegories*, 14–15.
80. Hopkins, "Talma Gordon," 273.
81. Hopkins, "Talma Gordon," 273.
82. Hopkins, "Talma Gordon," 273.
83. Hopkins, "Talma Gordon," 273.

nation as "a house divided" not between enslaved and free, but between white opponents and supporters of slavery.[84] Such descriptions of the Civil War as a white family divided over the issue of slavery, later made famous in Thomas Dixon's 1905 novel, *The Clansman*, were compounded by the rise of Social Darwinism and eugenics in the late nineteenth century. For eugenicists, white Americans were the only legitimate members of the American family, and the presence of Black people and immigrants within the nation threatened the "blood" of the family unit. Other contemporaneous conceptions of the national family nominally included Black people in the American family but insisted on their subservience to white family members. As historian Grace Hale shows, late nineteenth-century plantation fiction and Southern histories ensconced Black Americans in the sociocultural position of the "dependent" child as a way of naturalizing Black subordination in the guise of "family" and friendship.[85] Segregation was seen as a kind of childhood, out of which Black people may one day emerge into full adult citizenship. Exclusionary laws such as segregation and immigration restriction acts were justified as preventing the deterioration of American blood or protecting the nation's children from self-destruction. Whether these models of the national family employed biological or sociocultural visions of Black inferiority, they barred Black Americans from equal participation.

Hopkins observed this latter version of the national family in her reports for the *Colored American Magazine* on the exclusion of the NACWC from the General Federation of Women's Clubs (GFWC). In her reports, Lincoln's logic of familial reconciliation re-emerged in the justification one white member gave for this exclusion: "The North and the South are re-united; and we cannot afford to take any action that will lead to more bitter feeling. . . . We must not, and I feel that the delegates will not, do anything that threatens disruption of the federation of which we are all so proud."[86] Another white member defended this decision by declaring:

> This is not a question of color, it is a question of an embryonic race, not yet strong enough to stand with us. . . . The Negroes are by nature imitators. If we admit them to associations with us, they will lose their power of independent development and become merely followers of the whites. They have not yet reached a plane on which they can compete with us and maintain

---

84. Lincoln, "House Divided," 372. See also Kramer, *Nationalism in Europe and America*, 102–24.

85. Hale, *Making Whiteness*, 61, 75.

86. Hopkins, "Famous Women: Educators," 210. See also Hopkins, "Echoes from the Annual Convention," 712–13.

their own independence. The best thing we can do for them is to let them go on developing along their own lines. Then when they have . . . won their way up, where they can stand on equal footing with us, let us consider their admission.[87]

In her response, Hopkins asserted that "behind windy, grandiloquent speeches of belief in the equality of the human species" there "dwelt a spirit of perverseness that might at any moment break forth to our undoing."[88] In another article in the series, she further argued that when the world "tells us in derision that when we have proven our ability, then we shall be admitted to the brotherhood of men on an equal footing with other races," it demonstrates that it is "willfully blind and perverse."[89] In other words, Hopkins was well aware that statements "of belief in the equality of the human species" and "the brotherhood of man" could be used to exclude rather than include.[90]

Hopkins's editorials suggest that *Of One Blood*'s overarching metaphor of brotherhood and family was fashioned to resonate with both human sameness and racial difference precisely to differentiate itself from the exclusive and exploitative accounts of the national family then in circulation. In one of her later reports on the NACWC's exclusion from the GFWC, Hopkins drew on the language of human equality she had previously critiqued. However, her use of that language was quite different:

> We hope the time is not far distant when the women of African descent will meet in a General Federation, and pray, with unwavering trust in the Fatherhood of God and the brotherhood of man: "Lord, from the four corners of the world we have come to this convention, as representing the homes of the world. It is to these homes the effects of this meeting, for good or for evil, will go. May many homes be made stronger and sweeter, may many crooked ways be made straight, by what we shall do and say here."[91]

Hopkins's vision of the human family was one that includes the many "homes of the world." Likewise, there were frequent references throughout the first volumes of *Colored American Magazine* to "common brotherhood" and

---

87. Hopkins, "Famous Women: Educators," 210–11, ellipsis in original. See also Hopkins, "Famous Women: Club Life," 275.
88. Hopkins, "Famous Women: Educators," 212.
89. Hopkins, "Famous Women: Artists," 366.
90. On a similar point about the "falseness" of certain "affective appeal[s] to family" and "fraternal language" in *Contending Forces*, see Sawaya, *Modern Women, Modern Work*, 50–51.
91. Hopkins, "Echoes from the Annual Convention," 713.

the "brotherhood of man," many made by Hopkins herself, but such declarations of Black people's "equality with the rest of the sons of Adam" were always accompanied by declarations of race "pride" and "brotherly love" for the "race."[92] Indeed, the magazine's purpose, its first issue proclaimed, was to "intensify the bonds of that racial brotherhood, which alone can enable a people to assert their racial rights as men and demand their privileges as citizens."[93] For the magazine, as for Hopkins, "racial brotherhood" and "human brotherhood" were not mutually exclusive. As Du Bois would put it in his "Strivings of the Negro People" (1897): "Work, culture, liberty,—all these we need, not singly but together, not successively but together, each growing and aiding each, and all striving toward that vaster ideal that swims before the Negro people, the ideal of human brotherhood, gained through the unifying ideal of Race."[94] Without the public recognition of racial particularity, the ideal of "human brotherhood" served only as a mask for the continued exclusion and exploitation of Black people, much as *Plessy*'s publicly "colorblind" pretension revealed.

Like Hopkins's nonfiction, *Of One Blood* explores both the danger and the potential of "human brotherhood" by contrasting incestuous familial relationships with more appropriately brotherly ones. In the novel, so long as Black "blood" remains invisible, the ideal of "human brotherhood" functions as a duplicitous tool that maintains the exclusionary injustice of slavery in a new guise. Aubrey's relationship with Dianthe—a sister whom he has enslaved to his sexual will—is a repetition of Aubrey's father's relationship with Mira—his father's enslaved half-sister. The only difference between Aubrey's father and Aubrey is that Aubrey has acted under a "mask of friendship."[95] When Aunt Hannah insists that "dese things jes' got to happen in slavery," the novel suggests that what was done in the open under slavery may now require a "mask of friendship," but the underlying structure remains unchanged.[96] This was one of the key arguments made by the plaintiff in the *Plessy v. Ferguson* case, that segregation laws covertly imposed a "badge of slavery or servitude" upon Black people. Segregation may seem to be about "marking" rather than "hiding" Blackness, but *Plessy* preserved the inferior legal status of Black Americans by "hiding" that inferior status's relationship to the law. At a national level, then, the logic of segregation is the same as that of the "hidden self": Black Americans, cordoned off in separate train cars, are the "hidden self" of

---

92. Hopkins, "Famous Men," 358, 366; and Elliot, "Story of Our Magazine," 44–45.
93. "Editorial and Publishers' Announcements," 60.
94. Du Bois, *Souls of Black Folk*, 11.
95. Hopkins, *Of One Blood*, 148.
96. Hopkins, *Of One Blood*, 176, 148.

the nation, that part of the nation about which white Americans are publicly encouraged to feel "contempt and pity."[97] *Of One Blood* argues that taking Black Americans out of "hiding" by ending segregation laws would end the inequality that this structure creates.

Black Women and the "Brotherhood of Man"

Although Hopkins's use of the term *brotherhood* may seem to elide the experience of Black women, Reuel and Aubrey's family importantly includes a sister, and the patriarchal form that their abuse of Dianthe takes suggests that incest—or brothers and sisters acting unlike brothers and sisters—acts as much as a metaphor for white domination as it does for patriarchal domination. The novel's rejection of the Washingtonian model of "racial uplift" thus indicates a refusal to use white values as the standard by which Black communities must be judged, and patriarchal values as the standard by which Black women must be judged. As Kevin Gaines notes, "a central rhetorical strategy of racial uplift ideology" at the turn of the century "was its opposition of racism by invoking conventional gender hierarchies of sexual difference, as this was widely regarded as the behavioral measure of bourgeois civilization."[98] To varying degrees, Hopkins's associates within the NACWC accepted conventional notions of female virtue, domesticity, "respectability," and female deference, but they also did much to challenge these concepts, in part through their own activism.[99] In *Of One Blood*, Dianthe acts out the limitations of using female deference to oppose racism. After she loses her memory, Dianthe is a model of female deference, both "like a child" and treated like one: "With a laugh [Reuel] kissed away her anxieties. . . . 'Don't get excited. That you *must* guard against.'"[100] But Reuel's insistence on Dianthe's deference leads her straight into the abusive arms of Aubrey, whose disregard of his white fiancée Molly and rape of Dianthe are reminiscent of Wells-Barnett's 1895 claim that "no one who reads the record, as it is written in the faces of the million mulattoes in the South, will for a minute conceive that the southern white man had a very chivalrous regard for the honor due the women of his own race or respect for the womanhood which circumstances placed in his power."[101] Washingtonian policies were dangerous because they enabled public blindness

---

97. Du Bois, *Souls of Black Folk*, 5.
98. Gaines, *Uplifting the Race*, 135.
99. See Gaines, *Uplifting the Race*, 135–37.
100. Hopkins, *Of One Blood*, 34, 65, emphasis in original.
101. Wells-Barnett, *Red Record*, 274.

to the legal and historical causes of racial inequality, gave white individuals the power to bestow "merit" on Black communities, and asked Black communities to conform to racist and sexist standards of social organization to earn that recognition.

Reuel and Aubrey enact this form of white and patriarchal domination on Dianthe when they decide to keep her race hidden from her. Because Reuel initially looks at Dianthe's race with "contempt and pity," he claims that he is doing her a favor by refusing to inform her of her identity: "There is no sin in taking her out of the sphere where she was born."[102] As a result, Dianthe becomes entirely dependent on Reuel, asking him to give her "the benefit of" his "powerful will" in the absence of having one of her own.[103] When he proposes, she creeps "into his arms" with "the sigh of a tired child" because she "depended upon him," a dependence that is the direct result of his deceit.[104] That deceit also leads to the more villainous deceit by Aubrey, of whom the narrator eventually declares: "In desperation [Dianthe] tried to defy him, but she knew that she had lost her will-power and was but a puppet in the hands of this false friend."[105] The "contempt and pity" that motivates Reuel to "hide" Black "blood" leads Dianthe into sexual enslavement. Her incestuous abuse at the hands of Reuel and Aubrey shows Black women's vulnerability to white supremacist and patriarchal abuse.

Dianthe's treatment by Reuel also suggests the danger of silencing female voices within the Black community's advocacy for equality. When Reuel first meets Dianthe, it is to hear her sing: "All the horror, the degradation from which a race had been delivered were in the pleading strains of the singer's voice. It strained the senses almost beyond endurance. It pictured to that self-possessed, highly-cultured New England assemblage as nothing else ever had, the awfulness of the hell from which a people had been happily plucked."[106] Dianthe's voice communicates the history of slavery to a "self-possessed, highly cultured" audience accustomed to tuning that history out. Reuel's insistence on hiding Dianthe's identity from her, as a way of making her white and making her *his*, has the effect of silencing that voice: "The grand, majestic voice that had charmed the hearts from thousands of bosoms, was pinioned in the girl's throat like an imprisoned song-bird. Dianthe's voice was completely gone with her memory."[107] Although Reuel imagines that he is raising her "socially

---

102. Du Bois, *Souls of Black Folk*, 5; and Hopkins, *Of One Blood*, 43–44.
103. Hopkins, *Of One Blood*, 40.
104. Hopkins, *Of One Blood*, 56.
105. Hopkins, *Of One Blood*, 69.
106. Hopkins, *Of One Blood*, 15.
107. Hopkins, *Of One Blood*, 55.

above the level to which" she was born, the conformity with white patriarchal values that her "uplift" requires fundamentally negates her interests as a Black woman.[108] Dianthe repeatedly tries to restore her particularity, "to grasp" her "fleeting memories," but Reuel only "closed her lips with warm lingering kisses."[109] Silenced by the act of kissing, Dianthe is denied her equal right to speak. Reuel's incestuous kiss here indicates his misrecognition of Dianthe as his inferior, rather than as his equal, or his family. As Wells-Barnett showed in *A Red Record* (1895), chivalry is a mask for patriarchal violence.[110] Just as Dianthe's treatment points to the dangers of any program of racial uplift that silences Black perspectives in favor of white ones, so does her treatment point to the dangers of any program of racial uplift that silences the voices of Black women and, in so doing, subordinates their interests to the interests of men.

Although some critics have taken issue with Dianthe's weakness as a character, her weakness functions primarily to expose the "badge of servitude" that Hopkins argued was maintained by America's segregation laws. Dianthe may be "far from being a woman who supports herself and survives in the face of past tragedy and victimization like Sappho Clark," the protagonist of *Contending Forces*.[111] But Hopkins's more pessimistic characterization of this later character coincides with her increasingly vocal critique of Washington's self-help narratives, a critique which eventually led to her dismissal from the *Colored American Magazine* once Washington took control of the magazine.[112] Of primary concern to the editor operating under Washington's command was Hopkins's tendency to speak of Black people as a "proscribed race," which he saw as contrary to Washington's belief in self-help.[113] Considered in this context, Dianthe's "proscription" indicates that segregation is not progress "up from slavery" but a repetition of its abuses. *Of One Blood* shows that men who see progress in their individual ability to rise are only sustaining a system that exploits Black men and women. Of course, Dianthe's weakness is also in stark contrast to the apparent strength of Candace, the queen of the hidden African city of Telassar. While some critics have seen Hopkins's deification of Candace as part of a "patently escapist fiction meant to flee the brutality and racism of American history," she just as easily represents Hopkins's hope for America's

---

108. For a similar critique of "patriarchal strictures" in *Contending Forces* and *Iola Leroy*, see duCille, *Coupling Convention*, 32.
109. Hopkins, *Of One Blood*, 65.
110. See Wells-Barnett, *Red Record*, 274.
111. Rich, *Transcending the New Woman*, 100.
112. See Wallinger, *Pauline Hopkins*, 79–94.
113. Hopkins, "How a New York Newspaperman," 155.

future.¹¹⁴ As Melissa Daniels argues, Candace shows "that black women not only have the capacity for political work, but that they are critical conduits of ancestral and cultural knowledge."¹¹⁵ The deification of Candace, who rules over a Black, antimaterialist, and matriarchal African society, does not indicate Hopkins's retreat from American society but her demand that American society be restructured to represent rather than hide Black histories, Black political and philosophical thought, and Black women.

Another female character whose voice is "hidden" is Mira, Dianthe's mother. While Mira is enslaved by Aubrey Sr., he repeatedly throws her "into a trance-state . . . to amuse the guests."¹¹⁶ In this state, she transforms from one socially acceptable stereotype of Black female behavior—"a rather sad Negress, very mild with everyone"—into another one—"a gay, noisy, restless woman, full of irony and sharp jesting."¹¹⁷ Although the latter voice is more outspoken, Aubrey Sr. retains control of that voice by commanding her to "tell the company what you see."¹¹⁸ However, Mira diverges from these two socially acceptable expressions of the Black woman's voice, prophesizing the coming of the Civil War, the South's loss, and Aubrey Sr.'s death. She is punished for this verbal transgression by being "sold . . . just a few months before the secession of the Confederate States."¹¹⁹ Mira's similarity to Dianthe, who is likewise silenced by Reuel and Aubrey, suggests—as Hopkins argued elsewhere—that there is a strong relationship between slavery's and segregation's abuse of Black women. But Mira is not merely a victim of the "hiding" of Black history and Black women's voices; she is also the novel's primary figure for "unhiding." Mira, which means "light" in Hebrew and "look" in Spanish, repeatedly appears in ghost form to draw attention to her hidden existence and to a passage from the Bible that reads: "For there is nothing covered that shall not be revealed, neither hid that shall not be known."¹²⁰ The speaking and silencing of Mira and Dianthe suggest, as Anna Julia Cooper famously declared, that only the Black woman can say "when and where I enter, in the quiet, undisputed dignity of my womanhood, without violence and without suing or special patronage, then and there the whole *Negro race enters with me.*"¹²¹ A functional notion of common humanity must represent rather than

---

114. Sundquist, *To Wake the Nations*, 569.
115. Daniels, "Limits of Literary Realism," 171.
116. Hopkins, *Of One Blood*, 50.
117. Hopkins, *Of One Blood*, 51.
118. Hopkins, *Of One Blood*, 50–51.
119. Hopkins, *Of One Blood*, 51.
120. Hopkins, *Of One Blood*, 73, 168. For more on Mira's role in disrupting the social order, see Kassanoff, "'Fate Has Linked Us Together,'" 174–76.
121. Cooper, *Voice from the South*, 31.

repress Black women's interests, preserving rather than silencing Black female voices. For the Black community to overcome white structures of oppression, Black women must be represented, and they must do that representative work.

Dianthe learns her identity from the ghost of Mira and from Mira's mother, an elderly woman known as Aunt Hannah. Reuel learns his identity from the motherland of Ethiopia. This connection between Ethiopia and the Black mother further suggests that Black history and Black women are equally silenced by white supremacy. In passing fiction of the period, denying one's history often comes at the cost of one's mother. In *Of One Blood,* passing also comes at the cost of Africa, because it requires that Reuel win his social status through the perpetuation of Western imperialism. Contrary to those who see both the novel's and Reuel's final retreat to Africa as indicative of Hopkins's retreat from American politics, Reuel's new relationship with Africa reveals the extent to which Hopkins saw the relationship between African Americans and Africans—as between Black men and Black women, and as between white people and Black people—as containing both the risk of "false friend[ship]" and the potential for "mutual aid and comfort."[122] Transforming false friendship into friendship, the novel shows, depends on the visibility of historically produced particularities.

Where some readers have seen Reuel's ultimate return to "the Hidden City" as the fulfillment of a Black nationalist fantasy, and others have seen him spending "his days in teaching his people all that he has learned in years of contact with modern culture" as an imperialist fantasy, we might understand Reuel as a Du Boisian figure, "a co-worker in the kingdom of culture" who has merged his doubled consciousness in such a way that "neither of the older selves" is "lost": "He would not Africanize America, for America has too much to teach the world and Africa" and "would not bleach his Negro soul in a flood of white Americanism, for he knows that Negro blood has a message for the world."[123] Reuel's position at the end of the novel as an intermediary between America and Africa represents an attempt to merge their two perspectives into one wider whole that does not obscure the particularity of either position. Nevertheless, the novel refuses to give Reuel the unconditionally happy ending that such a reading might imply. Instead, Reuel "views . . . with serious apprehension, the advance of mighty nations penetrating the dark, mysterious forests of his native land."[124] Black history has been "unhidden." An alliance of African and African American leadership has been forged. Perhaps, as editor and novelist Jessie Fauset later hoped after attending the Second Pan-African

---

122. Hopkins, *Of One Blood,* 69, 92, 148; and Hopkins, *Primer of Facts,* 345.

123. Kassanoff, "'Fate Has Linked Us Together,'" 170–71; Hopkins, *Of One Blood,* 193; Harris, "Not Black and/or White," 387–88; and Du Bois, *Souls of Black Folk,* 5.

124. Hopkins, *Of One Blood,* 193.

Congress in 1921, this Black alliance will become "so powerful" that on "the day when black and white meet to do battle . . . the enemy will say, 'But behold! these men are our brothers.'"[125] But Reuel is less hopeful, "view[ing] with serious apprehension" the likelihood that the "mighty nations" advancing on Ethiopia will accept this more capacious vision of shared humanity, or if they will bring out into the open their acts of incestuous and fratricidal violence. As Kate Manne and Koritha Mitchell have shown, human recognition is no guarantee of humane conduct.[126]

Nevertheless, in making visible the hidden Blackness of Western civilization, Hopkins advances a theory of shared humanity that is not in conflict with a theory of racial difference but rather requires it, precisely to distinguish itself from theories of shared humanity that promote white supremacy by insisting on "sameness." In so doing, Hopkins simultaneously asserts a nonseparatist Black consciousness and a nonwhite universalism, or a political framework in which difference and commonality are simultaneously necessary. Hopkins's use of *blood* resonates both with biological discourse on race and biblical discourse on shared humanity to provide the term's doubled symbolic function in the text. "Blood" acts as something hidden, but that "something" could be either difference or commonality. Initially, it seems that what is hidden beneath Dianthe, Reuel, and Aubrey's common, phenotypically white exteriors is their racially distinct "blood." Eventually, it becomes evident that what is hidden beneath their now conceptually distinct exteriors is their common familial "blood," just as what is hidden beneath Charlie's and Jim's phenotypically distinct exteriors and Dianthe's, Reuel's, and Aubrey's differently gendered exteriors is the "brotherhood of man." If "blood" indicates both commonality and difference as properties that are capable of being hidden beneath the other, it demonstrates that abstract notions of shared humanity and historically produced notions of racial and gendered particularities are not mutually exclusive. So long as these particularities remain "hidden," the language of shared humanity will be race- and gender-specific—a mask for white patriarchal interests. It is only by taking these particularities out of hiding that the language of shared humanity can be rewritten to include rather than exclude. What white patriarchal supremacy hopes to hide—and what Hopkins believed her writing could reveal—is precisely this fact.

Soon after the final installment of *Of One Blood* appeared in January of 1903, ownership of *Colored American Magazine* was taken over by Washington

---

125. Fauset, "Impressions of the Second Pan-African Congress," 18.
126. See Manne, "Humanism," 407; and Mitchell, *From Slave Cabins*, 17.

and became an outlet for the very views on merit that Hopkins so strenuously opposed.[127] That same year, Du Bois republished his 1897 essay on the "Strivings of the Negro People" as the first chapter of *The Souls of Black Folk* (1903), which went on to become a touchstone publication in the growing field of African American letters. Du Bois and other Black men such as Alain Locke, James Weldon Johnson, and Carter G. Woodson are often seen as key architects of the "cultural turn" in Black politics—or the turn to art, literature, and history in the fight for racial equality—even though Black women such as Cooper, Matthews, Harper, and Hopkins were making similar arguments about the political value of the arts years before theirs.[128] By 1909 the *Colored American Magazine* had folded. As Du Bois later wrote, under Washington's leadership, the magazine became "so conciliatory, innocuous and uninteresting that it died a peaceful death almost unnoticed by the public."[129] One year later, Du Bois launched *The Crisis*, an NAACP-sponsored magazine that reemphasized the link between literature and Black liberatory activism that had been so central to Hopkins's prior editorial vision. Under the leadership of Jessie Fauset, who wrote book reviews for the magazine starting in 1912 and served as literary editor from 1919 to 1926, *The Crisis* became an important outlet for young Black writers, many of whom Fauset herself discovered or encouraged.[130] By 1925 the Black literary world was flourishing. Immediately following the landmark publications of Jean Toomer's *Cane* (1923) and Fauset's *There Is Confusion* (1924), Locke's Harlem issue of *The Survey Graphic* (1925) restated the hope that uniquely Black contributions to American culture, music, and literature might be the means through which Black political equality would finally be realized. And yet, even as these hopes became widely shared by artists and intellectuals as part of the emerging "New Negro Movement," the widespread concern that Black artistry would only accomplish this goal if it earned the "recognition" of white audiences repackaged the pseudo-universalist logic of "merit" in a new, but equally insidious, guise.[131]

---

127. In contrast to the magazine's earlier editorials, the first one following this shift in ownership echoed Washington's argument that Black people needed to prove themselves worthy of equal rights, arguing that "what the nation desires to know about the Southern Negro is . . . whether he is bringing himself into such a position that he can discharge his social and personal duties as an American citizen" ("In the Editor's Sanctum," 382). The change in ownership also resulted in the magazine moving away from literature in favor of a focus on Black "economic and industrial progress" and becoming "strikingly more male-focused and male-dominated" (Ammons, introduction to *Short Fiction*, 5–6).

128. See Du Bois, *Souls of Black Folk*, 3–12. For more on this "cultural turn," see English, *Each Hour Redeem*, 49–51; Warren, *So Black and Blue*, 25–41; and Jarrett, *Representing the Race*, 7–11.

129. Du Bois, "Colored Magazine in America," 33.

130. See Ammons, introduction to *Short Fiction*, 6.

131. Locke, "New Negro," 15.

CHAPTER 2

No Sanctuary

Plagiarism, Primitivism, and the Politics of Recognition

Five years after Alain Locke's special issue on Harlem for *The Survey Graphic* (1925), and on the heels of two successful novels of her own, Nella Larsen published a story in a mainstream magazine that stopped her career in its tracks. Three months after "Sanctuary" (1930) appeared in *The Forum*—a magazine that had never previously published a story by a Black author—the editors published one of many letters they had received accusing Larsen of plagiarizing the work of British author Sheila Kaye-Smith.[1] As *Forum* reader Marion Boyd put it, "Aside from dialect and setting, the stories are almost identical."[2] Boyd had seen Kaye-Smith's story eight years earlier in *The Century*, a magazine with such a similar audience to *The Forum* that the two magazines merged later that year.[3] Larsen denied any knowledge of the *Century* story, and *The Forum* eventually exonerated her based on "four rough drafts" that she submitted to them in her defense.[4] Nevertheless, the Harlem literary scene remained suspicious, with Harold Jackman writing to Countee Cullen that "no

---

1. *The Forum* invited Larsen to submit a story "of 1500 to 2000 words at $200 to $250 a piece" six months prior, with Larsen complaining to a friend in response, "I can't write short stories" (Nella Larsen to Carl Van Vechten, 28 July 1929, James Weldon Johnson Memorial Collection).

2. Boyd, "Nella Larsen's Story," 41. Kaye-Smith's story first appeared in *John O'London's Weekly* in 1921 and was reprinted in *The Century* (1922) and *Joanna Godden Married* (1926).

3. See Hutchinson, *In Search of Nella Larsen*, 344.

4. "Editor's Note," xli. These drafts have not been recovered.

one who has heard about Nella Larsen's steal has quite gotten over it."[5] According to Jackman, "The only difference is that Nella has made a racial story out of hers"; she "has just changed it to make it colored."[6] Scholars have been at pains to explain the scandal ever since, with some speculating that Larsen's public humiliation may have been behind her failure to publish again.[7]

However, although these allegations of literary theft were certainly the most dramatic of Larsen's career, the "Sanctuary" incident was not the first time she had been accused of producing art that was not authentically her own. In a *New Republic* review of Larsen's first major publication, *Quicksand* (1928), T. S. Matthews faulted Larsen's debut novel for dealing with reality "as falsely as its characters ape the envied and hated whites."[8] He claimed, "We still like to consider the Negro a child, if we think of him as a human being at all. And unself-conscious children, if they are of a happy disposition . . . are much more attractive than children who have copied some airs and graces from their elders."[9] After sarcastically quoting several lines of "fine writing," Matthews declared Larsen's novel ruined by its supposed imitation of her white "elders'" literary style.[10] For Black art to be authentic, in Matthews's view, both its content and its style needed to be recognizably "Black." By contrast, Larsen's publisher located *Quicksand*'s artistic authenticity in the very quality that made it inauthentic to readers like Matthews—its apparent lack of racial particularity. The inside flap of Knopf's 1928 edition declared Helga Crane to be "beset by problems, but they are the problems of the individual and not of a class or of a race" and "she confronts them like a human being."[11] Whereas Matthews viewed Larsen's "imitation-white" writing as a didactic effort to "make . . . you uncomfortable," Knopf described the book as "almost the only Negro novel of recent years which is wholly free from the curse of propaganda," a term that W. E. B. Du Bois observed was often used to denigrate Black art.[12] A review in the *Boston Evening Transcript* followed suit, declaring that Larsen's novel "deals with a universal story . . . a tragedy that is independent of social rank and racial distinction."[13] For such audiences,

---

5. Harold Jackman to Countee Cullen, 10 February 1930, quoted in Hutchinson, *In Search of Nella Larsen*, 345.

6. Harold Jackman to Countee Cullen, 27 January 1930 and 13 March 1930, quoted in Hutchinson, *In Search of Nella Larsen*, 345.

7. See Larson, "Surviving the Taint of Plagiarism," 83.

8. Matthews, "What Gods! What Gongs!," 51.

9. Matthews, "What Gods! What Gongs!," 50.

10. Matthews, "What Gods! What Gongs!," 50.

11. Inside front flap of the first edition, quoted in Hutchinson, *In Search of Nella Larsen*, 274.

12. Matthews, "What Gods! What Gongs!," 50; inside front flap of the first edition, quoted in Hutchinson, *In Search of Nella Larsen*, 274; and Du Bois, "Criteria of Negro Art," 66.

13. H.W.R. "Story of the Revolt," pt. 3, p. 2.

Quicksand addressed the "broad, universal problems that cling to humanity as a whole" only insofar as it avoided problems that were perceived as being particular to Black experience.[14] These polarized responses to Larsen's work demonstrate that Black writers were as likely to be accused of inauthenticity if their writing looked too *much* like "white" writing as if it looked too *little*.

These opposing doubts about the authenticity of Larsen's writing expose a double standard that stood in the way of one of the central goals of the Harlem Renaissance—the hope, Du Bois argued, that Black people would be "rated as human" as soon as "true Art emerge[ed]" and "compell[ed] recognition," or, as Alain Locke argued, that the "especially cultural recognition" that Black artists were poised to win might "prove the key to that revaluation of the Negro which must precede or accompany any considerable further betterment of race relationships."[15] As Langston Hughes would argue not long after, the hope embedded in what scholars now call this "politics of recognition" was deeply fraught because it depended on winning recognition from a white literary establishment that always already associated so-called universal artistic value with whiteness, or "the old subconscious" idea that "white is best."[16] Recognizably Black art that failed to appeal to the implicitly white standards of "universality" risked being dismissed as "particular," "propagandistic," or "primitive." The desire for recognition was further fraught because when Black art did appeal to those implicitly white standards of "universality"—whether by the adoption of Western literary forms or the avoidance of "racial" themes—it risked being dismissed as "imitative" or "inauthentic." Black artists found themselves in the impossible position of having to be both *universal* enough and *Black* enough at a time when these terms were broadly understood to be mutually exclusive.

Curiously, because Larsen's "Sanctuary" managed to imitate a white literary source in such a way that her only apparent innovation was to add Black characters and dialect, her story would have appeared artistically inauthentic on *both* grounds. Not only was "Sanctuary" a mere "imitation" of white art, but the story's focus on Black characters speaking in Black dialect about specifically Black concerns was evidence of its mere "particularity"; she had "just changed it to make it colored."[17] And yet, even though Larsen's story was judged and dismissed by this paradoxical logic, her story also internally disrupts that logic. On one hand, that the two stories were considered "almost

---

14. H.W.R. "Story of the Revolt," pt. 3, p. 2.
15. Du Bois, "Criteria of Negro Art," 67; and Locke, "New Negro," 15.
16. Taylor, "Politics of Recognition," 25; and Hughes, "Negro Artist and the Racial Mountain," 55, 58.
17. Harold Jackman to Countee Cullen, 13 March 1930, quoted in Hutchinson, *In Search of Nella Larsen*, 345.

identical" indicates the universalizing gesture of Larsen's rewriting, as it suggests there is some commonality between Black and white experiences—a direct challenge to the era's essentialist investment in absolute racial difference. On the other hand, the implication that Larsen considered "Mrs. Adis" worthy of retelling in a Black context indicates the particularizing gesture of her rewriting, as it suggests that Black characters, voices, contexts, and concerns are worthy of unique representation. By making these universalizing and particularizing gestures simultaneously, Larsen's story disrupts the Western critical conventions regularly used to denigrate Black artists. Although "Sanctuary" was still judged and dismissed by those conventions, the story should be understood as an attempt to reclaim Black artistic authenticity by insisting on its universality and its particularity *at the same time.*

Larsen was far from alone among Harlem Renaissance–era artists in troubling the white supremacist binary of universality and particularity. Like many others, she understood that so-called universal aesthetic values depended on the exclusion of Black people and Black aesthetic objects. As Elise Johnson McDougald argued in "The Task of Negro Womanhood," published in Locke's *The New Negro* (1925), the Black woman "realizes that the ideals of beauty, built up in the fine arts, have excluded her entirely."[18] However, in the process of un-whitening the concepts of art and humanity, writers of the Harlem Renaissance often found themselves beholden to definitions of Blackness that were as racially and sexually stifling as were white supremacist definitions of the universal. In this struggle over what counted as authentic humanity and authentic Blackness, Larsen pioneered a unique approach that is visible across her fiction. Taken together, *Quicksand* (1928), *Passing* (1929), and "Sanctuary" (1930) challenge essential, timeless, ahistorical, and constant conceptions of the universal and the particular—which were so often conceptualized in this period as the human and the racial—by coupling the assertion of racial specificity with a denial of racial authenticity.[19] As a direct refutation of the Harlem Renaissance–era obsession with authenticity, Larsen's fictions show that the concepts of art, universality, and humanity, like the concept of racial particularity, are not fixed and timeless but fluid and historically constructed. Her work argues that these concepts should be defined not by their supposed authenticity but by their creative, skillful, or artful mastery of artifice.

---

18. McDougald, "Task of Negro Womanhood," 369–70. See also Hughes, "Negro Artist and the Racial Mountain."

19. On "authenticity" in *Quicksand*, see Favor, *Authentic Blackness*, 81–110. On arguments about "authentic humanity" and "authentic Blackness" dating back to Phillis Wheatley, see Lewis, "Naming the Problem," 54–60.

Modernism, Primitivism, and Plagiarism

The two critical impulses by which Larsen's work was judged—that Black writing should be "Black" rather than "imitative" and the (supposedly) contrary insistence that it be "universal," or, as that term was practically deployed, "white"—stemmed, at least in part, from a contradiction in the modernist aesthetics that dominated the white literary establishment at the time. Michael Levenson argues that modernism was torn between two competing visions of itself, one being "modernism as a classicism," "a renewal of the Western tradition," or "the neo-classical," and the other being "modernism as an attempt to escape from the classical," "a rejection of that tradition," or "the neo-primitive."[20] While classicist and primitivist versions of modernism superficially appeared to oppose one another, they were both rooted in the colonial presumption that non-Western races were the historical, evolutionary, or "primitive" precursors of "modern" Western ones. White modernists like Gertrude Stein, T. S. Eliot, and James Joyce were able to yoke these two modernist impulses together for their own benefit. Stein's invocation of a Black voice in "Melanctha" (1909), for example, depended on her supposed distance from that "primitive" voice, ironically reinforcing the perception of her white aesthetic mastery by eschewing classical models of that mastery.[21] Both classicism and primitivism shored up perceptions of white artistic mastery and the "universality" and "modernity" of white art.

But where white modernists' turns to primitivism were seen as evidence of their personal artistic mastery, Black writers of the period were doubly marginalized—accused of imitation when they turned to the neoclassical, and accused of just being themselves, rather than artists, when they turned to the primitive.[22] In the 1918 edition of the *Cambridge History of American Literature*, for example, the author declared that Paul Laurence Dunbar's "dialect poems . . . are better than the poems that he wrote in standard English" because his "command of correct English was always somewhat meager and uncertain"; they were poor imitations.[23] A few years later, white art collector Albert C. Barnes argued in his contribution to Locke's *The New Negro* that Black people "had kept nearer to the ideal of man's harmony with nature" and that their "wild chants are the natural, naïve, untutored, spontaneous utterance" of "the human soul."[24] Rather than being perceived as the expression

---

20. Levenson, *Genealogy of Modernism*, 205.
21. See North, *Dialect of Modernism*, 72–73.
22. See Balshaw, "Harlem," sec. 3.
23. Smith, "Dialect Writers," 351.
24. Barnes, "Negro Art and America," 20–21.

of artistic skill and adaptation, Black artistic productions were perceived by white critics as weak "imitations" of Western art or as the unconscious, unthinking outpouring of "pure," "unmixed negro [sic] blood" or "the essence of the Negro soul."[25]

Scholarship by Kelli Larson and Hildegard Hoeller has begun to fit "Sanctuary" into this context by noting how Larsen's story was judged by one of these two contradictory standards. Larson and Hoeller both persuasively insist upon Larsen's intentionality in adapting "Mrs. Adis" to her own purpose. Larson points to similar forms of adaptation that were common in the Black theater of the time.[26] Hoeller points to Larsen's admiration of Gertrude Stein's "Melanctha" and her interest in telling the tale from a sixteenth-century Spanish novel in the "naïve manner" of a "Negro ruffian."[27] Larson and Hoeller therefore argue that while white writers took part in acts of appropriation and adaptation all the time, and without issue, the accusations against Larsen indicate that different standards applied to Black writers.[28] For Larson, "Sanctuary" fell victim to the long tradition of judging Black art as "derivative" or imitative of Western art.[29] For Hoeller, "Sanctuary" fell victim to the hypocrisy by which white modernists, but not Black modernists, were able to borrow from other cultures with impunity while maintaining their distance from the "primitive" mask.

This chapter argues that to fully understand the contours of the "Sanctuary" scandal, these two prohibitions on Black writing must be considered in tandem. After all, what the reviews of Larsen's *Quicksand* show are that the aesthetic double standards of the period barred Black art from being considered authentic both when it looked like an assimilationist attempt at neoclassicism, as Larson suggests, and when it looked like Black primitivism, as Hoeller argues. These double standards applied not just to Black writing that engaged in the explicit acts of adaptation and appropriation that Larson and Hoeller

---

25. Smith, "Dialect Writers," 351; and Barnes, "Negro Art and America," 20.

26. See Larson "Surviving the Taint of Plagiarism," 85–86. Deborah McDowell notes that Jessie Fauset's first short story, "The Sleeper Wakes" (1920), was "adapting Ibsen's *A Doll's House* to the special problems of a black woman" (McDowell, "Neglected Dimension," 90).

27. Hoeller, "Race, Modernism, and Plagiarism," 426–28. Beverly Haviland also notes that one of Larsen's next projects, a collaborative novel called "Adrian and Evadne," drew its title names from Greek and Latin mythology (Haviland, "Passing from Paranoia to Plagiarism," 307). See also Davis, *Nella Larsen*, 251, 404.

28. Examples given by Larson and Hoeller include Harriet Beecher Stowe's attempt to incorporate Harriet Jacobs's unpublished *Incidents in the Life of a Slave Girl* (1861) into her own book, *A Key to Uncle Tom's Cabin* (1853), and William Carlos William's verbatim use of a *Ladies' Home Journal* issue in his *Great American Novel* (1923). See Larson "Surviving the Taint of Plagiarism," 100; and Hoeller, "Race, Modernism, and Plagiarism," 433.

29. Larson, "Surviving the Taint of Plagiarism," 98.

consider, but to all Black writing. Given this, it seems less likely that Larsen wanted to participate in white modernist primitivism, as Hoeller claims, than that she was consciously continuing the critiques of primitivism and assimilationism that appear in her prior novels. After all, in *Quicksand*, Helga is torn between primitivist Denmark and assimilationist Harlem; in *Passing*, Irene represents the hypocrisies of a Black middle class that embraces what Locke described as a "racial awakening" alongside what Hughes described as an "urge within the race toward whiteness."[30] Ann duCille argues that "Clare and Irene—the exotic and the elite—may represent the dialectics of the renaissance moment itself"—one character representing the primitivist "fascination with sexuality . . . the foreign, and the forbidden," and the other representing the concern for the "propriety" and "social and racial uplift" that occupied so many among the Black bourgeoisie.[31] "Sanctuary" must be considered in this wider context—both in relation to modernist primitivism and neoclassicism, and also in relation to the struggles of contemporaneous Black writers against modernist injunctions on Black writing. "Sanctuary" is not an isolated literary experiment within Black writing of the time but one part in a larger effort on the part of Black writers to challenge the aesthetic double standards by which their work was judged and dismissed.

Kaye-Smith's "Mrs. Adis" and Larsen's "Sanctuary," each no more than a few pages long, follow a nearly identical sequence of dialogue and events. They begin by describing their setting—Kaye-Smith's on castle grounds located on the site of South East England's long-dead "iron industry," Larsen's alongside one of the American South's many "ruined plantations."[32] In both, a poor woman is approached late at night by her son's friend who has come to her house seeking refuge. Having been caught stealing (rabbits in Kaye-Smith's story, tires in Larsen's), he has shot his attempted apprehender and run. When the authorities come to the woman's house, she discovers that the murdered man was, unbeknownst to the thief, her own son; nevertheless, she hides her son's friend and murderer and lets him go free. In both stories, the sequence of events and the syntax of the descriptions and dialogue are almost identical (see the side-by-side comparison in table 1). Larsen even takes the name of Kaye-Smith's "old hammer woods" for her protagonist, Jim Hammer.[33] Both stories share an engagement with themes of Christian charity and class solidarity. But they differ in terms of nationality and race, which Larsen expresses

---

30. Locke, foreword to *The New Negro*, xxvii; and Hughes, "Negro Artist and the Racial Mountain," 55.
   31. DuCille, "Blues Notes on Black Sexuality," 438–39.
   32. Kaye-Smith, "Mrs. Adis," 190; and Larsen, "Sanctuary," 250.
   33. Kaye-Smith, "Mrs. Adis," 190.

TABLE 1. Comparing Sheila Kaye-Smith's "Mrs. Adis" and Nella Larsen's "Sanctuary"

KAYE-SMITH, "MRS. ADIS," 190–204 (1921)	LARSEN, "SANCTUARY," 250–55 (1930)
In Northeast Sussex a great tongue of land runs into Kent by Scotney Castle. It is a land of woods—the old hammer woods of the Sussex iron industry. (190)	On the Southern coast, between Merton and Shawboro, there is a strip of desolation some half a mile wide and nearly ten miles long between the sea and old fields of ruined plantations. (250)

He was a big, hulking man, with reddish hair and freckled face, evidently of the laboring class, but not successful, judging by the vague grime and poverty of his appearance. For a moment he made as if he would open the window, then he changed his mind and went to the door instead.
 	
    He did not knock, but walked straight in. (191–92)
	He was a big, black man with pale brown eyes in which there was an odd mixture of fear and amazement. The light showed streaks of gray soil on his heavy, sweating face and great hands, and on his torn clothes. In his woolly hair clung bits of dried leaves and dead grass.
	
	    He made a gesture as if to tap on the window, but turned away to the door instead. Without knocking he opened it and went in. (250–51)

"I'm in trouble." His hands were shaking a little.
    "What you done?"
    "I shot a man, Mrs. Adis."
    "You?"
    "Yes—I shot him."
    "You killed him?"
    "I dunno." (192)
	"Ah's in trubble, Mis' Poole," the man explained, his voice shaking, his fingers twitching.
	    "W'at you done done now?"
	    "Shot a man, Mis' Poole."
	    "Trufe?" The woman seemed calm. But the word was spat out.
	    "Yas'm. Shot 'im." In the man's tone was something of wonder, as if he himself could not quite believe that he had really done this thing which he affirmed.
	    "Daid?"
	    "Dunno, Mis' Poole. Dunno."
	    "White man o' ni**ah?"
	    "Cain't say, Mis' Poole. White man, Ah reckons." (251, redaction added)

But she did not come in. She merely unlocked the door, then crossed the kitchen with a heavy, dragging footstep and shut herself into the room where Tom was.
 	
    Peter Crouch knew what he must do—the only thing she wanted him to do, the only thing he could possibly do. He opened the door and silently went out. (204)
	Annie Poole had come into the room.
	
	    It seemed a long time before Obadiah's mother spoke. When she did there were no tears, no reproaches; but there was a raging fury in her voice as she lashed out, "Git outen mah feather baid, Jim Hammer, an' outen mah house, an' don' nevah stop thankin' yo' Jesus he done gibe you dat Black face." (255)

by changing the setting of the story and by changing key points in the characterization, dialogue, imagery, and plot.

In "Mrs. Adis," the titular character seems to be motivated at least partly by class solidarity. The mention of the Scotney Castle and the faded iron industry in the first sentence of the story draws the reader's attention to class relations, and the descriptions of both the murderer, Peter Crouch, and Mrs. Adis highlight their shared working-class status. He is "evidently of the laboring class, but not successful, judging by the vague grime and poverty of his appearance," while she looks older than her years because "life treats some women hard in the agricultural districts of Sussex, and [her] life had been harder than most."[34] Though set in Kent, his "reddish hair" may be intended to suggest Irish origins, although there is no explicit indication that she shares that origin, and Adis is a name common in both England and Ireland.[35] Just as likely, his "reddish hair" appears as an anti-Irish and antisemitic stereotype commonly used by English authors like Charles Dickens to demarcate untrustworthy characters, used here to signal Peter's moral difference from Mrs. Adis despite their common class background.[36] However, the murderer and Mrs. Adis share an open disdain for the keepers who guard the castle property on which they live, to the extent that she justifies hiding him on the basis that "shooting a keeper ain't the same as shooting an ordinary sort of man, as we all know."[37] The tragedy is that, rather than killing "one of them damned keepers," he has killed her son, one of their own.[38] Though she is briefly tempted to turn Peter in upon discovering this fact, putting "her hand into her apron pocket, where she had thrust the key of the lean-to," she decides to protect her son's friend as she had promised. Wordlessly, Christ-like, she forgives.[39]

In "Sanctuary," the Mrs. Adis figure—called Annie—is motivated by both race and class solidarity. The first question she asks of Jim Hammer is whether the person he killed was white or Black, and she agrees to hide him on the basis that "white folks is white folks" and he's "a po' ni**ah."[40] Since Jim believes he killed a white man, the threat of lynching is implicit throughout this exchange, both in the repeated references to "the horror that his capture meant" and in Annie's statement that to hide him constitutes a "dangerous

---

34. Kaye-Smith, "Mrs. Adis," 191–93.
35. Kaye-Smith, "Mrs. Adis," 191.
36. See MacDonald, "'red-headed animal,'" 53–54.
37. Kaye-Smith, "Mrs. Adis," 197.
38. Kaye-Smith, "Mrs. Adis," 201.
39. Kaye-Smith, "Mrs. Adis," 203. On this Christian theme, see Hathaway, "'Almost Folklore,'" 265.
40. Larsen, "Sanctuary," 252, redaction added.

risk" to herself.[41] Jim begs the woman to protect him "foh de Lawd's sake," but she insists that her duty to him is not religious but racial: "Ef de Lawd had gib you a white face 'stead o' dat dere black one, Ah shuah would turn you out."[42] The class solidarity of Kaye-Smith's version is recast as loyalty to the race. It is also on this basis that Jim—once he discovers that he has killed not a white man but a Black man—finally views that act as "wicked," a betrayal of "the Bible" and "the Lord" only because it is a betrayal of the race.[43] Ironically though, if Jim Hammer has sinned by betraying the sacred bonds of racial solidarity, Annie cannot do the same by handing him over to white authorities. Where Kaye-Smith's heroine lingers over her decision but lets the murderer go without a word, Larsen's heroine answers "promptly" and "unwaveringly," telling her son's murderer in the final line of the story to "nevah stop thankin' yo' Jesus he done gib you dat black face"—and voicing the special role that racial violence and racial solidarity play in the story's retelling.[44]

By drawing the threat of lynching into the story, Larsen draws "Sanctuary" into a larger literary tradition of fictional works about lynching that by 1930 included Charles Chesnutt's "The Sherriff's Children" (1889), Theodore Dreiser's "Ni**er Jeff" (1901), Du Bois's "Of the Coming of John" (1903), Paul Laurence Dunbar's "The Lynching of Jube Benson" (1904), Jean Toomer's "Blood-Burning Moon" and "Kabnis" (1923), and James Weldon Johnson's *The Autobiography of an Ex-Colored Man* (1912/1927).[45] These stories tend to use lynching either as an argument against white cruelty or as an argument for Black solidarity.[46] Larsen's story—much like Toomer's "Kabnis" and Johnson's *Autobiography*—uses the threat of lynching to consider the place of white violence in the formation of Black solidarity and to consider the costs and benefits of that solidarity. In "Sanctuary," it is the threat of white violence against Black bodies that turns Black individuals into Black communities, even when the solidarity of that community comes at a high price for Black individuals. Both "Sanctuary" and "Mrs. Adis," then, bring to the point of conflict the social pressures—class, race—that both unite and divide.

The correlation between their plots, structure, and syntax all suggests Larsen's familiarity with Kaye-Smith's version—her conscious playing with her

---

41. Larsen, "Sanctuary," 251–52.
42. Larsen, "Sanctuary," 251–52.
43. Larsen, "Sanctuary," 254.
44. Larsen, "Sanctuary," 255.
45. Redaction added. On plays and poetry, see Mitchell, *Living with Lynching*, 2; and Goldsby, *Spectacular Secret*, 34.
46. See Harris, *Exorcising Blackness*, 69–71.

source material.[47] In this, "Sanctuary" could be said to share as much with the modernist aesthetic techniques and commercial practices that Hoeller and Larson point to as it does with a literary model of repetition and revision that was well established within the Black community. Henry Louis Gates Jr. describes this model as the Black literary tradition of "Signifyin(g)," in which acts of "repetition and revision" govern the substance and form of Black oral traditions and texts, as well as "a principle of literary history" that describes the intertextual relationships among these texts.[48] Signifyin(g) can also take the form of satiric subversions of white aesthetic objects and forms. For example, the cakewalk was a dance that originated in slavery as a mockery of the "high manners of the folks in the 'big house,'" and as "a resonant instance of the subversion from within that defines the place of much African American cultural work with respect to the prevailing mainstream and typically exclusive norms of white culture."[49] The subversion was missed by white Americans, however, for whom the cakewalk was imagined as a sign of enslaved people's buffoonery, a view codified on the minstrel stage.[50] Although Larsen may have been inspired by modernist models of adaptation, she may have been equally inspired by the long-established Black tradition of repetition and revision to critique white aesthetic objects and their producers. If so, it is little surprise that the subversive thrust of Larsen's story, much like the subversive thrust of the cakewalk, went over the heads of white audiences.

Curiously, however, when *The Forum* confronted Larsen with Boyd's letter, Larsen did not admit to adapting the story from Kaye-Smith's but rather argued that she had heard it from "an old Negro woman" sometime between 1912 and 1915, ten years before Kaye-Smith's story was published. "In talking it over with Negroes," Larsen continued, she found that "the tale is so old and so well known that it is almost folklore. . . . A Negro sociologist tells me that there are literally hundreds of these stories. Anyone could have written it up at any time."[51] Although the close structural similarities between Larsen's story and Kaye-Smith's trouble this account of her story's origins, her attribution of the story to Black folklore acts as its own refusal of white claims to literary authority and originality. Moreover, as it turns out, Kaye-Smith's story did not

---

47. Newspapers from the mid-1920s indicate that Kaye-Smith was among the decade's most widely read novelists. See Ford and Ford, "Kind of Books"; Swinnerton, "Miss Kaye-Smith"; and "Miss Kaye-Smith."
48. Gates, *Signifying Monkey*, xxiv, 89. Gates writes his term with an "upper case" S and "a bracketed final g" to differentiate it from "the white term" (Gates, *Signifying Monkey*, 46).
49. Edmonds, quoted in Sundquist, *To Wake the Nations*, 278; and Sundquist, *To Wake the Nations*, 280.
50. See Sundquist, *To Wake the Nations*, 277–78.
51. Larsen, "Author's Explanation," xli.

originate with her either but was borrowed from a Christian parable written by a seventeenth-century bishop, a source that Kaye-Smith did not acknowledge until thirty-five years after her version was first published.[52] Given the story's origins in Christian writing, Larsen's claim that similar stories were popular in the Black community seems plausible. As Rosemary Hathaway demonstrates, "the central plot point here—'woman shelters son's murderer out of charity'—is so widely used" in folkloric traditions "as to have its own motif number" and "tale type" in the classification of global folktales.[53] She notes that "analogues for the tale type" appear "in sources from 13 different cultural traditions, ranging from Irish to Russian to Jewish to Sudanese."[54] It seems likely, therefore, that Larsen could have come across Kaye-Smith's story and recognized its resonance with Black folkloric traditions. In this way, both Larsen's version of Kaye-Smith's story and her attribution of the story to Black folklore challenge her readers' oversimplified understandings of artistic originality and authenticity.

Considered in these thematic, stylistic, and historical contexts, Larsen's story could be said to Signify on Kaye-Smith's story in several overlapping ways. First, it highlights the uniqueness of the Black experience in America—in particular, how the threat of racial violence informs racial solidarity. Second, it highlights the commonality of the underlying ethical affiliations and decisions that shape those experiences—the shared experience of two women who put the interests of their social group over and above other ethical imperatives. These structural parallels also point to the rough equivalence of what would most likely have been described as "universal" themes in Kaye-Smith's story—forgiveness, charity, and empathy—to what certainly would have been described as "particular" themes in Larsen's—racial solidarity and antilynching "propaganda."[55] Third, by drawing Kaye-Smith's non-Black story into a specifically Black tradition, "Sanctuary" points to the common ground—in many cases, the shared origins—of European and African American parables, linking Kaye-Smith's story to a prior tradition of lynching stories while linking those lynching stories to prior Christian parables. And fourth, because Larsen's story superimposes Black forms and themes on supposedly non-Black material, it shows that these aspects are not "the natural, naïve, untutored, spontaneous utterance" of Black souls, but are conscious artistic effects, just

---

52. See Yoon, "Art of Stealing," 20; Kaye-Smith, *All the Books*, 161–62; and Camus, "Upon Forgiving," 101–3.

53. Hathaway, "'Almost Folklore,'" 265.

54. Hathaway, "'Almost Folklore,'" 265.

55. On Kaye-Smith's supposed timelessness, see "Sheila Kaye-Smith's Sequel"; and "Miss Kaye-Smith."

as they are when deployed by white modernists.⁵⁶ In all of these ways, then, Larsen's story disrupts the primitivist and neoclassicist logics that the white literary establishment used to hold the universal and the particular—or the civilized and the primitive—at odds.

Imitation, Authenticity, and the Politics of Recognition

Although Larsen's story disrupts the modernist logics of the civilized and the primitive against which Black artists of the period struggled, the fact that Larsen had Signified on Kaye-Smith did not strengthen her position among other Black artists, and Larsen did not defend her story on those grounds. On the contrary, Larsen's Black peers proved to be some of the story's harshest critics, likely because Black writers—in response to centuries of accusations of "imitation" from the likes of David Hume, Immanuel Kant, Thomas Jefferson, and others—often tried to distance themselves from certain kinds of "repetition and revision" that scholars such as Gates would later reclaim.⁵⁷ It is significant, therefore, that Larsen defended herself from the accusation of plagiarism not by claiming her artistic right to repeat and revise but by locating her story's origins in the anonymous realm of African American folklore. Hoeller argues that Larsen's self-defense could be seen as a savvy attempt to move "her story out of white written culture into a black oral culture, where ownership and originality are not relevant concepts."⁵⁸ But it could also have been a savvy attempt in the face of literary ostracism to align herself with one of the central aesthetic goals of the Harlem Renaissance: to demonstrate that Black folk material offered fertile ground for contemporary Black artists and would be the key to enabling the cultural recognition of the beauty, depth, universality, and humanity of Black people's artistic expression.

An early example of this effort appears in Du Bois's *The Souls of Black Folk* (1903), which opens each chapter with quotations from "classic" poets (most white) followed by lines of music from African American spirituals, a juxtaposition that expresses the continuity between these forms while relying, rhetorically, on their perceived difference. Although Du Bois goes on to describe the experience of being Black in America as that of "measuring one's soul by the tape of a world that looks on in amused contempt and pity," his epigraphs suggest that world must begin measuring things differently.⁵⁹

---

56. Barnes, "Negro Art and America," 21.
57. Gates, *Signifying Monkey*, 113, 52.
58. Hoeller, "Race, Modernism, and Plagiarism," 424.
59. Du Bois, *Souls of Black Folk*, 5.

Similarly, in Johnson's *The Autobiography of an Ex-Colored Man,* first published in 1912 and rereleased in 1927, the protagonist pursues a similar goal of taking "modern ragtime" and "the old slave songs" and making them "classic," which he believes will "distinguish [him]self" as an artist and "help those [he] considered [his] people."[60] With Locke's 1925 collection *The New Negro,* these twin goals were codified as the central purpose of the "New Negro Movement." Locke argued that the art of the younger generation showcased an "increasing tendency to evolve from the racial substance . . . a distinctive contribution."[61] Du Bois and Johnson followed with similar essays, Du Bois arguing in the "Criteria of Negro Art" (1926) that Black material constitutes "the true and stirring stuff of which Romance is born," and Johnson arguing in "The Dilemma of the Negro Author" (1928) that the "Negro author" must "stand . . . on his racial foundation" and "fashion something that rises above race, and reaches out to the universal in truth and beauty."[62] For all of them, it was hoped that showing Black material to be both original, distinctive, or "particular," and also comparable to white "classics," or "universal," might negate the suppositions of Black inferiority that underwrote Jim Crow.[63] The "new literary generation," as William Stanley Braithwaite put it in his contribution to *The New Negro,* would be "racial in substance, but with the universal note."[64] It was only by producing racially distinctive art, in other words, that the Black community could stake its claim at being "a co-worker in the kingdom of culture," "a conscious contributor," and "a collaborator and participant in American civilization."[65]

However, championing original Black material as "classic" meant determining what kinds of Black art were original and authentic expressions of Black culture, and which were not. As Johnson put it in his 1931 preface to the revised edition of *The Book of American Negro Poetry,* "Negro dialect poetry had its origin in the minstrel traditions" and "these conventions were not broken for the simple reason that the individual writers wrote chiefly to entertain an outside audience, and in concord with its stereotyped ideas about the Negro."[66] "Herein," he argued, "lies the vital distinction between them and the folk creators, who wrote solely to please and express themselves."[67] For

---

60. Johnson, *Autobiography of an Ex-Colored Man,* 103–4, 107.
61. Locke, "Negro Youth Speaks," 51.
62. Du Bois, "Criteria of Negro Art," 63; and Johnson, "Dilemma of the Negro Author," 751–52.
63. See Warren, *What Was,* 80.
64. Braithwaite, "Negro in American Literature," 38.
65. Du Bois, *Souls of Black Folk,* 5; and Locke, "New Negro," 15.
66. Johnson, preface to revised edition, 4.
67. Johnson, preface to revised edition, 4.

Johnson, declaring certain Black material to be "classic" first required separating the "artificial folk stuff of the dialect school" from "genuine folk stuff."[68] In practice, though, critics both within and without the Black literary community often disagreed as to where books fell along the spectrum of authenticity. Novels that were deemed "authentic" by one might be deemed imitative or primitive by another, depending on what kinds of behaviors or styles a critic believed to be "authentically" Black. For instance, where T. S. Matthews saw "the breath of life" in Claude McKay's *Home to Harlem* (1928), Du Bois thought the same novel catered only to "that prurient demand on the part of white folk for a portrayal in Negroes of that utter licentiousness which conventional civilization holds white folk back from enjoying."[69] And where Matthews saw in *Quicksand*'s Helga "the stilted creature of a white man's culture," Du Bois saw her as "typical of the new, honest, young fighting Negro woman" and praised the fact that "white folk will not like this book."[70] Black art could be deemed "authentic" either when it appeared racially distinctive or when it refuted false white stereotypes about Black distinctiveness. Conversely, it could be deemed "artificial" either when it "imitated" white art or when it "imitated" white stereotypes about Black distinctiveness. As a result, accusations of inauthenticity quickly collapsed back into accusations of imitation.

Many Black leaders of the Harlem Renaissance believed they could skirt this familiar new obstacle by removing Black art from the influence of white gatekeepers. After all, the contradictory accusations of imitation that plagued Black artists were fundamentally driven and shaped by white audiences' preconceptions about whiteness as universal or "civilized" and Blackness as particular or "primitive." As Du Bois argued, it would be only once Black artists had found a way around the "white jury" of white publishers and white newspapers that their art could be "reviewed and acclaimed by our own free and unfettered judgment."[71] Indeed, Jessie Fauset, who began reviewing books for *The Crisis* in 1912 and became its literary editor in 1919, was motivated to write her first novel, *There Is Confusion* (1924), after being frustrated that an inauthentic "novel of Negro life" written by a white author was being taken

---

68. Johnson, preface to revised edition, 6. Similarly, in *Autobiography of an Ex-Colored Man*, the narrator views positively the act of taking ragtime and making it "classic," but sees turning classic music into ragtime as a "wast[e]" of his "time and abus[e]" of his "talent" (103–4). The former takes "genuine" Black art and reveals its universality, while the latter adds "artificial" color to white art. Despite Johnson's ambivalence about racial authenticity more broadly (see Favor, *Authentic Blackness*, 25–52; and Goldsby, *Spectacular Secret*, 164–213), he nevertheless relies on the concept to defend Black art.
69. Matthews, "What Gods! What Gongs!," 50; and Du Bois, "Two Novels," 202.
70. Matthews, "What Gods! What Gongs!," 50; and Du Bois, "Two Novels," 202.
71. Du Bois, "Criteria of Negro Art," 67.

"seriously by white readers" and the white press.[72] Arguing that "the portrayal of black people calls increasingly for black writers," she committed herself to cultivating, encouraging, and offering publishing pathways for young Black writers such as Larsen, Hughes, and others.[73] "Here," she said, "is an audience waiting to hear the truth about us. Let us who are better qualified to present that truth than any white writer, try to do so."[74] Magazines such as *The Crisis* (founded in 1910), *The Messenger* (founded in 1917), and *Opportunity* (founded in 1923), all operating under Black editorial leadership, seemed to offer a platform for this newly true and free self-expression.

Nevertheless, such editorial calls for Black freedom from white gatekeeping were compromised by those editors' ongoing interest in winning cultural recognition from white audiences. Rather than being constrained by "the psychology of imitation" that Locke associated with the "Old Negro," Black writers were now bound by the Black elite's often contradictory expectations of racial authenticity.[75] Locke, for example, would argue that "not all of our younger writers" were "deep enough in the sub-soil of their native materials" to achieve this authenticity; "too many are pot-plants seeking a forced growth according to the exotic tastes" of the public.[76] The need for cultural recognition thus renewed the gatekeeping power of white audiences and reinforced Black gatekeepers' concerns about Black art being imitative rather than authentic—a "shallow, truckling imitation" of Black folk material instead of "the true and stirring stuff" that "compells [sic] recognition."[77] The paradox at the heart of the Harlem Renaissance, then, was the claim that original Black art would emerge once it stopped seeking recognition from white audiences, and the simultaneous claim that once this art emerged, it would compel recognition from white audiences.

Black artists and intellectuals felt this renewal of the pressures of white recognition keenly. Indeed Fauset, whose first novel was described by Locke as "the novel that the Negro intelligentzia [sic] have been clamoring for," found it difficult to keep publishing novels on Black life "higher up the social pyramid" because, as her publisher informed her, "white readers just don't expect Negroes to be like this."[78] Writer George Schuyler and anthropologist Allison

---

72. Fauset, "Jessie Fauset," 218. DuCille also notes Fauset's skepticism toward "white culture keepers" within the novel itself (duCille, *Coupling Convention*, 76).
73. Fauset, "New Books," 177. See also Johnson, "Literary Midwife," 145–46, and the letters shared between Fauset and Hughes published in Banks, "Jessie Redmon Fauset," 221–28.
74. Fauset, "Jessie Fauset," 219.
75. Locke, "New Negro," 4.
76. Locke, "Art or Propaganda?," 313.
77. Locke, "Art or Propaganda?," 313; and Du Bois, "Criteria of Negro Art," 63, 67.
78. Du Bois and Locke, "Younger Literary Movement," 162; and Fauset, "Jessie Fauset," 219.

Davis subsequently worried that white publishers and patrons were simply paying for stereotypical images of Black particularity and that Black artists had to play up their primitiveness to be well received. In Schuyler's 1926 essay for *The Nation*, "The Negro-Art Hokum," he satirized the idea that "new art forms expressing the 'peculiar' psychology of the Negro were about to flood the market."[79] He argued that this investment in the "peculiarity" of Black art was grounded in the "baseless premise, so flattering to the white mob, that the blackamoor is inferior and fundamentally different."[80] Davis, writing in *The Crisis* in 1928, expressed similar concerns that the desire for Black artistic particularity was driven by the racist assumptions of white audiences and patrons who endorsed the "myth of the spiritual and artistic virtue of spontaneous emotion in the Negro."[81] Just as Johnson had worried about the pressure Black writers faced to conform with minstrel conventions, Davis worried about the pressure they faced to conform with primitivism. He refused to accept such images as authentic: "There is nothing more foreign to the Negro's imagination than this yearning for savage Africa, and it is a false note every time it is struck by a Negro poet."[82] His critique cast doubt on the newfound freedom of Black artists. In his words, "The untrammeled self-expression which the supporters of the movement claimed for it was actually freedom only to be as *primitivistic* as one liked. There was no freedom from the creed that a Negro poet ought to be barbaric."[83] So long as Black art was judged by the white audience's primitivist expectations of Black "authenticity," Schuyler and Davis argued, it would remain inauthentically constrained by those expectations.

While Schuyler and Davis worried that white patrons and audiences were pressuring Black writers into a superficial embrace of primitivistic stereotypes, many Black writers worried about the contrary pressure from the Black bourgeoisie to hide or avoid anything that might be perceived as reinforcing these stereotypes. Wallace Thurman would announce his refusal of such pressures in his short-lived journal, *FIRE!! A Quarterly Devoted to the Younger Negro Artists* (1926), writing in the journal's editorial comment that "any white person who would believe such poppy-cock probably believes it anyway. . . . It really makes no difference to the race's welfare what such ignoramuses think, and it would seem that any author preparing to write about Harlem or anywhere else . . . should take whatever phases of life that seem the most interesting to

---

79. Schuyler, "Negro-Art Hokum," 51. Schuyler's essay appeared June 16, 1926.
80. Schuyler, "Negro-Art Hokum," 54.
81. Davis, "Our Negro 'Intellectuals,'" 328.
82. Davis, "Our Negro 'Intellectuals,'" 329.
83. Davis, "Our Negro 'Intellectuals,'" 329, emphasis in original.

him, and develop them as he pleases."[84] Langston Hughes agreed, writing in *The Nation* in response to Schuyler's "Negro-Art Hokum" that for Black writers to achieve artistic freedom, they would have to stop caring what audiences thought of their work:

> We younger Negro artists who create now intend to express our individual dark-skinned selves without fear or shame. If white people are pleased we are glad. If they are not, it doesn't matter. We know we are beautiful. And ugly too. The tom-tom cries and the tom-tom laughs. If colored people are pleased we are glad. If they are not, their displeasure doesn't matter either. We build our temples for tomorrow . . . free within ourselves.[85]

Although these refusals of recognition were accompanied by a continued embrace of racial authenticity—Thurman refers to it as "sincerity"; Hughes, as "the eternal tom-tom beating in the Negro soul"—both writers understood the logic of cultural recognition as a renewal of the power of white audiences to judge the merit of Black art.[86]

These debates about the value of recognition, and what kind, shaped much of the conflict between the two most recognizable schools of Harlem Renaissance literature: racial uplift literature and literature inspired by Black folk traditions. But Larsen's novels never fit comfortably into these two schools of Harlem Renaissance literature. As Cheryl Wall notes, she is rarely associated with writers of the younger generation such as Thurman, McKay, Hurston, or Hughes because most of her writing focuses on the bourgeois communities from which those writers were so anxious to disassociate.[87] At the same time, although she is sometimes associated with writers like Jessie Fauset because of their shared attention to light-skinned heroines from bourgeois communities—common features of so-called uplift literature—Larsen's novels are also quite critical of those communities.[88] Like "Sanctuary," her novels also go out of their way to trouble the idea of Black authenticity. In Wall's words, "the tragedy" for Larsen's characters "is the impossibility of self-definition. . . . Passing

---

84. Thurman, "Fire Burns," 47–48. See also Thurman, "Negro Artists and the Negro," 38.

85. Hughes, "Negro Artist and the Racial Mountain," 59. Hughes's essay appeared in *The Nation* on June 23, 1926, one week after Schuyler's, and quickly won praise from Amy Jacques Garvey, who wrote in the Garveyite newspaper *The Negro World* that "from now on . . . we expect our artists to express their real souls" (Garvey, "On Langston Hughes," 46).

86. Thurman, "Negro Artists and the Negro," 38; and Hughes, "Negro Artist and the Racial Mountain," 58. On Hughes's somewhat essentialist embrace of racial authenticity, see Wall, *Women of the Harlem Renaissance*, 7–8.

87. See Wall, "Passing for What?," 97.

88. See Bone, *Negro Novel in America*, 97, 102–6.

for white, Larsen's novels remind us, is only one way this game is played."[89] Filled with characters who are passing for Black as much as they are passing for white, Larsen's work pioneered an intriguing response to the double bind that Harlem Renaissance–era artists faced. Instead of choosing between neoclassical and primitivist definitions of Black authenticity, she rejected the idea of authenticity that buttressed accusations of imitation and primitivism alike.

Troubling Authenticity with Artifice

In rejecting the idea of authenticity, Larsen sought to escape not only the constraints imposed on Black people by the twin logics of imitation and primitivism but also the constraints they imposed on Black women. As Wall argues, the ongoing feelings of constraint described by writers such as Hughes, Thurman, Davis, and Schuyler were especially prevalent among young Black female writers. In contrast to the freedom and optimism of Locke's introduction to *The New Negro*, much of the writing produced by Black women of the same era emphasizes, in Wall's words, feelings of "stasis and claustrophobia, not change and movement," conveying the "sense that the stereotypes Locke dismissed" as relics of the past "continue to haunt."[90] As duCille notes, this was a moment when "black female sexuality was either completely unwritten to avoid endorsing sexual stereotypes or sensationally overwritten to both defy and exploit those stereotypes."[91] In the writing of Black women living under these constraints, Wall writes, the "consequences of racial prejudice, gender bias, and class stratification" appear in consistent metaphors of "confinement and self-division," and suggest "major contrasts between the Harlem Renaissance memorialized by male writers and that remembered by women."[92]

Wall draws on Marita Bonner's 1925 essay, "On Being Young—a Woman—and Colored," published the same year as *The New Negro*, as exemplifying this feeling of constraint. In Bonner's words: "You decide that something is wrong with a world that stifles and chokes; that cuts off and stunts; hedging in, pressing down on eyes, ears and throat. . . . You long to explode and hurt everything white; friendly; unfriendly. . . . You get hard. [. . .] And many things in you can ossify."[93] For Bonner, suffocation, paralysis, and rage are inseparable from her experience as a Black woman, triply constrained by the forces of rac-

---

89. Wall, "Passing for What?," 98.
90. Wall, *Women of the Harlem Renaissance*, 4, 6.
91. DuCille, *Coupling Convention*, 109.
92. Wall, *Women of the Harlem Renaissance*, 9.
93. Bonner, "On Being Young," 229–30, bracketed ellipsis in the original.

ism, sexism, and classism: "Why do they see a colored woman only as a gross collection of desires, all uncontrolled. . . . Why unless . . . your taste runs to violent colors—impossible perfumes and more impossible clothes—are you a feminine Caliban craving to pass for Ariel?"[94] She feels trapped between stereotypical perceptions of Black female sexual primitivism and the assumption that Black women who do not fit that primitive stereotype are false imitators of white civility. Whereas Locke imagined that the "New Negro" was throwing off the shackles of "imitation," Bonner is still bound by her delicate status as a woman, wounded by insults that are "like pebbled sand on your body where the skin is thinnest and tenderest," and sharply aware that her physical and spiritual survival depends on performing "an empty imitation of an empty invitation. A mime; a sham; a copy-cat. A hollow re-echo."[95] Like Du Bois in *The Souls of Black Folk*, she sees beyond the "veil" of white stereotypes; but, unlike the endless "striving" that Du Bois describes, Bonner is motionless.[96] She sits, "weighted as if your feet were cast in the iron of your soul . . . motionless on the outside. But inside? Silent," her only consolation that "perhaps Buddha is a woman."[97] Frozen between primitivist stereotypes and a stifling "politics of respectability," she has no access to Locke's "spiritual emancipation," but recasts the stillness and silence of her confinement as signs of her wisdom and strength as she weathers the storm of white ignorance.[98]

These doubled constraints had real-life impacts on the careers of Black women writers of the Harlem Renaissance, many of whom were displaced by Black male peers. For example, in 1924 more than a hundred Black and white writers, editors, and publishers gathered at New York's Civic Club to celebrate the publication of Jessie Fauset's *There Is Confusion,* one of the first book-length works of fiction published during the Harlem Renaissance. Hosted by *Opportunity* editor Charles S. Johnson, the event diminished Fauset's role in the program to almost nothing, instead becoming a well-orchestrated "debut of the younger school of Negro writers," most of them male, that was presided over by Alain Locke.[99] Indeed, in a private letter before the event, Johnson assured Locke that the event would not feature Fauset: "The matter has never rested in my mind."[100] Johnson and Locke may have been motivated

---

94. Bonner, "On Being Young," 229.
95. Locke, "New Negro," 4; and Bonner, "On Being Young," 230, 229.
96. Du Bois, *Souls of Black Folk*, 4–5.
97. Bonner, "On Being Young," 231.
98. Higginbotham, *Righteous Discontent*, 14; and Locke, "New Negro," 4.
99. Johnson, "Debut of the Younger School," 143. See also Wall, "Jessie Fauset," 149–50.
100. Charles S. Johnson to Alain Locke, 7 March 1924, quoted in Hutchinson, *Harlem Renaissance in Black and White,* 390. See also Wall, "Jessie Fauset," 150.

to downplay Fauset's achievement as a writer because of Locke's sense, as he would later put it, that her work was "too mid-Victorian," and therefore not representative of the modern Black sensibility he and Johnson wished to promote.[101] In so doing, they not only discounted the complicated negotiations of "New Negro womanhood" in Fauset's writing, but they diminished her achievements as one of the most important "midwi[ves]" of the movement who, despite the supposedly conservative sensibilities of her fiction, personally discovered and "championed" many of the "the young rebels of the Harlem School."[102] Johnson anointed Locke, rather than Fauset, as "'Dean' of this younger group," and the two men used her novel's launch event to solidify that position, securing not only Locke's role as master of ceremonies for the evening but subsequently as editor of the special issue on Harlem for *The Survey Graphic*, which led to the publication of *The New Negro* and Locke's position as the movement's spokesman.[103] Fauset was privately livid but publicly polite, bound by the ongoing expectations of Black female "propriety and reserve" that were used paradoxically to characterize her work as "outdated."[104]

For Wall, Johnson and Locke's treatment of Fauset is "emblematic of ways in which African Americanist historians and literary scholars long treated female artists," in no small part because of their disregard for the value of her fiction's attention to the experience of Black women.[105] Moreover, where Fauset's work has been dismissed as too "genteel"—a feminine posture Robert Bone would describe as "orient[ed] toward white opinion"—those Black female writers who defied genteel sensibilities were similarly disparaged and accused of courting white audiences.[106] Zora Neale Hurston, for example, a writer closely associated with the younger "Harlem School," was openly criticized by several Black male peers for supposedly playing into white audiences' primitivist desires. As Hughes claimed in *The Big Sea* (1940), she "was always getting scholarships and things from wealthy white people" who "paid her just to sit around and represent the Negro Race for them" in "a racy fashion."[107]

---

101. Locke "Saving Grace of Realism," 9.
102. Sherrard-Johnson, *Portraits of the New Negro Woman*, 55; Hughes, *Big Sea*, 218; and Bone, *Negro Novel in America*, 101.
103. Charles S. Johnson to Alain Locke, 7 March 1924, quoted in Hutchinson, *Harlem Renaissance in Black and White*, 390. See Hutchinson, *Harlem Renaissance in Black and White*, 392.
104. Goldsmith, "Jessie Fauset's Not-So-New Negro Womanhood," 270, 259. See Jessie Fauset to Alain Locke, 9 January 1933, quoted in Hutchinson, *Harlem Renaissance in Black and White*, 390; and Johnson, "Debut of the Younger School,"143.
105. Wall, "Jessie Fauset," 152.
106. Bone, *Negro Novel in America*, 97.
107. Hughes, *Big Sea*, 239.

Dorothy West, one of Hurston's mentees, would later describe how "hurt" she was by Hurston's treatment, claiming that "the Renaissance men were jealous of Zora" because she was "getting grants and so forth."[108] Margaret Walker, another mentee, put it more strongly: "I think they were more than jealous of her; they hated her."[109] As a result of such sidelining of Black female writers, by the time *Black World* published a Harlem Renaissance retrospective in 1970, Fauset and Hurston had both been forgotten. In West's words, "not one black wom[an was] included."[110] Accused of producing outdated "imitations" no matter what they wrote, and no matter their "reserve" or their "raciness," they were both slowly silenced.

Much like Bonner's essay, Larsen's fiction explores this double-edged experience of confinement, her characters being constrained both by the stifling puritanism of white middle-class respectability and by stereotypes about Black female primitive licentiousness. In *Quicksand*, Helga is forced to choose between bourgeois Harlem society, which she perceives as "ap[ing]" the "clothes . . . manners, and . . . gracious ways" of white people, and life as an "exotic" in Denmark, where she feels forced to occupy white stereotypes of Black behavior: they "had known that in her was something, some characteristic, different from any that they themselves possessed. Else why had they decked her out as they had?"[111] Rejecting both, Helga thinks she has found an "authentic" Black lifestyle in the rural and religious South—one in line with Johnson's appraisal of African American spirituals as representative of the "genuine folk." But that lifestyle proves disastrous for her mind and her body. Although "this one time in her life, she was convinced, she had not clutched a shadow and missed the actuality," she soon feels trapped again, "determined" but unable "to get herself out of this bog into which she had strayed. . . . Her suffocation and shrinking loathing were too great."[112] Helga's situation can be read as a metaphor for the aesthetic impasses faced by Harlem Renaissance–era artists, torn between the respectable novels of Jessie Fauset and the so-called primitivist novels of Claude McKay, and troubled by the "imitative" relationship of each to white writing and white stereotypes. If some recourse to the "folk" was meant to offer a way out of this double bind, as Johnson's appeal to African American spirituals implies, Helga's tragic end

---

108. West, "Alive and Well and Living," 30. When asked if she had felt "constrained" by the movement's "predominantly white audience," West noted the fragile position of Black women in this respect: "You don't know what we had to go through back then. . . . Women were just like excess baggage or fair game" (West, "Conversations with Dorothy West," 273).
109. Walker, "Reflections on Black Women Writers," 46.
110. West, "Alive and Well and Living," 29.
111. Larsen, *Quicksand*, 48, 68, 83.
112. Larsen, *Quicksand*, 118, 134.

in the "quicksand" of the South suggests otherwise. *Quicksand* shows that the neoclassical approach, the primitivist approach, and Johnson's neoclassical reclamation of the "primitive" folk were each incapable of repudiating the incapacitating notion of authentic Blackness. That Helga's search for authenticity ends with her exile from "sophisticated" and aesthetically "agreeable" urban spaces further indicates authenticity's negative impact on modern Black art.[113]

Passing takes this critique of authenticity even further in that it complicates the erroneous equation of Blackness with primitivism and whiteness with bourgeois respectability. Of course, passing itself is a kind of "imitation" that both troubles and reinforces definitions of "authentic Blackness," simultaneously pointing to the arbitrariness of the line that separates the races, while also reinforcing the idea that you are "really" one thing and are falsely pretending to be something else.[114] Larsen's *Passing*, however, is written from the perspective of Irene, whose unreliability unsettles any claims that she makes about what "thing" might define who you really are.[115] In *Passing*, it is Clare, the woman who is passing for white, who is the novel's most "exotic" character: she is "catlike"; she writes in "purple ink" on "foreign paper" in a way that is "a shade too unreserved in the manner of its expression"; she smiles in a way that "was too provocative for a waiter"; she dresses "conspicuous[ly]"; and she wears "an expression so dark and deep and unfathomable" that Irene had "the sensation of gazing into the eyes of some creature utterly strange and apart."[116] Meanwhile, Irene, the woman who loudly proclaims her loyalty to the race, is concerned with issues of sexual, social, and economic respectability that point to her self-restraint.[117] To a certain degree, this dynamic is also present in *Quicksand* in the relationship between Helga and Anne Grey, the latter of whom is named to suggest the middle space that Anne occupies between her self-proclaimed loyalty to the Black community and what Helga sees as Anne's white assimilationism. But the association between Helga's discomfort in each locale and her torn identification between white and Black parents has led many critics to read her as simply too Black for Denmark and too white for Harlem (a modern tragic mulatta).[118] *Passing* deflects such readings by making the only difference between Clare and Irene that one has chosen to pass and

---

113. Larsen, *Quicksand*, 135.
114. On this "paradox," see Moynihan, *Passing into the Present*, 9.
115. Larsen, *Passing*, 206.
116. Larsen, *Passing*, 161, 144, 143, 182, 203, 172.
117. See Wall, "Passing for What?," 108.
118. See, for example, Watson, "Tragic Mulatto Image," 62–71; and Thornton, "Sexism as Quagmire." See also McDowell, introduction to *"Quicksand" and "Passing,"* xvii.

the other has not, while also insisting that "Blackness" can be associated with bourgeois respectability and that "whiteness" can be associated with primitive exoticism.[119]

Clare's association with both assimilationism and exoticism further frustrates the reader's tendency to hold the "primitive" and the "civilized" apart. Reading through Irene's eyes, Clare is a problem for both reasons: both because of her assimilationism (she has rejected the Black community to join the white one) and because of her exoticism (which always seems to be the real reason behind Irene's discomfort). Irene, by contrast, represents racial uplift ideology: she has affirmed her commitment to the Black community in part by rejecting any association with anything sexual or vulgar that might reinforce stereotypes of Black primitivism.[120] As a result, Irene often characterizes her relationship with Clare as one of differences: "They were strangers. Strangers in their ways and means of living. Strangers in their desires and ambitions. Strangers even in their racial consciousness. Between them the barrier was just as high, just as broad, and just as firm as if in Clare did not run that strain of black blood."[121] And yet, as Wall notes, "Larsen minimizes these differences to great effect," with both characters passing as white in the novel's opening scene, and with both proving to be just as materialistic, selfish, ambitious, and "[un]safe" as the other.[122] That the novel makes it impossible to tell Clare and Irene apart further frustrates our desire to hold the "primitive" and the "civilized" at odds.

The real difference between Clare and Irene is their respective comfort with the instability of their racial identities. This is also the difference between Helga and Audrey Denney in *Quicksand*. Audrey is another light-skinned Black woman who (like Clare) mixes freely with both white and Black people; as a result, Anne Grey dismisses her as a race traitor (just as Irene dismisses Clare). Helga, however, feels "for the beautiful, calm, cool girl who had the assurance, the courage, so placidly to ignore racial barriers and give her attention to people . . . not contempt, but envious admiration."[123] While Helga and Irene are psychologically destroyed by the contradictory pulls of primitivism and assimilationism, Audrey and Clare move freely between white and Black communities and identities.[124] In *Quicksand* and *Passing*, there is no such thing as "authentic" Blackness, just people who recognize the artifice of race

---

119. See Tate, "Nella Larsen's *Passing*," 142–43.
120. See Jenkins, "Decoding Essentialism," 149.
121. Larsen, *Passing*, 192.
122. Wall, "Passing for What?," 107; and Larsen, *Passing*, 210.
123. Larsen, *Quicksand*, 62.
124. See Larsen, *Quicksand*, 61; and Larsen, *Passing*, 199.

and are driven mad by it (like Helga and Irene), and people who recognize this artifice and move between racialized performances with comfort and ease (like Audrey and Clare).

Just as Helga's search for authenticity leads to the loss of her aesthetic and intellectual spirit in the "quicksand" of the South, so does Clare's death function as an aesthetic loss: "Gone! The soft white face, the bright hair, the disturbing scarlet mouth, the dreaming eyes, the caressing smile, the whole torturing loveliness that had been Clare Kendry. That beauty that had torn at Irene's placid life. Gone!"[125] Clare's death (possibly at Irene's hands) serves as another metaphor for the aesthetic impasse faced by Harlem Renaissance–era writers. Throughout the novel, Irene vacillates between seeing Clare as a problem because Clare holds "so low an opinion of her loyalty" to the race and because she shows a "new tenderness, this avowed yearning" for her "own people."[126] If we see Clare as a kind of art object (as Irene's obsession with Clare's beauty often suggests), then Irene's equal discomfort with Clare's whiteness and her Blackness mirrors the dismissal of Harlem Renaissance–era art for being both too "white" and too "Black." The pairing of Audrey and Helga in *Quicksand* and Clare and Irene in *Passing* reveals the kind of aesthetic fluidity that Larsen desired, coupled with her awareness that fluidity was not tolerated by either neoclassicist or primitivist critical perspectives.

In Larsen's novels, the responses that Larsen's protagonists have to primitivist and assimilationist constrictions on their identity are, as Wall notes, those of "asphyxiation, suffocation, and claustrophobia."[127] In "Sanctuary," this feeling of suffocation reappears at a key moment in the text, which is also the moment that departs most significantly from Larsen's source. In "Mrs. Adis," the woman hides the man in "the small lean-to of the cottage"; in "Sanctuary," she hides him in her "feather baid" with his "soiled body and grimy garments" lying "between her snowy sheets" and covered with "piles of freshly laundered linen."[128] Beverly Haviland reads this moment as a reference to miscegenation, but it can also be read as a kind of "passing"—a Black body dressed in white sheets.[129] Hidden in these white sheets when he hears "wheels in the road outside," Jim begins to suffocate, cramped in both by his desire to escape the white law and by the method of "passing" that Annie has concocted to protect him:

---

125. Larsen, *Passing*, 239.
126. Larsen, *Passing*, 163, 182.
127. Wall, "Passing for What?," 105.
128. Kaye-Smith, "Mrs. Adis," 194; and Larsen, "Sanctuary," 252.
129. Haviland, "Passing from Paranoia to Plagiarism," 305–6.

> Fear clutched so tightly at him that he almost leaped from the *suffocating* shelter of the bed in order to make some active attempt to escape the horror that his capture meant. There was a spasm at his heart, a pain so sharp, so slashing that he had to suppress an impulse to cry out. He felt himself falling. Down, down, down. . . . Everything grew dim and very distant in his memory. . . . Vanished. . . . Came rushing back.[130]

As Kelli Larson notes, "Larsen's verbal image approximates the physical and psychological effects of lynching," equating the symbolically suffocating shelter of the bed with the literally suffocating experience of being lynched.[131] Jim also equates Annie with the white sheriff, Bill Lowndes, by describing them both as "a hard one."[132] Later, when the true victim of his crime is revealed, Jim again feels equally trapped, hemmed in by his transgression of white law and by his transgression of racial solidarity: "He was paralyzed. He couldn't move hand or foot. He moaned again. It was all there was left for him to do. For in the terror of this new calamity that had come upon him he had forgotten the waiting danger which was so near out there in the kitchen."[133] Like Helga and Irene, Jim Hammer is as physically and psychologically threatened by violent white attitudes toward his Blackness as he is by the Black community's restrictive expectations of the kind of behaviors that his Blackness requires.

Annie's decision to cover Jim's "soiled body and grimy garments" in the "snowy white sheets" of her feather bed also draws attention to the sexualized components of these racialized stereotypes.[134] The clean white sheets connote the sexual puritanism and respectability of the Black bourgeoisie, concealing any "soil" or "grime" that could be seen as reinforcing primitivist stereotypes about Black sexuality, savagery, and immorality.[135] Lying in the bed under those clean white sheets, "his whole body went taut. His feet felt frozen, his hands clammy, his tongue like a weighted, dying thing."[136] His stillness protects him from the violent gaze of the white world, but it is stifling. Once the threat of the white gaze is removed by Annie's choice to protect him, his suffocation ends: "Jim Hammer caught his breath."[137] When the white men leave, his cold stillness ends, though it is quickly replaced with a new feeling of

---

130. Larsen, "Sanctuary," 252, ellipses in the original, emphasis added.
131. Larson, "Surviving the Taint of Plagiarism," 94.
132. Larsen, "Sanctuary," 252–53.
133. Larsen, "Sanctuary," 254.
134. Larsen, "Sanctuary," 252.
135. See Haviland, "Passing from Paranoia to Plagiarism," 305–6.
136. Larsen, "Sanctuary," 253.
137. Larsen, "Sanctuary," 254.

constraint: "With the sound of the door closing on the departing men, power to move came back to the man in the bedroom. He pushed his dirt-caked feet out from the covers and rose up, but crouched down again. He wasn't cold now, but hot all over and burning. Almost he wished that Bill Lowndes and his men had taken him with them."[138] Like Harlem Renaissance artists, like Helga, and like Marita Bonner, Jim finds himself doomed to physical or spiritual death by opposing sets of racialized and sexualized images: cold and hot, clean and dirty, still and wild.

Whereas Jim is paralyzed by these opposing images and experiences, Annie moves between them with skill and ease. Like Clare, she is willing to dirty her sheets, muddying the story's white characters' perceptions of her and her son as "good" and Jim as "bad." As Bill Lowndes describes Jim, he "never was no 'count. Thievin' an' sly," an affirmation of white prejudices about Black particularity.[139] By contrast, the sheriff says that Annie's son "was a mighty fine *boy*. Ef they was all like him—," praising him for being willing to die protecting white property while looking down upon him as a "boy."[140] In protecting Jim, Annie refuses to endorse this paternalistic perspective. She also refuses to see Jim's behavior as more "authentically Black" than her son's. Annie parrots Bill Lowndes early in the story when she claims that she "shuah don' see nuffin' in" Jim "but a heap o' dirt," but she says so with "a look of irony, of cunning, of complicity" on her face, mirroring the "ugly, cunning smile" that graces Jim's face later in the story and suggesting that she is more like him than not.[141] Even though she ostensibly saves Jim only because her "good" son "allus set such a heap o' store by" him, she thereby maintains an ironic relationship to both her own and her son's "goodness" and Jim's "badness."[142] By covering Jim in white sheets, she protects him in the same way that her son had protected himself—by assimilating with white norms—a performance that she carries out not with the sincerity or hypocrisy of Anne or Irene but with the "cunning" of Audrey or Clare.[143] "Sanctuary"—both a regional Black story that is too particular and a copy of a white story that is too assimilationist—mirrors Annie's tolerance for both Jim and her son, even as the story's merging of these two things disrupts their individual coherence and their presumed opposition.

---

138. Larsen, "Sanctuary," 254–55.
139. Larsen, "Sanctuary," 254.
140. Larsen, "Sanctuary," 254, emphasis added.
141. Larsen, "Sanctuary," 251, 253.
142. Larsen, "Sanctuary," 251.
143. Larsen, "Sanctuary," 251, 253.

Although they embody a kind of defiance in the face of racialized and sexualized constraints, Audrey, Clare, and Annie do not discount the suffocating experiences of characters like Helga, Irene, and Jim, nor do they suggest that individuals can simply overcome the suffocating effects of racism and sexism on their own. In Larsen's novel, Audrey's and Clare's freedom to move between racialized identities and spaces is also a sexual freedom. It is precisely that sexual freedom that Helga and Irene so desire, even though they are terrified of and paralyzed by the racist ways that claiming such freedom would be perceived.[144] Importantly, in the novels, this sexual freedom is not tolerated but punished: Audrey is shot; Clare falls to her death from a window. If these characters' tragic fates arguably align them with the trope of the tragic mulatto, as scholars sometimes argue, they also arguably align them with the trope of the scarlet letter. But by placing Helga and Irene at the center of these two stories, rather than the more openly transgressive characters of Audrey and Clare, the novels shift our attention away from those tropes' traditional uses. Rather than focusing on the consequences for individuals who refuse to follow the rules of racial and sexual propriety, as in traditional tragic mulatto and scarlet letter stories, Larsen's novels focus on the equally suffocating consequences for those who do. Helga—after finally experiencing one liberating sexual experience in a storefront church and pursuing a respectable marriage to its reverend—is doomed to the child-bearing bed.[145] Irene, finally free of Clare's threats to her respectable life in the Black bourgeoisie and her sexless marriage to her husband, ends up in a suffocating state of heaviness, drowning, and darkness: "She moaned and sank down, moaned again. Through the great heaviness that submerged and drowned her she was dimly conscious of strong arms lifting her up. Then everything was dark."[146] Annie is left at the end of "Sanctuary" in a "raging fury," a grieving mother whose son found no sanctuary, despite his and her efforts to stay safe by doing all the "right" things.[147]

The Harlem Renaissance was centrally devoted to finding ways to challenge the legal and political dehumanization of Black people by demonstrating the universality of Black art. To do so, they sought to challenge the implicit association of "universal" art with whiteness by creating art that could be recognized as both particular to Black experience and "universal." Nevertheless, their efforts to dismantle racist conceptions of the universal were often replaced with conceptions of "authentic" Blackness that Black writers found

---

144. See duCille, *Coupling Convention*, 87.
145. See Larsen, *Quicksand*, 113–14, 135.
146. Larsen, *Passing*, 242.
147. Larsen, "Sanctuary," 255.

just as suffocating. Larsen's innovation, across her work, was to insist that disrupting the concept of authentic Blackness was the only way to disrupt the aesthetically and politically incapacitating logic that equated racial particularity with Black inferiority and universality with white superiority—a logic that underwrote Jim Crow laws and restricted Black participation in American democracy. Larsen not only challenged the prevailing view of universality and racial particularity as essential and ahistorical constants but also insisted on the incredible power that these concepts had in shaping American identities, aesthetics, and politics. Indeed, although "Sanctuary" represents a continuation of Larsen's argument with authenticity, the way that the story was read in its own time demonstrates just how persistently her readers clung to the notions that her fiction so consistently undermined.

Larsen's skepticism toward authenticity aligns her with another contrarian figure of the Harlem Renaissance: Zora Neale Hurston, whose well-known "Characteristics of Negro Expression" (1934) also repudiated the concepts of "authentic humanity" and "authentic Blackness."[148] In response to the stereotype that Black people were "natural" mimics—simultaneously "primitive" and "imitative"—Hurston refused to insist on an alternative ground for Black artistic "authenticity." Instead, she questioned the possibility of "originality" as an alternative to "imitation" by arguing that repetition has always been at the heart of artistic labor. She wrote: "It is obvious that to get back to original sources is much too difficult for any group to claim very much as a certainty. What we really mean by originality is the modification of ideas. The most ardent admirer of the great Shakespeare cannot claim first source even for him. It is his treatment of the borrowed material."[149] For Hurston, there was no transcendent concept of originality that can authenticate art; rather it is *both* the repetition of shared material *and* the particular treatment of that material—its repetition *with* a difference—that makes art "authentic."

Since both Larsen's and Kaye-Smith's stories depended on what Hurston called the repetition of shared or "universal" material with some "particular" difference, it is likely, then, that Hurston would have recognized Larsen's racialized treatment of Kaye-Smith's story as art—just as she might have recognized Clare and Audrey as sources of aesthetic admiration rather than contempt, not because they are "authentically" Black or "authentically human" but because perceptions of "authenticity" are always the effect of artifice, as in the

---

148. See Hoeller, "Race, Modernism, and Plagiarism," 431–32.
149. Hurston, "Characteristics of Negro Expression," 86.

sense of artful performances, productions, and skills. However, where Larsen represented the twin pressures of primitivism and assimilationism as suffocating constraints—both despising the pressure to "play the primitive" and longing for the sexual and cultural freedom to do so—Hurston's work emphasized less the stifling pressure to perform than the pleasurable connotations of "play."[150] As Wall has argued, Hurston's work both mocks and finds pleasure in the primitivist stereotypes of her day. She understands that she must hide this pleasure, but she also insists on retaining her "access to the feelings she suppresses."[151] In Hurston's folklore collections and folklore-inspired fictions of the late 1930s, such internal experiences of pleasure and pain became narrative opportunities to explore the material constraints of racism, sexism, and classicism, and to imagine embodied experiences not yet mediated by those structures.

---

150. See the use of this phrase in Retman, *Real Folks*, 46; and Hughes, *Big Sea*, 316, 325. See also Thurman, *Infants of the Spring*, 142; Patterson, *Zora Neale Hurston*, 8–9; and Huggins, *Harlem Renaissance*, 130–32.

151. Wall, *Women of the Harlem Renaissance*, 29.

CHAPTER 3

Folk in the Flesh

Insides, Outsides, and the Object of Anthropology

At the height of the Harlem Renaissance, Zora Neale Hurston was recognized by her peers as an exemplar of what Alain Locke had called "the ambition and promise of Negro artists to make a distinctive contribution" to American letters.[1] And yet, when her now best-known novel, *Their Eyes Were Watching God*, was first published just over a decade later in 1937, its reception was decidedly mixed. In the white press, reviewers praised the novel for going beneath "mere national or racial characteristics . . . to gain universal human meaning."[2] Lucille Tompkins of the *New York Times Book Review* wrote that although Hurston's novel "is about Negroes, and a good deal of it is written in dialect . . . really it is about every one, or at least every one who isn't so civilized that he has lost the capacity for glory."[3] Such praise for the novel stemmed largely from what white reviewers' saw as the novel's avoidance of the so-called race problem: her characters were not like the "self-conscious, self-pitying and over-idealized Negro of most such literature" nor "the sullen, persecution-crazed hulks that Faulkner drives to nothingness."[4] For

---

1. Locke, "Negro Youth Speaks," 51.
2. Knickmeyer, "Notable Studies of Negro Life," 4H.
3. Tompkins, "In the Florida Glades," 29.
4. Leverty, "Beauty, Freshness, Poetry," 16; and Lockhart, "Zora Hurston Pens Novel," sec. 4, p. 9.

these reviewers, Hurston had presented the most "real and believable colored folks" they had "yet encountered in books"; "the negroes [sic] here are human beings."[5]

Writers for the Black and radical press, on the other hand, were suspicious of the novel's crossover appeal. By 1937 the African American literary community was increasingly radicalized, which meant that a novel that might have been embraced ten years earlier was now out of step with expectations of Black art among Black writers. Alain Locke—who in 1925 had looked to "the very heart of the folk-spirit" for the "essential forces" of "social change and progress"—now felt that Hurston's "gift for poetic phrase, for rare dialect, and folk humor keep her flashing on the surface of her community and her characters and from diving down deep . . . to the inner psychology of characterization."[6] In a review for the *New Masses,* a young Richard Wright put it more bluntly, arguing that Hurston's use of dialect aligned her novel with "the minstrel technique that makes the 'white folks' laugh."[7] While one white reviewer claimed that "the roots" of the novel's "vibrant Negro lingo" touched "deeper levels of human life," both Wright and Locke believed that the novel's "highly-charged language" and depiction of "entertaining pseudo-primitives" had left it mired in stereotype and superficiality.[8] For them, her novel lacked a "sharp analysis of the social background" and therefore showed "no desire whatever to move in the direction of serious fiction."[9] The apparent avoidance of sociopolitical issues that gave the novel its "universal" appeal among mainstream white reviewers marred the novel for Black reviewers.

It was a critique that would plague Hurston throughout her career, from Langston Hughes's retrospective claim that she played the primitive for "wealthy white people," to Roi Ottley's denunciation of her as a "handkerchief head" because of her controversial opposition to the *Brown v. Board* decision in 1955.[10] If Hurston's contemporaries were divided as to whether her depiction of rural Black folk culture was an expression of universal humanism or primitive stereotypes, later critics would reinterpret her representation of Black folk culture again, now as an expression of proto–Black nationalism. By the 1970s, Alice Walker was in a position to view both Hurston's folk fiction

---

5. Leverty, "Beauty, Freshness, Poetry,." 16; and Lockhart, "Zora Hurston Pens Novel," sec. 4, p. 9.

6. Locke, foreword to *The New Negro,* xxv; and Locke, review of *Their Eyes,* 18. Hurston's furious unpublished response is quoted in Hemenway, *Zora Neale Hurston,* 241–42.

7. Wright, "Between Laughter and Tears," 25.

8. Hibben, "Vibrant Book," 2; Wright, "Between Laughter and Tears," 25; and Locke, review of *Their Eyes,* 18.

9. Locke, review of *Their Eyes,* 18; and Wright, "Between Laughter and Tears," 25.

10. Hughes, *Big Sea,* 239; and Ottley, "Handkerchief Head, Female," 8.

and her 1955 opposition to *Brown v. Board* not as pandering to segregationist public opinion but as positive symptoms of growing up in the self-sufficient, all-Black community of Eatonville, Florida.[11] Drawing on Hurston's argument that "it is a contradiction in terms to scream race pride and equality while at the same time spurning Negro teachers and self-association," Walker would help inaugurate the more recent characterization of Hurston as "an early black nationalist" who would have been less out of step with the intellectual circles of the 1960s Black Power movement than she was with her own.[12]

Even now, however, few critics have been able to reconcile this reading with what Walker also describes as Hurston's "unpredictable and occasionally weird politics," and Walker would decide that "we are better off if we think of Zora Neale Hurston as an artist, period—rather than as the artist/politician most black writers have been required to be."[13] For Hurston's biographer, Robert Hemenway, the "chaos" of Hurston's thought is related to her failure to see the radical implications of her ideas, a failure to "transform . . . her observations about the distinct culture of black people into the idea of a distinct black political movement or a collective alternative to capitalism."[14] As Leigh Anne Duck summarizes, Hurston has been "celebrated as an artist whose work resisted racism by emphasizing the holistic, communal values of traditional African-American culture" and "dismissed as a writer whose representations of the 'folk' accommodated the racism of a nation quick to exploit 'undeveloped' peoples."[15] Very often, she is seen in both of these ways at once.[16]

This chapter demonstrates that what has made Hurston's work appear incoherent or contradictory in these ways is her troubling of the critical association of rural Black folk culture with a "natural," "organic," "spiritual," "mythic," "anti-historical," or "nostalgic" past that represents an absolute contrast with a modern, bourgeois, and white-coded Western present.[17] Drawing on but also critiquing the anthropological discourse of her day, Hurston represents Black folk cultures as complex, fluid, and hybrid social structures capable of both

---

11. See Walker, "Looking for Zora," 302.
12. Hurston, "Court Order," 958; and Hemenway, *Zora Neale Hurston*, 5. See also Washington, "Zora Neale Hurston," 19.
13. Walker, "On Refusing to Be Humbled," 1, 3.
14. Hemenway, *Zora Neale Hurston*, 6, 334.
15. Duck, "'Go There tuh *Know* There,'" 265.
16. See, for example, Baker, *Blues, Ideology*, 58; and Carby, "Politics of Fiction," 82.
17. Maroto, "'So This Was a Marriage!,'" 81; Levy, "'That Florida Flavor,'" 86; Baker, *Workings of the Spirit*, 92; Wall, "*Mules and Men* and Women," 667; Gilroy, *Black Atlantic*, 91; and Carby, "Politics of Fiction," 79. For counter-readings, see Duck, "'Go There tuh *Know* There,'" 265–66; Kaplan, "Erotics of Talk," 127; and Davie, "Free Mules, Talking Buzzards," 448. On the value of Black historical nostalgia, see Ahad-Legardy, *Afro-Nostalgia*, 1–26.

reinforcing and resisting racist, sexist, and bourgeois ideologies. Moreover, her use of natural imagery is not aligned with folk characters or communities, as is so often presumed, but with cross-cultural experiences of physical pleasure and pain. In *Their Eyes Were Watching God*, these embodied experiences of pleasure and pain become narrative opportunities to imagine (if not instantiate) human identities and relationships beyond the rigid binaries and patterns of domination that she describes as present in all of the human communities the novel represents.

By using natural imagery to explore the pleasures and pains of the flesh, *Their Eyes Were Watching God* also opens up the imaginative space necessary to explore what Black feminist theorist Joan Morgan has more recently called a "politics of pleasure," which entails the "recognition of black women's pleasure (sexual and otherwise) as not only an integral part of fully realized humanity," but also as "capable of intersecting, challenging, and redefining dominant narratives about race, beauty, health and sex."[18] Considered through this lens, Hurston's famous construction of "insides" and "outsides" reads not just as a reference to the insider/outsider status of the anthropological observer, as is often argued, but as an effort to find new ways to speak openly about the intimate, "fleshy," and culturally "shameful" pleasures and pains that make us human. Although *Their Eyes Were Watching God* is often characterized as torn between opposing commitments to bourgeois/individualist and folk/communal ideologies, this chapter argues that the novel is better understood as exploring the limitations of these intersecting ideologies in order to begin the work of imagining a Black feminist politics of pleasure.

Anthropology, Cultural Relativism, and the Folk

Hurston moved from Eatonville to New York in 1925 after one of her short stories and a play won prizes in an *Opportunity* contest. In New York, she became a central member of what she and fellow-writer Wallace Thurman self-mockingly deemed Harlem's "Ni**erati," and was soon offered a funded place at Barnard College, where she studied with anthropologist Franz Boas, a white anthropologist intent on developing a diverse circle of students and peers that included Hurston, Margaret Mead, Ruth Benedict, and Arthur Fauset (brother of Jessie Fauset), who trained in Philadelphia with Boas's former student, Frank Speck.[19] Before Hurston and Fauset, only a handful of Black

---

18. Morgan, "Why We Get Off," 44.
19. Hughes, *Big Sea*, 238, redaction added. See Hemenway, *Zora Neale Hurston*, 20–21; King, *Gods of the Upper Air*, 10; Plant, "Benedict-Hurston Connection," 436; and Baker, *From Savage to Negro*, 153–63.

writers, scholars, and intellectuals had done serious Black folklore collection.[20] Boas was excited about the work of these early Black folklorists, and in the 1920s he began to recruit Black graduate students to support his own efforts because he believed that they, as people "on the 'inside,'" might be able to elicit more open and "authentic" displays of Black folklore and folk manners.[21] In 1927 Hurston went to Florida on a research fellowship to record Black folklore in Eatonville and surrounding areas.[22] The fieldwork that she conducted from 1927 to 1932 was eventually published as *Mules and Men* (1935), a book that defied the conventions of traditional "folk" ethnographies by blurring the lines between observer and observed, objective and subjective, fact and fiction, authenticity and artifice, science and art.[23] After parting ways with Alan Lomax over one of his colleague's insistence on photographing an Eatonville resident eating watermelon, Hurston received a 1936 Guggenheim Fellowship to conduct research in Jamaica and Haiti, where she wrote *Their Eyes Were Watching God* and collected material for her second folklore collection, *Tell My Horse* (1938).[24]

As Hurston's entrée into the field of folklore collection suggests, the 1920s and 1930s saw major shifts in the field of anthropology, shifts that impacted American theories of race and folk culture. Dominant scientific and anthropological discourses of the nineteenth and early twentieth centuries constructed Black people as "primitive, uncivilized, and/or quaint and simple 'others'" as part of an effort "to buttress constructions of whites as inherently civilized, modern, rational, and ultimately superior beings endowed with the right and responsibility to rule over and/or be separated from inferior nonwhite others."[25] Boas's work exposed the bias underlying such theories, positing instead an influential theory of cultural difference that described all human cultures as equally dynamic, complex, and shaped by environmental and historical, rather than biological or essential, determinants.[26] And yet, although this approach is often referred to as "cultural relativism," Boas was not a pure relativist. Rather, he argued that it was "one of the fundamental aims of scientific anthropology to learn which traits of behavior" are "due to the culture

---

20. Early Black folklorists included Anna Julia Cooper and several others associated with the Hampton Folklore Society. See Lamothe, *Inventing the New Negro*, 23–32; Moody-Turner, *Black Folklore*, 3–8; and Hemenway, *Zora Neale Hurston*, 86–87.
21. Baker, *From Savage to Negro*, 151; and Lamothe, *Inventing the New Negro*, 5.
22. See Hemenway, *Zora Neale Hurston*, 87.
23. See Retman, *Real Folks*, 154.
24. See Hemenway, *Zora Neale Hurston*, 212, 230–31; and Stewart, *Long Past Slavery*, 165–66.
25. Moody-Turner, *Black Folklore*, 6.
26. See Boas, *Mind of Primitive Man*, 103; Boas, *Anthropology and Modern Life*, 57; and Kadlec, "Zora Neale Hurston and the Federal Folk," 477.

in which we live" and which are "organically determined and are, therefore, the common property of mankind."[27] To do this, he argued, the ethnographer "must endeavor to divest himself entirely of opinions and emotions based upon the peculiar social environment into which he is born.... The more successful he is in freeing himself from [this] bias ... the more successful he will be."[28] By separating "nature" from "nurture" via rigorous and objective scientific observation, Boas aimed to disprove the claims of racist pseudoscientists and provide positive scientific evidence for "a wider concept of humanity."[29]

Boas's anthropological model not only depended centrally on the ideal of scientific objectivity, but it also presented the (Western) scientific observer as having unique access to that superior objective outlook.[30] As Boas would write:

> A long and difficult step was taken when the acquired knowledge was first systematized and conscious inquiry was attempted intended to expand the boundaries of knowledge. In early times imagination was drawn upon to supply the causal links between the phenomena of nature, or to give teleological explanations that satisfied the mind. Gradually the domain for the play of imagination has been restricted and the serious attempt is being made to subject imaginative hypotheses to the close scrutiny of observation.[31]

Although Boas dismissed most assertions of Western cultural superiority as cultural bias, he considered "the rapid development of science and ... scientific knowledge" to be "impressive indications of the progress of modern civilization," and he associated these knowledge systems unproblematically with the West.[32] "Modern civilization," he wrote, had improved on the knowledge systems of "primitive" societies by moving from understanding the world through the mere "play of imagination" to understanding the world through the more rigorous and objective "scrutiny of observation," and this shift had brought with it an "increase in our knowledge and in the control of nature."[33]

---

27. Boas, *Anthropology and Modern Life*, 114. See also Lewis's introduction to Boas, *Anthropology and Modern Life*, xx–xxi.

28. Boas, *Mind of Primitive Man*, 98.

29. Boas, *Anthropology and Modern Life*, 57, 127. Indeed, the first fieldwork Boas asked Hurston to do was "measurements of Harlem physiognomy," a sign of the troubling depth of Boas's "commitment to 'objective research'—the skulls must be measured" (Hemenway, *Zora Neale Hurston*, 88).

30. See Jacobs, "From 'Spy-Glass' to 'Horizon,'" 330–31; and West, "Subversions of Boasian Anthropology," 157.

31. Boas, *Anthropology and Modern Life*, 121.

32. Boas, *Anthropology and Modern Life*, 120.

33. Boas, *Anthropology and Modern Life*, 121–22.

In these areas, he believed, it was possible to see cultural differences not in relative terms but in progressive, evolutionary, hierarchical terms, leading "from simplicity to complexity."[34] In this way, Boas embraced the legacy of a colonial framework that saw Western knowledge systems as more objective, advanced, and superior to folk or "primitive" knowledge systems.

Hurston's folklore work, by contrast, reveals a playful skepticism toward the objectivity of the anthropological method and the role of the scientific observer, distinguishing her approach from that of the white mentors and colleagues—Boas, Mead, and Benedict—with whom she is often aligned.[35] As Suzanne Clark argues, "in *Mules and Men* . . . the persona of the anthropologist—objective, professional, and disinterested—is the subject of a narrative that will not work to get field data."[36] Hurston's work also reveals a playful skepticism toward Boas's association of "cultural progress" with both Western knowledge systems and the concepts of domination and control.[37] In *Tell My Horse*, she aimed to show that voodoo—which Boas would have classified as a folk belief system based on "the play of imagination"—was based "not on superstition but on knowledge of nature."[38] As Hurston wrote in a letter to her funding agency: "I think that I will be doing medical science a great service to identify these weeds so that antidotes can be prepared. The greatest power of voodoo rests upon this knowledge."[39] Hurston's analysis of voodoo also suggests that knowledge of nature does not lead naturally to the domination or control of nature, as Boas assumed. Rather, voodoo unites the "scientific understanding of plants and animals" with a "religious belief in the superiority of Nature over human will."[40] Hurston's engagement with the nature-versus-nurture debate refutes not only primitivist and eugenicist discourses about Black people's biological inferiority but also colonial investments in Western intellectual superiority and domination that lingered in Boas's anthropological framework.

By refusing Boas's objectivity, Hurston placed herself out of step with both the field of anthropology and with the documentarian and social realist

---

34. Boas, *Anthropology and Modern Life*, 121.

35. On their alignment, see King, *Gods of the Upper Air*, 10–11; and Plant, "Benedict-Hurston Connection," 455. On their differences, see West, "Subversions of Boasian Anthropology," 158; and Moody-Turner, *Black Folklore*, 158. Moody-Turner also notes that Hurston's skepticism toward objectivity aligns more closely with the approach of the early Black folklorists of the Hampton Folklore Society (*Black Folklore*, 158–59).

36. Clark, "Narrative Fitness," 46.

37. Boas, *Anthropology and Modern Life*, 120.

38. Boas, *Anthropology and Modern Life*, 121; and Clark, "Narrative Fitness," 59.

39. Zora Neale Hurston to Henry Allen Moe, Guggenheim Foundation principal administrator from 1925 to 1963, 10 June 1936, in Kaplan, *Zora Neale Hurston*, 382, quoted in Hemenway, *Zora Neale Hurston*, 229.

40. Clark, "Narrative Fitness," 59.

aesthetics of the 1930s and '40s.⁴¹ In many ways, Boas's progressive valuing of diverse cultures mirrored the central strategy of the mid- to late 1930s leftwing antifascist coalition known as the Popular Front, with which many Black writers became involved. The Great Depression had meant that white philanthropists and consumers had less disposable income to spend in Harlem, and many Harlem Renaissance artists joined the Communist Party of the United States of America (CPUSA), took up employment with the New Deal Works Progress Administration (WPA) Federal Writers' Project documenting the history and cultures of the United States, and increasingly aligned themselves and their writing with leftist politics, organizations, and themes.⁴² But while Black writers began to critique the Black "folk" art of the prior generation as having pandered to the primitivist stereotypes of the white elite, versions of those stereotypes continued to persist in these leftist coalitions.⁴³ Indeed, when the white-dominated CPUSA adopted the strategy of the Popular Front in 1934, the image of the "folk" was embraced precisely because its opaque referent was usefully vague enough to help build a broad coalition of leftists. As Michael Denning argues, the Popular Front's populism often depended on the elision of racial difference and an implicit appeal to a white-identified American nationalism.⁴⁴ When nonwhite folk figures were embraced by ethnographers, folklorists, and other prominent figures in the Popular Front, it was most often by drawing on the primitivist fantasies of the prior decade to represent those nonwhite others as representatives of a primitive, closer-to-nature past.⁴⁵ Sonnet Retman summarizes:

> African Americans were often represented as exotic, domestic "others." Poor rural whites, alternatively, were made to symbolize a nostalgic and "traditional" Anglo-Saxon identity. Each group may have been assigned its specific place in the Edenic past but the groups certainly were not treated equally. These representations shored up white privilege, providing a folksy precapitalist antecedent to the white figure of the "standard" citizen-consumer in the 1930s.⁴⁶

---

41. See Kadlec, "Zora Neale Hurston and the Federal Folk," 477; and Retman, *Real Folks*, 28.
42. See Jones, "Black Excesses and Deprivations," 33–34.
43. See Wright, "Between Laughter and Tears," 25; and Hughes, *Big Sea*, 325.
44. See Denning, *Cultural Front*, 267.
45. See, for example, folklorists John and Alan Lomax's treatment of Black singer Huddie "Lead Belly" Ledbetter in Filene, *Romancing the Folk*, 58–63.
46. Retman, *Real Folks*, 14.

Although "folk" aesthetics appealed to many Black writers' cultural and class interests, the differential treatment of Black and white folk populations in the ethnographic, documentarian, and populist imagination of the period suggests that "folk" aesthetics were used just as often to maintain as to disrupt racial and economic disparities.

Hurston's fiction, folklore, and essays offer a playful response to both anthropological and Popular Front efforts to exclude Black folk, art, and experience from their respective universalist frameworks. Furthermore, where other Black female writers of the Harlem Renaissance such as Nella Larsen and Marita Bonner often focused on the pain caused by such exclusions, Hurston used pleasure as an entry point into opening new ways to imagine and describe human experience. As she famously wrote in 1928, "I do not belong to the sobbing school of Negrohood who hold that nature somehow has given them a lowdown dirty deal and whose feelings are all hurt about it."[47] Sorrow and pain were not the tools Hurston wanted to assert her rightful place in the world; she was "too busy sharpening [her] oyster knife," a tool and a phrase that poet Eve L. Ewing argues "at once implies luxury, opulence, eroticism," and even "the potential for violence."[48] By centering within her subjectivity the radical pursuit of physical pleasure, Hurston cuts through the narratives of respectability and primitivism that kept Black women from the full expression and enjoyment of their bodies, along with Western thought's most beloved binary oppositions: mind/body, civilization/primitive, human/animal, and culture/nature.

Nature/Nurture, Insides/Outsides

The scene in *Their Eyes* that most directly addresses the relationship of nature to nurture is one in which Sam Watson and Lige Moss debate "whut is it dat keeps uh man from gettin' burnt on uh red-hot stove—caution or nature?"[49] Lige takes the position that it must be caution, or culture, since "if it was nature, nobody wouldn't have tuh look out for babies touchin' stoves, would they?"[50] Sam one-ups that position by arguing that "it's nature, cause nature makes caution."[51] At first glance, Lige's position that nurture trumps nature appears to mirror Boas's argument that cultures are environmentally and

---

47. Hurston, "How It Feels," 827.
48. Hurston, "How It Feels," 827; and Ewing, "On 'What I Mean.'"
49. Hurston, *Their Eyes*, 64.
50. Hurston, *Their Eyes*, 64.
51. Hurston, *Their Eyes*, 65.

historically rather than biologically produced. But for Boas, environmental and historical determinants were the cause of cultural difference; here, the focus is on what it is that makes "uh man" *similar* to all others. After all, Sam argues, whether the behavior is learned or innate, most humans familiar with stoves will avoid touching them. If learned, it is an experience that all humans learn from in the same way; if innate, it again implies universality across the human species.[52] Sam's point, then, correlates with Boas's interest in those "natural" traits that humans share in common, and the debate between Sam and Lige—which is interrupted and never resolved—highlights Boas's interests in separating environmentally and naturally determined human traits, and in using naturally determined human traits as the basis for any conceptualization of shared humanity.

Lige and Sam never resolve their differences, but the novel itself tests Sam's proposal that caution—or culture—follows from nature. If, in the case of the stove, the thing that is common to us all is pain, the novel recasts the debate in terms of pleasure. If we learn naturally from our environment how to decrease pain, don't we also learn how to increase pleasure? This is the conclusion that Janie comes to at the dawning of her "conscious life," which begins with an intimate experience of nature.[53] In her innocence, Janie connects natural processes with known cultural institutions: "She saw a dust-bearing bee sink into the sanctum of a bloom; the thousand sister-calyxes arch to meet the love embrace and the ecstatic shiver of the tree from root to tiniest branch creaming in every blossom and frothing with delight. *So this was a marriage!*"[54] Her view is like Sam's: that cultural institutions follow from natural feelings, marriage from sexual pleasure. Moments later, however, Janie experiences "the end of her childhood," when she discovers that pleasure is not socially sanctioned.[55] Her culture does not follow from nature but pulls in the opposite direction—turning, in Koritha Mitchell's words, "away from pleasure and toward propriety."[56]

For many critics, Janie's loss of innocence is therefore solidified by her entry into the bourgeois social order represented by her economically motivated marriages to Logan and Joe.[57] For these critics, Janie's subsequent search

---

52. Admittedly, Sam does not here account for the more complicated possibility that one might "receiv[e] pleasure from physical pain," as in masochism (Musser, *Sensational Flesh*, 7).
53. Hurston, *Their Eyes*, 10.
54. Hurston, *Their Eyes*, 11, emphasis added.
55. Hurston, *Their Eyes*, 12.
56. Mitchell, *From Slave Cabins*, 112.
57. See, for example, Gates, *Signifying Monkey*, 185–91; Lamothe, "Vodou Imagery," 163; Menke, "'Black Cat Bone,'" 132; and Maroto, "'So This Was a Marriage!,'" 77–78.

for the lost liberation of her youth is also associated with her growing participation in folk culture, represented by her rejection of Joe and her relationship with Tea Cake. After all, it is Tea Cake who teaches Janie the "maiden language," an image that refers as much to the pleasure of sex as it does to the pleasure of self-expression.[58] But while it is true that Nanny's claim that "mouf kissin' is on uh equal and dat's natural" runs in direct contrast to Joe's concern that Janie is "gettin' too moufy," and finds temporary fulfillment in Tea Cake's "maiden language," similar imagery also appears in *Tell My Horse* as a rebuke of Black folk wisdom, where Hurston writes that "it is assumed" that the female "mouth . . . was made" for nothing but "to supply some man . . . with kisses."[59] And of course, Janie's "folk" sojourn with Tea Cake to the muck ends not in pleasure but in pain. As Leigh Anne Duck writes, "Because critics correctly think of Hurston as an artist devoted to the representation of 'folk' culture, they often overlook the extent to which her critique of patriarchy connects it with bourgeois, as well as 'folk,' ideology."[60]

The natural imagery that the novel uses to describe Janie's search for liberation is better understood not as a metaphor for Black folk culture but as a literal reference to nature, the natural needs and desires of human bodies, and humanity's place in the natural world. It is not, after all, with the "folk" that young Janie identifies, but with a pear tree. Neither are Janie's physical pleasures mere metaphors for linguistic pleasures, as some critics have argued.[61] As Sharon Davie suggests, "Janie, 'stretched on her back beneath the pear tree,' has a visionary experience that comes to her in an 'inaudible voice.' The experience escapes words, and it is orgasmic, not cerebral."[62] In direct refutation of the Enlightenment's mind-over-body binary, Janie's coming-of-age experience highlights the centrality of the body, in all its pleasures and pains, to human desire and subject-formation. Primitivist stereotypes of the 1920s and 1930s may have encouraged readers to attach nature to Black folk culture, but Hurston's novel asks that we think beyond these colonial stereotypes to understand nature as a distinct force that drives and constrains all human behavior.

Considered through this lens, Janie's recurring troubles are caused by her movement through various communities that want to control her "nature" or her desire for sensual pleasure—in particular, by restricting her access to sensually construed forms of sexual, linguistic, and imaginative "play." In Hurston's novel, then, "the play of imagination" that Boas dismissed as a

---

58. Hurston, *Their Eyes*, 115.
59. Hurston, *Their Eyes*, 23, 75, 115; and Hurston, *Tell My Horse*, 327, 326.
60. Duck, "'Go There tuh *Know* There,'" 280.
61. See, for example, Kaplan, "Erotics of Talk," 117.
62. Davie, "Free Mules, Talking Buzzards," 455.

"primitive" form of knowledge is reconfigured as a physically pleasurable and natural activity; likewise, Boas's idea that progress is defined by our ability to "control" this nature—an idea that is voiced in Hurston's novel by characters such as Nanny and Joe—is challenged by Janie's repeated refusals to see the pleasures and pains of her physical body controlled or determined by cultural norms.[63] For example, when Eatonville residents demand Janie "pay . . . de right amount uh respect tuh [her] dead husband," she refuses because her internal feelings do not match this public expectations: "Ah ain't grievin' so why do Ah hafta mourn?"[64] And when Tea Cake succeeds in courting Janie, it is not by speaking of cultural expectations such as "honor and respect" like her other suitors, but by speaking of his personal "desire."[65] Efforts to control these feelings and desires are figured in Hurston's novel not as progressive, but as oppressive.

In the novel, Janie's thwarted desire for sensual pleasure emerges most often as a conflict between insides and outsides. As the novel notes when Janie's marriage to Joe turns sour because of his overbearing sense of social propriety, "she had an inside and an outside now and suddenly she knew how not to mix them."[66] Although critics sometimes argue that the novel sublimates the longing for sex for the "longing to talk," the novel's construction of insides and outsides serves as a useful metaphor for how Janie is forced to repress her "flesh and blood" desires for the sake of cultural norms:

> She stood there until something fell off the shelf inside her. Then she went inside there to see what it was. It was her image of Jody tumbled down and shattered. But looking at it she saw that it never was the *flesh and blood* figure of her dreams. Just something she had grabbed up to drape her dreams over. . . . She had no more blossomy openings dusting pollen over her man, neither any glistening young fruit where the petals used to be. She found that she had a host of thoughts she had never expressed to him, and numerous emotions she had never let Jody know about. Things packed up and put away in parts of her heart where he could never find them. . . . She bathed and put on a fresh dress and head kerchief and went on to the store before Jody had time to send for her. That was a bow to the outside of things.[67]

Faced with a husband and a community that inhibits her "flesh and blood" desires, Janie does not deny their existence but rather "packed [them] up and

---

63. Boas, *Anthropology and Modern Life*, 120–21.
64. Hurston, *Their Eyes*, 113.
65. Hurston, *Their Eyes*, 93.
66. Hurston, *Their Eyes*, 72.
67. Kaplan, "Erotics of Talk," 117; and Hurston, *Their Eyes*, 72, emphasis added.

put [them] away"; they become a private part of her "insides" that she packs away to protect them from the scrutiny of a hostile "outside" world.[68] Far from being purely linguistic, these "insides" are actively associated with flesh, blood, bodies, and the natural world—with Janie's "blossomy openings" and "glistening young fruit where the petals used to be."[69] Janie's "bow to the outside of things" represents her momentary acquiescence not just to cultural barriers against female self-expression but to cultural barriers against their expression of physical pleasure and bodily desire.[70]

In making the pursuit of physical "flesh and blood" pleasures central to Janie's self-actualization, Hurston challenges Western conceptions of humanity grounded in the human mind and in the mind's control over the body (a control animals were presumed to lack). In this, she prefigures more recent theoretical turns away from Enlightenment conceptions of selfhood as defined by the sovereign control of one's body. As Alvin Henry explains, "The idea of the self as subjectivity . . . adopted the key tenets of liberal humanism, giving primacy to the notion of sovereignty over the self and of self-possession, since ownership over the body founds the first act of sovereignty."[71] This is a definition that has always proven problematic for "enslaved or marginalized people" who "are assumed to lack heroic agency or full self-determination," and thereby, by the terms of liberal humanism, "become dehumanized."[72] Following Saidiya Hartman's argument that even when liberal humanism does recognize Black humanity, that recognition operates more to "tether, bind, and oppress" than to "liberate the flesh," scholars have turned to Hortense Spillers's reclamation of the "flesh" itself—or the body not conceptualized as a sovereign body—for alternative ways of theorizing Black liberation.[73] But where scholars typically associate the flesh with pain, Hurston associates it as strongly with pleasure.[74] In this way, she prefigures Morgan's call "to articulate a politics of pleasure that positions pleasure not only as [a] desirable goal and a social and political imperative, but also as an under-theorized resistance strategy for black women."[75] As Morgan writes, "a great deal of energy has been spent disputing deeply entrenched and dehumanizing stereotypes" about Black female sexuality.[76] The "upside" of this has been "a sorely needed, compassionate

---

68. Hurston, *Their Eyes*, 72.
69. Hurston, *Their Eyes*, 72.
70. Hurston, *Their Eyes*, 72.
71. Henry, *Black Queer Flesh*, 1–2.
72. Henry, *Black Queer Flesh*, 2.
73. Hartman, *Scenes of Subjection*, 5; and Spillers, "Mama's Baby, Papa's Maybe," 67.
74. Spillers, "Mama's Baby, Papa's Maybe," 67–68; Weheliye, *Habeas Viscus*, 12–14; Musser, *Sensational Flesh*, 20; and Henry, *Black Queer Flesh*, 5.
75. Morgan, "Why We Get Off," 44.
76. Morgan, "Why We Get Off," 36.

rendering of the difficult and compromised space black women's sexuality occupies."[77] On the other hand, "the downside has been a mulish inattentiveness to black women's engagements with pleasure—the complex, messy, sticky, and even joyous negotiations of agency and desire that are irrevocably twinned with our pain."[78] Under the twin historical threats of sexual exploitation and sexual stereotypes, Black female sexuality and desire have become virtually unspeakable—hidden for the sake of Black female survival. Hurston's fiction, however, places sexual desire at the center of her Black female protagonist's interiority and uses the fictional form to narrate the sociocultural race, class, and gender obstacles that prevent Janie from expressing these "insides" to the "outside" world. As Catherine Knight Steele insists, such expressions of sexuality reclaim for Black women the "freedom granted at birth to those occupying white, cis, male bodies—those whose humanity goes unchallenged in our society."[79]

Hurston would explore these obstacles to the expression of Black women's full, fleshy humanity in her nonfiction narratives as well. Most famously, in "How It Feels to Be Colored Me" (1928), Hurston uses the nominal topic of defining Black identity to narrate the incompatibility of her internal "feelings" with rigid and fixed sociocultural classifications. Far from always "feeling . . . colored," Hurston describes her feelings as shifting and complex: "I remember the very day that I became colored," "I do not always feel colored," "I feel most colored when," "at certain times I have no race."[80] Throughout the essay, Hurston's feelings contend with the rigid classifications and stereotypes of the outside world that looks upon her complex humanity and sees only "a little colored girl": "I found it out in certain ways. In my heart as well as in the mirror, I became a fast brown—warranted not to rub nor run."[81] Despite her shifting and complex "feelings," the outside world has no trouble placing her into a simple, static category.

Notably, in the essay, the outside world also threatens Hurston's expression of physical pleasure by reducing those pleasures to primitivist stereotypes about "color." "For instance," she writes, "when I sit in the drafty basement that is The New World Cabaret with a white person, my color comes."[82] Listening to jazz music in white company, she feels the tension between the physical pleasure the music evokes "within" her and the cultural taboos surrounding the expression of such pleasures:

---

77. Morgan, "Why We Get Off," 36.
78. Morgan, "Why We Get Off," 36.
79. Steele, "Black Feminist Pleasure," 464.
80. Hurston, "How It Feels," 829, 826, 828, 828, 829.
81. Hurston, "How It Feels," 827.
82. Hurston, "How It Feels," 828.

[The music] constricts the thorax and splits the heart with its tempo and narcotic harmonies. This orchestra grows rambunctious, rears on its hind legs and attacks the tonal veil with primitive fury, rending it, clawing it until it breaks through to the jungle beyond. I follow those heathen—follow them exultingly. I dance wildly inside myself; I yell within, I whoop. . . . I am in the jungle and living in the jungle way. . . . But the piece ends. . . . I creep back slowly to the veneer we call civilization with the last tone and find the white friend sitting motionless in his seat, smoking calmly. "Good music they have here," he remarks, drumming the table with his fingertips. Music! The great blobs of purple and red emotion have not touched him. He has only heard what I felt. . . . He is so pale with his whiteness then and I am *so* colored.[83]

As Cheryl Wall notes, Hurston's use of "exaggerated" jungle metaphors seems to "parody the myth of exotic primitivism" even as Hurston simultaneously insists "that the power of the music . . . is genuine."[84] Hurston describes feeling the pleasures of the music in her "thorax" and her "heart," but she also demonstrates that in the company of a white person, the primitivist assumptions that place physical pleasure and emotion beyond "the veneer we call civilization" can only be understood in racialized terms: "He is so pale with his whiteness then and I am *so* colored."[85] Nevertheless, she refuses to deny herself the pleasures of the music, dancing "wildly inside myself."[86] For Wall, Hurston's "wholly internalized" response to the music's "undefinable and unspeakable" physical and emotional power allows her to claim the pleasures of those feelings, while also acknowledging that too often "the key to survival" for Black women is to "keep one's feelings safely hidden" or controlled.[87]

Hurston's folkloric and fictional work straddles this tension between expressing and hiding Black women's inner feelings, pleasures, and sexuality. In her introduction to *Mules and Men*, Hurston famously describes her culture as "fitting me like a tight chemise," a sexually charged image for the tight but distinct relationship between her physical body and its cultural significance.[88] It is not until she goes to college that she can view this garment from an "outside" perspective: "I could see myself like somebody else and stand off and look at my garment. Then I had to have the spy-glass of Anthropology to look through at that."[89] For Karen Jacobs, the "spy-glass" that Hurston is

---

83. Hurston, "How It Feels," 828–29, emphasis in original.
84. Wall, *Women of the Harlem Renaissance*, 29.
85. Hurston, "How It Feels," 828–29.
86. Hurston, "How It Feels," 828.
87. Wall, *Women of the Harlem Renaissance*, 29.
88. Hurston, *Mules and Men*, 9.
89. Hurston, *Mules and Men*, 9.

encouraged to turn on herself and her community "evokes not just the penetrating male gaze of science, but also the imperial white gaze of colonialism" with all of its voyeuristic, exploitative, and primitivist connotations.[90] The "spy-glass of anthropology" may give her an "outside" perspective on her culture, but it also threatens to reduce the fleshy complexity of the individuals within that culture to rigidly racialized, sexualized, and controlled objects of scientific and colonial knowledge.

In *Their Eyes Were Watching God*, it is not merely the white connoisseur of Black culture and the white anthropologist who threaten to observe and fix complex Black feelings into rigid stereotypes and scientific classifications, but all the communities with which Janie interacts. Her very first conscious experience is defined by the conflict between who she feels herself to be on the "inside" and how she is seen on the "outside." As a six-year-old living in Mrs. Washburn's backyard, Janie doesn't see any difference between herself and the other children with whom she plays: "Ah was wid dem white chillun so much till Ah didn't know Ah wuzn't white."[91] But when she sees a photograph of herself she is forced to occupy an "outside" perspective for the first time: "There wasn't nobody left except a real dark little girl with long hair. . . . Dat's where Ah wuz s'posed to be, but Ah couldn't recognize dat dark chile as me."[92] The scene is remarkably similar to the "revelation" described by W. E. B. Du Bois in the opening pages of *The Souls of Black Folk* (1903), in which being dismissed by a white girl "with a glance" leads him to "see himself through the revelation of the other world": "I was different from the others; or like, mayhap in heart and life and longing, but shut out from their world by a vast veil."[93] Likewise, Janie is only able to recognize the distinction between herself and the other children when she moves from her "inside" perspective to the "outside" perspective made available to her by the photograph. Of course, Hurston famously rejected Du Bois's theory of double consciousness by claiming that she had "no separate feelings about being an American citizen and colored. I am merely a fragment of the Great Soul that surges within the boundaries."[94] In *Their Eyes,* then, the veil does not result in the "twoness" of being "an American" and "a Negro," but rather divides Janie's internal experience of self—that fragment of the Great Soul—from her culturally and hierarchically bounded exterior (both "American" and "Negro"). In other words, like the "spy-glass of Anthropology," the photograph allows Janie

---

90. Jacobs, "From 'Spy-Glass' to 'Horizon,'" 330.
91. Hurston, *Their Eyes*, 8.
92. Hurston, *Their Eyes*, 9.
93. Du Bois, *Souls of Black Folk*, 4–5.
94. Hurston, "How It Feels," 829.

to "see [herself] like somebody else," but that outside perspective is notably inconsistent with her internal one: "Before Ah seen de picture Ah thought Ah wuz just like de rest."[95] In contrast to Boas's investment in "objective" observation, Hurston's folklore and fiction reveal a persistent skepticism about the ability of such "outside" observations to capture the complexity of interior human experience without distorting it to fit rigid and oversimplified social classifications, expectations, and stereotypes.

Hurston's folklore and fiction tread a careful line between exploring the physicality of Black women's interiority and narrating the rigid social expectations that constrain its expression. In her 1950 essay, "What White Publishers Won't Print," Hurston would express her frustration with the "Anglo-Saxon's lack of curiosity about the internal lives and emotions of the Negroes," which she attributed to their racist belief that Black people have no interiority at all but are mere "types." As she put it:

> The answer lies in what we may call THE AMERICAN MUSEUM OF UNNATURAL HISTORY. This is an intangible built on token belief. It is assumed that all non-Anglo-Saxons are uncomplicated stereotypes. Everybody knows about them. They are lay figures mounted in the museum where all may take them in at a glance. They are made of bent wires without insides at all.[96]

Here, Hurston describes the colonial practice of the natural history museum, which acquired human and nonhuman "specimens" through raid and conquest and displayed them as evidence of the collector's (often the anthropologist's) "alleged distance" from "the societies that produced them."[97] Satirizing the museum's "unnatural" treatment of human beings as nonhumans, Hurston points to the dehumanizing effects of this ideological framework. As she would write in her autobiography, *Dust Tracks on a Road* (1942): "It seemed to me that the human beings I met reacted pretty much the same to the same stimuli. Different idioms, yes. Circumstances and conditions having power to influence, yes. Inherent difference, no."[98] But the "American Museum of Unnatural History" prevented white Americans from recognizing this shared humanity: "As long as the majority cannot conceive of a Negro or a Jew feeling and reacting inside just as they do, the majority will keep right on believing

---

95. Hurston, *Mules and Men*, 9; and Hurston, *Their Eyes*, 9.
96. Hurston, "White Publishers Won't Print," 950–52.
97. MacKenzie, *Museums and Empire*, 4.
98. Hurston, *Dust Tracks on a Road*, 713.

that people who do not look like them cannot possibly feel as they do."[99] For Hurston, dismantling this misperception requires the revelation of Black people's interior emotional lives—an expression to which she argues fiction, rather than the "objective" systems of classification and control of the sciences, is uniquely suited.

Although Hurston shared Boas's investment in identifying those traits that were natural to all humans in order to establish a broader vision of common humanity, her explicit critique of human efforts to control this nature represents a significant challenge to Boas's worldview. Boas did acknowledge the significant role that nonrational emotional experience played in human behavior; indeed, an important piece of his overarching critique of eugenics was that eugenics "treats the problem of procreation from a purely rationalistic point of view, and assumes that the ideal of human development lies in the complete rationalization of human life."[100] The anthropologist, he writes, agrees with the eugenicist in seeing "the steady advance of the rational knowledge of mankind" as "a source of satisfaction to him no less than to the biologist," but also sees that "our everyday habits . . . present endless proofs of the fact that our actions are the results of emotional preferences" and therefore that he "cannot acknowledge such a complete domination of emotion by reason."[101] This tension between reason and emotion lies unresolved in Boas's work. On the one hand, he sees human progress in the domination or control of nature; on the other hand, he also sees human emotions as a constant of human nature that cannot be fully dominated or controlled. But where Boas sees emotion as a fact of nature that limits the "steady advance of . . . rational knowledge," Hurston suggests that "cultural progress" might be possible if we began to see ourselves as part of the natural world, rather than trying to control and dominate our natures and the natural world alike.[102]

Pleasure, Pain, and Power

Hurston's use of natural imagery has led *Their Eyes Were Watching God* to be read through a primitivist lens that flatly perceives Black people and Black folk culture as being closer to nature and closer to our "animal" origins.[103]

---

99. Hurston, "White Publishers Won't Print," 952–53.
100. Boas, *Anthropology and Modern Life*, 61.
101. Boas, *Anthropology and Modern Life*, 61.
102. Boas, *Anthropology and Modern Life*, 61, 120.
103. On these primitivist claims' foundation in the work of Enlightenment philosophers such as Hume and Kant, see Davie, "Free Mules, Talking Buzzards," 449. See also Gates, "Writing 'Race,'" 8–11.

However, in numerous ways, Hurston's novel refutes this evolutionary and hierarchical view of the relationship of the human to the natural and animal world. Boas, though revolutionary for his time in his refutation of scientific racism, continued to invest in a binary relationship between humans and other animals. For Boas, "the differences between the minds of the animal and of man . . . are so striking that little or no diversity of opinion exists."[104] But he also admitted this perspective was limited to Western knowledge systems, arguing that "to the mind of primitive man . . . the dividing-line between man and animal is not sharply drawn."[105] Where Boas considered it merely "striking" and "peculiar" that "concepts that appear to us alike and related" are, in other knowledge systems, "separated and rearranged," Hurston's fiction and folklore disrupt Western presumptions about a static and hierarchical animal/human binary and exposes human beings' failed attempts to control and deny their animal natures.[106] Refusing a primitivist logic that associates Black communities alone with the animal, while also refusing Western attempts to deny human enmeshment in the shifting power relationships of the natural and animal world, Hurston instead imagines all human experience to be borne out of our natural, animal, embodied, and fully human experiences of sex and death, or pleasure and pain.

Whereas the primitivist understanding of human–animal relations that persists in Boas's work assumes a flat animal world that is evolutionarily inferior to humans, animals in Hurston's fiction and folklore, and in African American folklore in general, occupy a complicated and shifting social hierarchy. Although Henry Louis Gates Jr. has interpreted the animals of the "Signifying Monkey" stories in linguistic terms—with the monkey standing for the rhetorical use of language and the lion standing for the literal use of language—it is essential to those stories that these animals also occupy different positions of linguistic and physical power.[107] The monkey's linguistic besting of the lion is impressive because the lion is physically stronger than the monkey. The animal who bests the other with rhetorical language is also not fixed. There are plenty of Br'er Rabbit stories where the rabbit is bested by the fox, and where the pleasure of the storytelling is found in the back-and-forth over who ends up on top. In *Mules and Men*, dueling stories such as "How the 'Gator Got His Mouth," "How Brer 'Gator Got His Tongue Worn Out," "How the 'Gator Got Black," "How Brer Dog Lost His Beautiful Voice," and "What the Rabbit Learned" compete with one another over the relationship between gators, dogs, and rabbits, painting the relationships of the animal world as

---

104. Boas, *Mind of Primitive Man*, 96.
105. Boas, *Mind of Primitive Man*, 198.
106. Boas, *Mind of Primitive Man*, 198.
107. Gates, *Signifying Monkey*, 55.

playful, shifting, and importantly nonbinary, where the dog bests the gator in one story and the rabbit bests the dog in the next. The animals in *Their Eyes* occupy a similarly rich natural world: the wild bees that help Janie discover her sexuality are different from the domesticated mule that helps her understand her burdens and the mad dog who must die so that she can survive. The natural world in the novel is similarly dynamic: the pear tree that marks Janie's consciousness of sexual pleasure and human connection to the natural world does not serve the same narrative function as the hurricane, which marks Janie's consciousness of human insignificance. Hurston's natural world is not a flat terrain whose purpose is to be dominated and controlled by humans, but a shifting landscape in which humans and other animals do not always have the upper hand.

Human social relationships in Hurston's fiction and folklore are similarly dynamic. Nanny's observation in *Their Eyes Were Watching God* that "De ni**er woman is de mule uh de world" is oft-repeated by Hurston scholars, but in the folklore that permeates the novel, the place of both mules and women in the world's social hierarchy is repeatedly contested in and through folkloric exchanges.[108] As Wall writes, "Hurston's narrative strategies allow her to represent, first, the ways in which women are relegated to subordinate roles in the culture she otherwise celebrates and, second, the means by which women in that culture gain access to creative expression and power."[109] In the exchanges surrounding one of the most striking stories in *Mules and Men*, "Why Women Always Take Advantage of Men," one female storyteller named Mathilda Moseley suggests that *men* are the mule of the world. Although one male listener claims that "we got all de strength and all de law and all de money and you can't git a thing but whut we jes' take pity on you and give you," Mathilda calls this evidence of women's superior intellect and advantage.[110] Her story explains why "de man makes and de woman takes" and concludes that it is men, not women, who occupy the position of the laboring mule: "You men is still braggin' 'bout yo strength and de women is sittin' on de keys and letting you blow off till she git ready to put de bridle on you."[111] Likewise, although the title of *Mules and Men* seems to "privilege . . . the male," even this phrasing highlights a linguistic disruption of static social hierarchies—readable as either contrasting or equating mules and men or, when layered with Nanny's linking of women to mules, contrasting or equating women and men.[112] In

---

108. Hurston, *Their Eyes*, 14, redaction added.
109. Wall, "*Mules and Men* and Women," 661.
110. Hurston, *Mules and Men*, 34–35.
111. Hurston, *Mules and Men*, 38.
112. Wall, "*Mules and Men* and Women," 661.

other words, the title identifies the strategies by which men attempt to distinguish themselves from "mules" and "women" alike, and the ironic futility of those efforts.

Moments such as this could be described as aligning with what Victoria Googasian calls "the classic reading of Hurston" which "construe[s] voice as the key to personal and political agency" and presumes that "giving speech to the speechless affirms the humanity of the speaker."[113] For example, Wall argues that in this particular folkloric exchange, women momentarily "become subjects in their own discourse rather than the objects they generally are in the discourse of black men and white men and women."[114] And yet, as Wall herself notes, the problem with such readings is that having a "voice" doesn't necessarily translate into material power: these "discursive transformations do not make [women] the subjects of their own lives. Before the scene is concluded, more stories are told, but, between men and women, nothing is changed."[115] Moreover, the appeal to "voice" as a source of agency and subjectivity problematically depends on and reinforces the hierarchical binaries of liberal humanism that Hurston's work shows have been used to dehumanize Black people, denying their humanity by turning them into "tongueless, earless, eyeless . . . brutes."[116] In fact, while Mathilda does claim a "voice" for herself in the storytelling exchange, the story itself has little to do with the power of voice and everything to do with the instability of the disempowered category of the "brute": "Let 'im keep his strength," woman decides, but "de man had to mortgage his strength to her to live."[117] Seamlessly moving "strength" from an association with agency and ownership to an association with the captive brute, Mathilda shows that the binary oppositions of patriarchal, colonial, and liberal humanist power structures are not as stable as those who are traditionally empowered by those structures would like to pretend.

The shifting power relations in Hurston's representation of the human, animal, and natural world similarly illuminate the shifting power relations that govern the social dynamics of *Their Eyes*. Critics often talk about Janie's "oppression" and "empowerment" in the novel but rarely discuss how these two versions or deployments of power intersect and conflict. Davie is one of few critics to note that Janie's empowering exchange with Joe depends on her making him "trade places with her": "Joe is imaged as a female ('When you pull down yo' britches, you look lak de change uh life'). . . . Janie now has more

---

113. Googasian, "Zora Neale Hurston," 24. See also Henry, *Black Queer Flesh*, 2.
114. Wall, "*Mules and Men* and Women," 667.
115. Wall, "*Mules and Men* and Women," 667.
116. Hurston, *Their Eyes*, 1.
117. Hurston, *Mules and Men*, 38.

power than Joe does, an indication that women can signify their way out of oppression. But Joe is brought down only when Janie labels him a menopausal woman, an echo of the cultural devaluation of women."[118] Here, Janie empowers herself not by dismantling the male/female social hierarchy, but by making Joe occupy the female position. As a result, her self-empowerment has "an uncomfortable edge."[119] Communal expressions of empowerment in the novel are often similarly fraught. For example, for both the Eatonville community at the start of the novel and the "muck" community in the trial scene, "killing tools out of laughs" and "tongues cocked and loaded" are understood to be "the only real weapon left to weak folks."[120] Just as the "folk" on the muck redirect their anger at "white folks" toward a weaker "ni**er woman," the "folk" on the porch redirect their daily economic and social frustrations on "lesser things": "These sitters had been tongueless, earless, eyeless conveniences all day long. Mules and other brutes had occupied their skins. But now, the sun and the bossman were gone, so the skins felt powerful and human. They became lords of sounds and lesser things. . . . They sat in judgment."[121] Much as Janie empowered herself by making Joe feel "lesser," the Eatonville community insists on their humanity by occupying the position of the oppressor; they feel "powerful and human" by becoming "lords" over "lesser things."[122] Similarly, on the muck, Tea Cake beats Janie when he is threatened by Mrs. Turner's light-skinned brother because it "reassured him in possession" of her.[123] Much as Janie does with Joe, when these characters feel disempowered, they empower themselves by asserting their power over others.

What, then, if anything, differentiates Janie's self-empowerment from these other, potentially more sinister, expressions of power? The difficulty critics have had in answering this question may be wrapped up in one-sided ways of thinking about power. As feminist theorist Amy Allen argues:

> Feminists have traditionally talked about power in one of two ways: either by focusing on the ways in which men have power over women—that is, on power understood as domination—or by concentrating on the power that women have to act—that is, on power understood as empowerment. . . . [But] neither of these one-sided feminist conceptions of power can do justice to the complex ways in which women can be both dominated and

---

118. Davie, "Free Mules, Talking Buzzards," 451.
119. Davie, "Free Mules, Talking Buzzards," 451.
120. Hurston, *Their Eyes*, 2, 185–86.
121. Hurston, *Their Eyes*, 186, 1, redaction added.
122. Hurston, *Their Eyes*, 1.
123. Hurston, *Their Eyes*, 147.

empowered at the same time and in the context of one and the same practice, institution, or norm.[124]

Allen proposes instead that we begin thinking of power in more situated, shifting, and complex terms such as "power-over, power-to, and power-with," which "are not best understood as distinct types or forms of power" but as "analytically distinguishable features of a situation" that may all be present in any given interaction.[125] Hurston's fiction and folklore showcases such complex operations and exchanges of power—not fixed, classified, or simplified into pure representations of empowerment or domination, but shifting, relational, and impossible to pin down.

In *Their Eyes*, the pleasure and play of storytelling depend on this continual shifting of social power dynamics, in which individuals use the power of words to continually reclassify social roles and keep those dynamics fluid rather than fixed. This pleasure is disrupted only when this rotating exchange of power is substituted for fixed, static, and rigid power dynamics—or when the "play of imagination" is replaced with classification, stratification, domination, and control.[126] For example, where porch talk is one of the key strategies by which women in Hurston's work can challenge their social subordination, "Joe had forbidden [Janie] to indulge. He didn't want her talking after such trashy people."[127] By keeping Janie from participating in the porch talk, he attempts to fix in place her gendered subordination to him while using her to demonstrate his class superiority over the rest of the town.

Janie's situation as the "mule of the world" is further illustrated by the verbal exchanges related to Matt Bonner's mule, a poor creature who is mistreated by his owner, Matt Bonner, and subsequently becomes the town's favorite subject; the mule "was next to the Mayor in prominence, and made better talking."[128] At first, Janie "loved the conversation" about the mule, especially when the primary target of the teasing is the mule's abuser, Matt.[129] But when the "mule talk" at Matt's expense turns to "mule-baiting" at the expense of the mule, Janie gets angry: "A little war of defense for helpless things was going on inside her. People ought to have some regard for helpless things."[130] Joe's response is to do something that words alone cannot do: much as he "builds a high chair for

---

124. Allen, "Rethinking Power," 22.
125. Allen, "Rethinking Power," 37.
126. Boas, *Anthropology and Modern Life*, 121.
127. Hurston, *Their Eyes*, 53–54.
128. Hurston, *Their Eyes*, 53.
129. Hurston, *Their Eyes*, 53.
130. Hurston, *Their Eyes*, 53, 56, 57.

[Janie] to sit in and overlook the world," he buys and "free[s]" the mule.[131] In some ways, the freeing of the mule seems to upset rigid human/animal hierarchies: "Dat's uh new idea 'bout varmints," Sam says.[132] But in other ways, it solidifies both those hierarchies and Joe's social status. As Janie says, "Freein' dat mule makes uh mighty big man outa you. Something like George Washington and Lincoln. Abraham Lincoln, he had de whole United States tuh rule so he freed de Negroes. You got uh town so you freed uh mule. You have tuh have power tuh free things and dat makes you lak uh king uh something."[133] For Davie, "This part of the free mule story in a sense supports the hierarchical status quo. Like Lincoln, the white man who frees black people, Joe, the black man, frees the mule."[134] The moment reminds us that Joe's power depends not on the play of words but on his economic and social power. And while the town continues to enjoy its "free mule" stories, the stories mock the mule's freedom and its pretension of being "like the other citizens."[135] At the mule's mock funeral, Joe uses its "distended belly" as a platform, and Sam mocks the idea of a "mule-heaven" where "mule-angels would have people to ride on."[136] The town "mock[s] everything human in death," and leaves the mule for the buzzards, just "like all other dead brutes."[137] The rigid social order—human/animal, man/woman, white/Black, rich/poor—is restored.

However, the buzzard funeral that immediately follows the mule's mock funeral counters human pretensions to dominate the natural world and fit human life into rigid hierarchical categories. Just as the humans mocked the mule's freedom, citizenship, and access to heaven by giving him a funeral and then leaving him for the buzzards, these creatures turn the tables: they call the mule a "man" and proceed to "pick . . . out the eyes in the ceremonial way."[138] Googasian argues that buzzards are already "terrifying to those who insist on strict hierarchies among these categories" of "human, animal, and thing (food)."[139] Davie further suggests that "the description of the ceremonies" shows "that human beings create hierarchies, systems of control, to defend against death and exert power over life."[140] But despite Joe's pretension to stand above the mule and above death itself, the buzzards remind readers of the

---

131. Hurston, *Their Eyes*, 62, 58.
132. Hurston, *Their Eyes*, 58.
133. Hurston, *Their Eyes*, 58.
134. Davie, "Free Mules, Talking Buzzards," 449.
135. Hurston, *Their Eyes*, 58.
136. Hurston, *Their Eyes*, 60–61.
137. Hurston, *Their Eyes*, 59–60.
138. Hurston, *Their Eyes*, 62.
139. Googasian, "Zora Neale Hurston," 33.
140. Davie, "Free Mules, Talking Buzzards," 450.

inevitability of death and the final place of human bodies in the natural world. The buzzards and other animals will one day stand on the bellies of mules and men. The town's efforts to demonstrate man's superiority over animals are undercut by the role the buzzard plays in nature, which reminds readers of the complex power dynamics among different kinds of animals and that humans are just one of these animals. Joe may be a "big voice," but he also has a body.[141] Like the hurricane that later drives Janie off the muck and the mad dog that bites Tea Cake, the buzzards are another force of nature that remind Hurston's human characters of their lack of control over the natural world.

By refusing to give her characters control over the natural world, Hurston defies the objectifying perspective of Western science and its "Museum of Unnatural History." As Janie describes her desires early in the novel, she had hoped for a "great journey to the horizons in search of *people*. . . . But she had been whipped like a cur dog, and run off down a back road after *things*."[142] Turning away from anthropological classification and control to the fictional and folkloric "play of imagination," Hurston insists on a dynamic representation of Black women's humanity, sexuality, and desire.[143] Carla Kaplan notes that Janie has long since "reject[ed] her grandmother (and, implicitly, the cultural politics of many of her contemporaries) because Nanny gives up on female desire. Nanny, as Janie describes it, had taken the horizon—or desire itself—and 'pinched it in to such a little bit of a thing that she could tie it about her granddaughter's neck tight enough to choke her.'"[144] Janie, by contrast, concludes her narrative by flashing her "oyster knife": "She pulled in her horizon like a great fish-net. Pulled it from around the waist of the world and draped it over shoulder. So much of life in its meshes! She called in her soul to come and see."[145] Capturing life for its food, sustenance, and physical and emotional pleasure, Hurston reminds us of folklore's kinship with the flesh.

Boas's anthropological approach may have given Hurston powerful ways to resist the civilized/primitive and Black/white binaries of colonial frameworks, but it retained a Western colonial investment in the superiority of its own "objective" perspective, "rational" classification system, and rigid hierarchies regarding humanity's relationship to the animal and natural world. Hurston's more complicated take on the natural world instead resists static classifications and acknowledges contextually and temporally shifting power dynamics among humans and other animals. As Barbara Johnson writes, "There is

---

141. Hurston, *Their Eyes*, 46.
142. Hurston, *Their Eyes*, 89, emphasis in original.
143. Boas, *Anthropology and Modern Life*, 120.
144. Kaplan, "Erotics of Talk," 127.
145. Hurston, "How It Feels," 827; and Hurston, *Their Eyes*, 193.

no point of view from which the universal characteristics of the human, or of the woman, or of the black woman, or even of Zora Neale Hurston, can be selected and totalized. Unification and simplification are fantasies of domination, not understanding."[146] In refusing the dominating power and control of the colonial gaze, Hurston also opens up new ways of conceptualizing Black female subjectivity—not as an expression of essentialist and primitivist stereotypes, nor as dependent on the respectable control of the body and its desires, but as an emotional, embodied, and enfleshed experience that is all at once painful, pleasurable, pitiful, and powerful.

In 1936, one year prior to the publication of *Their Eyes Were Watching God*, the CPUSA-affiliated National Negro Congress brought together a broad coalition of Black organizations, unions, and fraternal organizations in support of a platform that included economic, racial, and gender equality.[147] By this point, many of the most prominent Black male artists had "committed to a leftward shift in their writing," and while some writers like Zora Neale Hurston and Sterling Brown kept their eye on working-class Black people of the rural South, the majority turned their attention to the urban Black experience.[148] To buttress these efforts, many Black writers also began to draw increasingly on what Stacy Morgan describes as "emerging scholarship in the sociology of race and class."[149] In many ways, the data-driven approach of this emerging academic field appealed to the materialist, class-oriented politics of this new generation of Black writers. However, as with anthropology's investment in the "objective" observer, sociology's investment in normative race, class, and gender assumptions meant that it tended to judge Black communities with a Western (white, middle-class, and male) measuring stick. As Black female writers such as Ann Petry took up the call to document the experience of urban, working-class Black women, they did so in the context of a white literary and critical establishment primed to read Black lives no longer as "primitive," but now "pathological."

---

146. Johnson, *World of Difference*, 170.
147. Mullen, *Popular Fronts*, 4.
148. Mullen, *Popular Fronts*, 10. See also Morgan, *Rethinking Social Realism*, 2–3.
149. Morgan, *Rethinking Social Realism*, 246.

CHAPTER 4

Networks of Care

Sentiment, Sociology, and the Protest Fiction Debate

In 1946 Ann Petry published *The Street,* the first novel by an African American woman to sell more than a million copies. Almost immediately, the novel drew comparisons to Richard Wright's *Native Son* (1940), which had also broken sales records when it was published six years earlier, selling half a million copies in its first six months. Not only had both books "broke[n] the rule that first novels rarely are successful," but they both made use of a seemingly naturalistic mode in which "the cards are stacked against" their protagonists.[1] A decade later, literary critic Robert Bone codified such views by describing Petry as part of the "Wright School," a set of "disciples" whose work shared the "urban realism," "literary naturalism," and "impulse to protest" that characterized *Native Son*.[2] And yet, whenever Petry was asked "to what extent" her "writing of *The Street*" was "influenced by Richard Wright's *Native Son*," her responses ranged from expressing polite "admiration" for his work alongside that of many other writers, to a more acerbic "It wasn't," or "I am not a follower of the

---

1. Petry, "First Novel," 35–36; and M.P., "Evil Results of Crowding," 4. One reviewer also compared Petry's novel to Wright's work more broadly, writing that "*The Street* might have been entitled *Black Girl* as a counterpart to Richard Wright's *Black Boy,*" the memoir Wright released in 1945, because *The Street* was just as "honest" and just as "bitter" (North, "*Wasteland*'s Realism," 4S).

2. Bone, *Negro Novel in America,* 157. A few years earlier, Richard Gibson had written with slightly more hostility that Petry was one of several "puerile imitators of Richard Wright" ("No to Nothing," 254).

tradition of Richard Wright."³ When given the opportunity, she described for herself a quite different literary trajectory: "I regard myself as a survivor and a gambler, writing in a tradition that dates back to 1859 when *Our N*g*, the first novel written by a black woman in this country, was published."⁴ Nevertheless, despite Petry's efforts to correct the narrative, she is still often described as Wright's follower—even as Wright's Black male mentees, James Baldwin and Ralph Ellison, are widely credited with breaking away from Wright's mold.⁵ Not only has this narrative obscured Petry's place in a lineage of Black female writers, it has also resulted in her fiction receiving less and less critical attention the further it moved from the so-called Wright School.

Wright first articulated the literary aims associated with the "Wright School" in his well-known essay "Blueprint for Negro Writing" (1937), in which he called upon Black writers to develop an analytic "perspective" on the "structure" of society, a perspective he found first in Communism and later in sociology.⁶ Wright famously broke from the Communist Party not long after, but his work over the next decade, including his introduction to St. Clair Drake and Horace R. Clayton Jr.'s sociological study, *Black Metropolis* (1945), shows the ongoing influence of sociology on his thinking—and with it, his embrace of the field's normative heteropatriarchal gender politics.⁷ In fact, even in his earliest essays, Wright was already grounding both his critique of systemic racism and his interest in a newly analytic "perspective" in troublingly masculinist language. In "Blueprint for Negro Writing," for example, he wrote:

> Generally speaking, Negro writing in the past has been confined to humble novels, poems, and plays, prim and decorous ambassadors who went a-begging to white America. They entered the Court of American Public Opinion dressed in the knee-pants of servility, curtsying to show that the Negro was not inferior, that he was human, and that he had a life comparable to that of other people.⁸

---

3. Janet Binette to Ann Petry, 8 October 1992, Ann Petry Papers; Petry, "*MELUS* Interview," 80; Ann Petry to Janet Binette, 14 October 1992, Ann Petry Papers; and Ann Petry to Matthew Bruccoli, editor of *Bibliography of American Fiction*, 3 January 1991, Ann Petry Papers.

4. Petry, "Ann Petry," *Contemporary Authors*, 253, redaction added.

5. See, for example, Bryant, "Wright, Ellison, Baldwin," 179; Gates, *Signifying Monkey*, 105–7; and Reid-Pharr, *Once You Go Black*, 99–100.

6. Wright, "Blueprint for Negro Writing," 103.

7. See Wright's "I Tried to Be a Communist" (1944), versus his praise for sociology in his introduction to *Black Metropolis* (1945).

8. Wright, "Blueprint for Negro Writing," 97.

Far from being received as "co-worker[s] in the kingdom of culture," Wright believed that prior "prim and decorous" Black artists had been received as "French poodles who do clever tricks"—not as humans but as trained animals, and the most feminized breed.[9] "Dressed in knee-pants" and "curtsying" to address white audiences, these writers appeared dehumanized to Wright because they were being seen not as men but as boys or women. In his later essay "How 'Bigger' Was Born" (1940), Wright again critiqued prior genres of Black writing, this time by pointing to their emotional appeal to white female readers: "I found that I had written a book which even *bankers' daughters* could read and weep over and feel good about. I swore to myself that if I ever wrote another book, no one would weep over it."[10] Refusing to see himself or his characters as objects of pity for white women, he wrote that his next book "would be so hard and deep" that readers "would have to face it without the consolation of tears."[11] In place of emasculating supplication and sentiment, Wright advocated for a masculine commitment to "hard and deep" truths—"a concrete vision" he found in the "honest science" of sociology.[12]

Wright's dismissal of "feminine" modes of reading and writing in "Blueprint for Negro Writing" also corresponded with his treatment of Black female peers in the circumstances leading up to the essay's publication. The essay was originally published in a small literary magazine run by Dorothy West, the youngest writer of the Harlem Renaissance. West started the magazine under the name *Challenge* in 1934 because the Harlem "movement was over" and she wanted "to give the younger generation a chance."[13] It was "the first little magazine of the Depression that sought to bridge the divisions among the older aesthetes . . . and the emerging social realists," attracting submissions from West's older New York circle as well as notable young writers like Pauli Murray, who published her first poems there in 1934 and 1935.[14] When Wright moved to New York in 1937, he became interested in the magazine by way of his friendship with Marian Minus, a leftwing writer who was Wright's mentor and West's intimate partner.[15] According to Wright's peer Margaret Walker, Minus was also "one of the few women who persisted" in Wright's South Side Writers Group in Chicago aside from herself.[16]

---

9. Du Bois, *Souls of Black Folk*, 5; and Wright, "Blueprint for Negro Writing," 97.
10. Wright, "How 'Bigger' Was Born," 454, emphasis added.
11. Wright, "How 'Bigger' Was Born," 454.
12. Wright, "How 'Bigger' Was Born," 454; and Wright, introduction to *Black Metropolis*, xviii. On the sentimental mode of American racial melodramas, see Williams, *Playing the Race Card*, 10–44.
13. West, "Conversations with Dorothy West," 271; and West, "Alive and Well," 38.
14. Ferguson, "Dorothy West." See Murray, "Song"; and Murray, "Inquietude."
15. See McCarthy, "Blues in Print," 208.
16. Walker, *Richard Wright, Daemonic Genius*, 91.

As a favor to Minus, West agreed to let Wright and Minus act as associate editors on a more radical reboot of her magazine called *New Challenge*.[17] Almost immediately, the collaboration went sour. West's magazine had already been criticized by some friends and readers as "pale pink" rather than red, or in Wallace Thurman's words, "too pink tea and la de da."[18] Wright similarly aligned his new leftist vision for the magazine with masculinity, telling Langston Hughes that his goal was to give the magazine "balls."[19] West, for her part, immediately saw that Wright and his mostly male writing group back in Chicago were trying to take control of the magazine, an assessment with which Margaret Walker, from her perspective within that group, later agreed.[20] Walker would also describe Wright's essay as a "group expression under his signature," hinting that he had muscled out voices from within that group as well, including her own.[21] West, for her part, responded to the attempted takeover by shutting down the magazine altogether. As she later explained: "It was very hard for one little woman back then . . . I was small and my voice soft. So when the Chicago group started having meetings about the direction of the magazine, I remember deciding to give it up."[22] But despite West's act of protest, the single issue of *New Challenge* "did for Wright in 1937 what *The Survey Graphic Number* did for Locke in 1925: it led contemporaries and later scholars to appoint Wright as dean of a black cultural renaissance," displacing in the process an important Black female editorial voice and the labor of several Black women writers.[23]

Likewise, whereas West's and Walker's critiques of Wright have been largely erased or dismissed from the literary historical record, the critiques emanating from Wright's Black male peers have dominated literary historical understandings of the period.[24] As early as 1963, Irving Howe's "Black Boys and Native Sons" had centered Baldwin's and Ellison's critiques of the "Wright School" of protest fiction in literary critical understandings of mid-twentieth-century

---

17. See McCarthy, "Blues in Print," 208.
18. West, "Dear Reader," 38; and Wallace Thuman to Dorothy West, 2 September 1934, quoted in McCarthy, "Blues in Print," 208.
19. Richard Wright to Langston Hughes, 29 May 1937, quoted in McCarthy, "Blues in Print," 209.
20. Walker, *Richard Wright, Daemonic Genius*, 91.
21. Walker, *Richard Wright, Daemonic Genius*, 77. See also McCarthy, "Blues in Print," 206.
22. West, "Conversations with Dorothy West," 271. Elsewhere, she elaborated: "The minute they decided they were gonna take over the magazine, I stopped it, and that was the end of that. I had no choice" (West, "Alive and Well," 39).
23. Jarrett, *Deans and Truants*, 118–19.
24. See, for example, Cruse, *Crisis of the Negro Intellectual*, 185–87; and Fabre, "Margaret Walker's Richard Wright," 434.

Black writing—with those critiques notably focusing not on protest fiction's treatment of Black women but on its "pathological" characterization of Black men.[25] Perhaps because Howe also interpreted the protest fiction debate as a debate among men about men—or, in Ellison's words, a "modern version of the Biblical myth of Noah . . . and Ham"—he did not mention West, Walker, or Petry in his essay, even though West and Walker played pivotal roles in Wright's early career, and even though Petry's "The Novel as Social Criticism" (1950) marked her intentional entry into the protest fiction debate.[26] Like Wright, Petry was also active in leftwing circles in the late 1930s and early 1940s, working in New York as a journalist for *Amsterdam News* and *People's Voice* and as an actor for the American Negro Theatre.[27] And although she left New York in 1948, her retreat was not unusual among her peers, including Wright, Baldwin, and Ellison.[28] Petry's exclusion from Howe's account of the protest fiction debate—like other exclusions of West and Walker—has less to do with her noninvolvement with or departure from the leftwing Black literary scene, as is sometimes argued, than with what Candice Jenkins calls "the extraordinary lapse of vision" evidenced by the "male critical establishment in regard to black women's writing of the era."[29]

While Petry's male peers debated protest fiction's treatment of Black men without much concern for its treatment of Black women, Petry's work challenged the patriarchal norms that her peers took for granted. In her best-known novels, *The Street* and *The Narrows* (1953), Petry interrogates the normative race, gender, and class politics of mid-twentieth-century sociology by exploring the tragic consequences of her characters' investment in individualistic models of agency, respectability, and uplift. Rejecting normative politics, her novels demand that we reattend to the race, gender, and class politics of sentiment and justice. Rather than refusing a feminized vision of sentiment or embracing a masculinized vision of justice, as so many of her male peers did, Petry formulates an alternative model of interracial and intraracial empathy grounded not in sentiment but in action—one that is based not on prevailing models of white female sympathy, but rather on a Black feminist network

---

25. Howe, "Black Boys and Native Sons." See also Gibson, *Five Black Writers*; Bryant, "Wright, Ellison, and Baldwin"; and Inge, Duke, and Bryer, *Black American Writers*, all of which focus on Wright, Ellison, and Baldwin, with the occasional inclusion of Langston Hughes or Amiri Baraka. On the elevation of these Black male writers and their aesthetic conflicts in major anthologies of African American literature, see Washington, *Other Blacklist*, 10–11.

26. Ellison, "World and the Jug," 157.

27. See Rubin and Smethurst, "Ann Petry's 'New Mirror,'" 25.

28. See Petry, "*MELUS* Interview," 80. Ellison moved to Vermont in 1945 to begin work on *Invisible Man*. Wright left for Paris in 1946 and Baldwin followed in 1948.

29. Jenkins, *Private Lives, Proper Relations*, 40.

of care. In Petry's fiction, Black women's resistance to normative racial, gendered, and class-based social structures are not signs of pathology or degeneracy, but signs of resistance, survival, and mutual care.

Race, Gender, and the Protest Fiction Debate

One year after she published *The Street,* Petry published an essay in *Negro Digest* called "What's Wrong with Negro Men?" (1947). The essay was one of several that the magazine published from 1947 to 1951 on the relationship between Black men and Black women, with Petry's essay followed closely by Pauli Murray's "Why Negro Girls Stay Single" (1947), and journalist Roi Ottley's "What's Wrong with Negro Women" (1950) followed by Black sociologist St. Clair Drake's "Why Men Leave Home" (1950) and Gwendolyn Brooks's rejoinder, "Why Negro Women Leave Home" (1951). In their essays, Petry, Murray, and Brooks all took issue with what Petry described as Black men's investment in the "God-given superiority of the male."[30] Petry argued that "the average Negro male" will "boast about being a progressive in politics," but "before you take him at his word, observe his actions at home."[31] For her, the intellectual and progressive credibility of a man who carries "a union card . . . as proof of his advanced thinking," or who "flatters himself [that] he is an expert on . . . diverse subjects," is belied by the fact that he "will run like a rabbit if his wife suggests he prepare a simple meal."[32] Brooks similarly argued that any woman would leave home if her husband treated "her as though she were a chattel or a slightly idiotic child" instead of "respect[ing] her as a person" and treating her "like a human being."[33] Murray, naming Petry as her precursor in this "growing literature of revolt," named this "system of discrimination based upon sex" that they were describing "Jane Crow" because "it is so strikingly similar to 'Jim Crow,'" or prejudice based upon race.[34] She closed her essay with a demand: "We desire that the Negro male accept the Negro female as his equal and treat her accordingly" and cease participating in the "aggression" and "exploitation" that were "made possible by her admittedly inferior position as a social human being in the United States."[35]

---

30. Petry, "What's Wrong with Negro Men?," 6.
31. Petry, "What's Wrong with Negro Men?," 4.
32. Petry, "What's Wrong with Negro Men?," 4–5.
33. Brooks, "Why Negro Women Leave Home," 28, 26.
34. Murray, "Why Negro Girls Stay Single," 8, 4.
35. Murray, "Why Negro Girls Stay Single," 8.

Drake's and Ottley's essays, by contrast, focused solely on rebuking racially essentialist stereotypes, which they did by invoking essentialist gender stereotypes. For Ottley, for example, there wasn't much difference between the races "which a little more freedom, opportunity and money won't fix pronto," but the differences between the genders dated back to the "Garden of Eden."[36] Drake, one of the co-authors of *Black Metropolis*, similarly argued that "Negro men leave home not because they are Negroes, but because they are men."[37] Drawing on previous sociological work by Black sociologist E. Franklin Frazier, whose book *The Negro Family in the United States* (1939) had focused on the disruption of "a stable pattern of family relations," Drake argued that racist employment and segregated housing practices had made it impossible for the Black man to align himself with the "ideal picture of the American husband" as "a good provider," a norm he described as "deeply set in human culture."[38] Because racist employment practices meant that, in Black families, it was "frequently the woman" rather than the man "who has a steady job," Drake argued that Black men were being forced into "weak," "unimportan[t]," and "shame[ful]" positions—positions that were all of these things because "for almost a million years" they were occupied by women.[39]

Ottley and Drake's embrace of essentialist gender norms was deeply embedded in early to mid-twentieth-century sociological frameworks. For example, in a preface to Frazier's earlier book, *The Negro Family in Chicago* (1932), Ernest W. Burgess—co-founder with Robert E. Park of the Chicago School of sociology—argued that it was the failure of Black men and women to conform to white patriarchal norms of "family life" that constituted the "chief handicap from which the Negro suffers," a claim that pathologized Black people by shifting the effects of systemic racism from American laws and practices to Black people's "disorganized family life."[40] Drake and Frazier both insisted that this "disorganization" was due to the environmental constraints Black families faced.[41] Nevertheless, their continued reliance on normative accounts of gender fed Daniel Moynihan's later deeply damaging report, "The Negro Family: The Case for National Action" (1965), which renewed Burgess's pathologizing of Black families, and blamed "the 'dominating position'

---

36. Ottley, "What's Wrong with Negro Women," 75, 71.
37. Drake, "Why Men Leave Home," 26.
38. Drake, "Why Men Leave Home," 26. See also Frazier's chapter on "Fathers on Leave" in *Negro Family in the United States*, 325–41.
39. Drake, "Why Men Leave Home," 26.
40. Burgess, preface to *Negro Family in Chicago*, xii. See also Jenkins, *Private Lives, Proper Relations*, 45.
41. See Platt, "E. Franklin Frazier," 269–73.

of the black mother," rather than racism, for Black "disorganization" and "delinquency."[42] In the long term, the very tool that 1930s- and 1940s-era Black sociologists and protest writers believed could be used to expose racist social structures functioned instead to shift the blame back to Black "pathology," or Black people's supposedly degenerate or inferior humanity, with these ideas becoming "more invidious" as they became more embedded in "scientific, 'objective' scholarship" and "more difficult simply to dismiss."[43]

Black writers were concerned that sociological approaches to the study of Black life were a double-edged sword long before Moynihan's report. Indeed, a central issue in the protest fiction debate was whether sociologically inspired protest fictions exposed systemic racism or pathologized Black characters. Wright had aligned with Black sociologists because he believed their focus on the sociological impact of racism offered a path toward structural change. As he put it, embracing the idea that "the Negro's conduct, his personality, his culture, his entire life flow naturally and inevitably out of the conditions imposed on him by white America" made it possible to critique the environmental "conditions which produce Bigger Thomases."[44] For Wright, sociologically informed protest fiction represented an important break from the sentimental protest tradition typified by Harriet Beecher Stowe's *Uncle Tom's Cabin* (1852), which invoked a dehumanizing and "condescending form of pity" that scholars argue "reinforce[d] the very patterns of economic and political subordination responsible for such suffering."[45] For Baldwin, by contrast, sociology represented not a break from this sentimental discourse but its continuation. Americans, Baldwin argued, "do not know what to do with [the black man] in life; if he breaks our *sociological* and *sentimental* image of him we are panic-stricken and we feel ourselves betrayed."[46] If in *Uncle Tom's Cabin*, the novel's "only black man" had been "robbed of his humanity" by being "divested of his sex," Baldwin insisted that he "needed only to drop the title 'Uncle' to become violent, crafty, and sullen, a menace to any white woman who passed by."[47] It was this opposing stereotype that Baldwin saw brought to life in *Native Son*'s Bigger Thomas. For Baldwin, both sentimental and sociological protest fictions dehumanized Black male characters—*Uncle*

---

42. Moynihan, "Negro Family," ch. 2, ch. 4. See also Jenkins, *Private Lives, Proper Relations*, 9–10.

43. Jenkins, *Private Lives, Proper Relations*, 45.

44. Wright, introduction to *Black Metropolis*, xxix; and Wright, "How 'Bigger' Was Born," 444.

45. Spelman, *Fruits of Sorrow*, 7. For an overview of such critiques of the concepts of sentiment, sympathy, empathy, and compassion, see Davis, *Beyond the White Negro*, 6–8.

46. Baldwin, "Many Thousands Gone," 25, emphasis added.

47. Baldwin, "Everybody's Protest Novel," 18; and Baldwin, "Many Thousands Gone," 28.

Tom's Cabin because it castrated Uncle Tom, and *Native Son* because it made Bigger Thomas into the myth used to justify lynch mob castrations.

Where Baldwin was concerned with the limits that protest fiction placed on Black male characters, Ellison worried about the limits it placed on Black male writers. He explained:

> I had undergone, not too many months before taking the path which led to writing, the humiliation of being taught in a class in sociology at a Negro college (from Park and Burgess, the leading textbook in the field) that Negroes represented the "lady of the races." . . . Well, I had no intention of being bound by any such humiliating definition of my relationship to American literature.[48]

Ellison refused not only Park and Burgess's insistence that he was the "lady of the races" but also Howe's later insistence that "clenched militancy" was necessary to the expression of Black experience, or that he and Baldwin were not living up to Wright's manliness.[49] Like Baldwin, Ellison saw emasculating and hypermasculine stereotypes as bound up in white efforts to dehumanize Black men; like Wright, his effort to protest those racial stereotypes—to refuse the insult of being called a "lady"—depended on a tacit embrace of misogynistic stereotypes about women.

In her entry into the protest fiction debate, Petry challenged pathologizing interpretations of Black life and Black protest fiction without resorting to the gender stereotypes so frequently adopted by her male peers. Petry had her own share of experience with white readers' patronizing responses to her work, including one reader who wrote to express the hope that Petry would make the characters "in her next book . . . more human" or, as the reader went on to explain, "more like the white reader."[50] The reader continued: "Placing too much emphasis on outward differences is apt to confuse the essential sameness of what lies underneath."[51] In her essay "The Novel as Social Criticism," Petry debunked such notions that in order to be "universal," art should avoid "outward differences," arguing instead that the novel, "like all other forms of art, will always reflect the political, economic, and social structure of the period in which it was created."[52] Making her case on the basis of

---

48. Ellison, introduction to *Shadow and Act*, 57. For the passage that offended Ellison, see Park and Burgess, *Introduction to the Science of Sociology*, 136.
49. Howe, "Black Boys and Native Sons," 109; and Ellison, "World and the Jug," 156–57.
50. Lucia Barker to editor Dorothy Hillyer, 21 February 1946, Ann Petry Collection.
51. Lucia Barker to editor Dorothy Hillyer, 21 February 1946, Ann Petry Collection.
52. Petry, "Novel as Social Criticism," 33.

white authors like George Eliot, Charles Dickens, and William Faulkner, Petry argued that "the moment the novelist begins to show how society affected the lives of his characters, how they were formed and shaped by the sprawling inchoate world in which they lived, he is writing a novel of social criticism whether he calls it that or not."[53] The trick, she wrote, was to do this without allowing the characters to become "pawns in the hands of a deaf, blind, stupid, social system" who bear no "responsibility for their actions" and thereby lose their "vitality."[54] Echoing Du Bois's famous claim that "all Art is propaganda and ever must be," Petry refused the distinction between "art . . . for art's sake" and protest fiction and debunked the claim that protest is especially suited to Black literature.[55] Instead, she described writing as a balancing act to represent both the limits on and possibilities of agency in a social world shaped by such "outward differences" as race, gender, and class.

Petry's fiction similarly echoes this interest in balancing the exploration of systemic oppression with an exploration of human complexity and agency, in part to resist Chicago School sociology's pathologizing tendencies. But where her fiction mirrors that of her male peers in exploring the relationship between systemic racism and dehumanizing stereotypes, it also insists on seeing Black women as more than mere objects or antagonists in the plight of Black men. In *Native Son*, Bigger's downfall comes from his replication of America's most violent visions of male agency, often at the expense of Black women, visions that sociologists would later describe as pathological despite their ubiquity in white American culture. In *The Street*, Lutie is triply stripped of agency by her race, gender, and class positions. But her downfall, in contrast to Bigger's, comes from her attempt to replicate America's most normative vision of female respectability, the very values sociologists typically criticized Black women for failing to uphold. As a result, Petry's novel challenges the normative race, gender, and class politics of mid-twentieth-century sociology by questioning Lutie's investment in bourgeois, respectable notions of individual uplift; her failure to invest in alternative support networks for Black female survival; and the tragic role that her choice to pursue normativity plays in her downfall.

Three years after she wrote "The Novel as Social Criticism," Petry published another novel called *The Narrows*. *The Narrows* announced its ongoing interest in the protest fiction debate by featuring a leftwing photographer as a main character and thus making the role and responsibility of the politically motivated artist a central theme of the novel. In alignment with Petry's essay, *The Narrows* asks how artists can protest inhuman conditions without

---

53. Petry, "Novel as Social Criticism," 33.
54. Petry, "Novel as Social Criticism," 36.
55. Du Bois, "Criteria of Negro Art," 66; and Petry, "Novel as Social Criticism," 33.

representing their characters as something less than human, or as oversimplified villains and victims. But *The Narrows* shifts our attention away from whether sociologically driven protest novels dehumanize the very people they are trying to redeem—the question that concerned Wright, Baldwin, and Ellison—and toward how attempts of such protests to humanize certain people too often depend on the dehumanization of others. By highlighting the way that several kinds of dehumanizing stereotypes—against Black men and against Black and white women—are put in conflict with one another, *The Narrows* not only challenges the gender normativity of mid-twentieth-century sociology, but also challenges binary models of race, gender, and class "justice" in favor of a historically nuanced and complex ethics of care.

Taken together, *The Street* and *The Narrows* transformed what was primarily a debate over the relationship of political protest to the dehumanization of Black men into a debate about the relationship of political protest to the dehumanization of Black men *and* women. Moreover, unlike pre-existing models of white female sentiment that Wright complained offered white readers the catharsis of tears while doing little to upset white power, Petry's novels center the caring work of Black women. Where eighteenth- and nineteenth-century sentimental philosophers and writers emphasized the potential power of emotion, Petry's work emphasizes the real power of care. Much like later theorists such as Joan Tronto, who defines care as "a species of activity that includes everything we do to maintain, contain, and repair our 'world' so that we can live in it as well as possible," Petry is less interested in emotions that may or may not lead to action than in actual actions of care, or, as she puts it, the "idea that man is his brother's keeper."[56] In this, Petry also challenges masculinist value systems that "give prime value to individual agency" and are averse to "dependency," stressing instead the ethical value of what Maria Puig de la Bellacasa calls "interconnection and interdependency."[57] For Petry, Black women's embrace of interconnection and interdependency are not signs of female weakness but strategies for resistance and survival in the face of racism, sexism, and economic exploitation.

The Street, Individual Respectability, and the Failure of Care

The Street is better understood not as a follower of *Native Son* but as a critique of the earlier novel's problematic gender politics. Indeed, although *Native Son*

---

56. Tronto, *Moral Boundaries*, 103; and Petry, "Novel as Social Criticism," 34.
57. Puig de la Bellacasa, *Matters of Care*, 4.

is "seen in some quarters" as "'the model' for contemporary black novelists," Wright's work has been described in other quarters as promoting a masculinist "assumption that racism is a crime against the black man's sexual expression rather than an economic, political, and psychological crime against black people."[58] As Abdul JanMohamed observes, "Bigger's victory over death is severely compromised because he has not won it by struggling directly against the master; rather, he has won it by killing two women who are, in their own, different ways, also socially dead and, in some ways, in weaker positions than Bigger."[59] Baldwin's early complaints about the novel were similar, arguing that it is only through the "murder and . . . rape" of women that Bigger comes, "through this violence, we are told . . . to a kind of life, having for the first time redeemed his manhood."[60] For Farah Jasmine Griffin, Bigger's attitude toward Black women is especially problematic: "Bigger is not acting out of fear here; he kills Bessie out of hate—hate for what she as a black woman represents to him. Unlike Mary, she is not the future to which he aspires but the past from which he flees."[61] While some scholars such as Paul Gilroy and Cheryl Higashida have argued that these readings incorrectly equate Bigger's misogyny with Wright's, many agree that Wright's work supports the pathologizing of Black women.[62] In Wright's novels, Jane Davis argues, "virtually all relationships between men and women . . . are plagued by the men's fear of women's power over them and their attempt to escape from or rebel against this power."[63] For Trudier Harris, his novels are deeply committed to the pathologizing perspective that Black women bear "responsibility for the plight of black men."[64]

Like *Native Son*, *The Street* deploys a seemingly naturalistic style to depict a murder that is caused as much by the protagonist's oppressive environment as it is by her hopeless desire to be free of that environment. As Lutie thinks, "It was that street. It was that god-damned street."[65] "My aim," Petry said in an interview following the novel's publication, "is to show how simply and easily the environment can change the course of a person's life."[66] However, as Petry

---

58. Williams, "Papa Dick and Sister-Woman," 396–97.
59. JanMohamed, *Death-Bound-Subject*, 136–37.
60. Baldwin, "Everybody's Protest Novel," 22.
61. Griffin, "On Women, Teaching, and *Native Son*," 79.
62. See Gilroy, introduction to *Eight Men*, xiv; Gilroy, *Black Atlantic*, 176–77; and Higashida, "Aunt Sue's Children," 397. See also Guttman, "What Bigger Killed For," 170–71; and Johnson, "Re(a)d and the Black," 120–25.
63. Davis, "More Force than Human," 82.
64. Harris, "Native Sons and Foreign Daughters," 64.
65. Petry, *The Street*, 436.
66. Petry, "Ann Petry Talks about First Novel," 49.

continued, her aim was also to "create . . . characters who are real, believable, alive" because she was "of the opinion that Americans regard Negroes as types—not quite human—who fit into a special category and I wanted to show them as people with the same capacity for love and hate, for tears and laughter, and the same instincts for survival possessed by all men."[67] Indeed, although scholars have frequently compared the two novels, several have observed that *The Street* departs from *Native Son* not only by making its protagonist a woman but by complicating the typical environmental determinism of the naturalist mode.[68] Petry's choice of a female protagonist forces readers to see violence against women not just as a "redemptive" response to racial oppression, but as an interrelated form of oppression to which Black women are doubly susceptible, a focus that Ayesha Hardison notes marks the novel's departure "from the conventions of the protest novel" set by Wright.[69] *The Street* also "moves beyond the naturalist tradition" by emphasizing its protagonist's "choices"—especially her choices to pursue normative bourgeois respectability and to protect her propriety by investing in property, choices that she discovers lead her to the very fate (or worse) that she was trying to escape.[70]

Although Lutie's commitment to bourgeois respectability is unsettled by the novel's tragic conclusion—her murder of a man and subsequent abandonment of her son—most scholars note that her investment in respectability politics is not entirely naïve. Candice Jenkins describes this commitment as a "salvic wish," which she defines as "the desire to rescue the black community from racist accusations of sexual and domestic pathology through the embrace of bourgeois propriety."[71] As Cherene Sherrard-Johnson and Hardison both argue, Lutie knows that the Chandlers, the white family she serves, are corrupt, but she still desires the protection of their material wealth because she recognizes firsthand "the power of economics to shape the truth, even though she knows the Chandler home is a dysfunctional space."[72] Citing the work of José Esteban Muñoz, Hardison describes Lutie as desiring the white ideal, but desiring it "with a difference."[73] For Lutie, this "salvic" commitment to respectability politics is an act of defiance against a racist racial order that prohibits her participation in that politics.

---

67. Petry, "Ann Petry Talks about First Novel," 49.
68. On Wright's own complicating of naturalism, see Goldstein, "Richard Wright's *Native Son.*"
69. Hardison, *Writing through Jane Crow,* 60. See also Shinn, "Women in the Novels of Ann Petry," 110.
70. Hardison, *Writing through Jane Crow,* 60.
71. Jenkins, *Private Lives, Proper Relations,* 43.
72. Sherrard-Johnson, "City Place/Country Place," 71.
73. Hardison, *Writing through Jane Crow,* 61, quoting Muñoz, *Disidentifications,* 15.

Nevertheless, as many scholars have noted, Lutie's enchantment with Benjamin Franklin as a model for individual uplift—her "feeling of self-confidence and [how] she went on thinking that if Ben Franklin could live on a little bit of money and could prosper, then so could she"—is odd for someone of her race, gender, and class position.[74] Bernard Bell explains that "while . . . myths of the Founding Fathers like Benjamin Franklin, who is the colonial paradigm of the successful self-made man, are available to all Americans, black Americans rarely refer to them."[75] Lutie, too, seems aware of this disconnect, reminding herself to remember that she's "in Harlem."[76] Still, as Vernon Lattin argues, she refuses to "resign herself to 'Negro' or 'female' roles," struggling instead "to fulfill the rags-to-riches formula" of the "American Dream."[77] It is only after "several harrowing experiences," Keith Clark writes, that "Lutie ultimately realizes, albeit too late, what the 'Emersonian' Invisible Man must also face: Hackneyed beliefs based on a prescription of 'hard work' and 'self-reliance' are not panaceas for black folks."[78] In Lattin's words, the American Dream has both "prevented her from seeing the reality of her trap" and acted as "the spring that operates the trap."[79] Coupling Lutie's pursuit of the American Dream with her ultimate act of murder, which she understands as devastating that dream, *The Street* pushes back against Bigger's effort to claim agency by dominating women in *Native Son*—Bigger's claim that he "didn't know I was really alive in this world until I felt things hard enough to kill for 'em."[80] *The Street* also pushes back on the normative claims of mid-twentieth-century sociology; whereas sociologists blamed Black people for their failure to conform to white social norms, *The Street* shows that such models not only are unavailable to Black individuals and communities but are dangerous to them as well.

By the end of the novel, Lutie's efforts at linear uplift have become a series of entrapping circles. Rather than pick herself up by her bootstraps, like Franklin, she has found herself worse off than when she started, having committed murder—ironically, of a man named Boots—out of a combination of self-defense and pent-up rage. Fleeing New York on a train to Chicago, and leaving behind the son she had tried so hard to protect, she begins to draw circles on the train's window:

---

74. Petry, *The Street*, 64.
75. Bell, "Ann Petry's Demythologizing," 106.
76. Petry, *The Street*, 64.
77. Lattin, "Ann Petry and the American Dream," 69.
78. Clark, "Distaff Dream Deferred?," 497.
79. Lattin, "Ann Petry and the American Dream," 69.
80. Wright, *Native Son*, 429.

> As the train started to move, she began to trace a design on the window. It was a series of circles that flowed into each other. She remembered that when she was in grammar school the children were taught to get the proper slant to their writing, to get the feel of a pen in their hands, by making these same circles.
>
> Once again she could hear the flat, exasperated voice of the teacher as she looked at the circles Lutie had produced. "Really," she said, "I don't know why they have us bother to teach your people to write."
>
> Her finger moved over the glass, around and around. The circles showed up plainly on the dusty surface. The woman's statement was correct, she thought. What possible good has it done to teach people like me to write.[81]

Scholars often read this scene as evidence of the novel's naturalism, and indeed, the theme of circles as a sign of containment, bondage, and entrapment weaves itself throughout the novel: "It was like a circle. No matter at what point she started, she always ended up at the same place"; "She was running around a small circle, around and around like a squirrel in a cage"; "So it was a circle, and she could keep on going around it forever and keep on ending up in the same place."[82] The obstacles Lutie faces because of her race, class, and gender have kept her moving in a circle, rather than following the linear path of Franklin made possible by his privilege.

In making it clear that Franklin's model of individual uplift is not available to poor Black women, *The Street* also underscores the consequences of Lutie's ill-fated clinging to the politics of respectability. As Petry described it, she made Lutie "an intelligent, ambitious, attractive woman with a fair degree of education" who "lives in the squalor of 116th Street" but "retains her self-respect and fights to bring up her little son decently."[83] But because the environment's obstacles are a far greater force than Lutie's small acts of defiance, her choice to pursue bourgeois respectability only succeeds in cutting her off from alternative support networks. As Jenkins argues, Lutie does have an alternative support network in her father's home, but she makes the decision to leave that home because she disapproves of her father's wife Lil. In Jenkins's words, "Lutie seems to believe that she can create a 'safer' intimate space in the midst of such materially unpleasant surroundings than she can while living with Lil," whose immodest dress, drinking, and smoking Lutie sees as "a more indelible source of peril."[84] Again, in depicting this as an active choice

---

81. Petry, *The Street*, 435–36.
82. Petry, *The Street*, 183, 323, 407. See, for example, Wurst, "Ben Franklin in Harlem," 21–22; Hicks, "Rethinking Realism," 102; and Dingledine, "It Could Have Been Any Street," 99.
83. Petry, "Ann Petry Talks about First Novel," 49.
84. Jenkins, *Private Lives, Proper Relations*, 54.

on Lutie's part, Jenkins continues, "Petry's text makes Lutie's unwitting contribution to her own victimization quite clear."[85] Her commitment to "bring[ing] up her little son decently" cuts her off from alternative modes and networks of care.[86]

The streets are a death sentence for Lutie because she tries to apply the logic of the suburbs to life on the street, much as sociologists blamed Black communities for failing to conform to suburban logic, rather than recognizing the ways in which they were foreclosed from the privileges that made that logic work for white people. As George Lipsitz argues:

> The national spatial imaginary is racially marked. . . . Segregation serves as a crucible for creating the emphasis on exclusion and augmented exchange value that has guided the contemporary ideal of the properly-ordered, prosperous private [white] home . . . [while] prevent[ing] people of color from equal opportunities to accumulate assets that appreciate in value and that can be passed down across generations.[87]

In other words, white cultural ideals that emphasize the values of privacy and private property are inseparable from a long history of "concrete policies and practices" that have both enabled and encouraged "well-off communities to hoard amenities and resources, exclude allegedly undesirable populations, and maximize property values in competition with other communities."[88] Far from the dirty, crowded street where Lutie finds herself, the Chandlers live down a "smaller road where there were big gates and a sign that said 'private road.'"[89] There, she discovers, they also have "an entirely different set of values . . . strange values."[90] Unlike the "filth" of Lutie's later apartment, the Chandlers are able to keep their home "clean" by virtue of Lutie's labor, all while pursuing a different kind of filth: "to be rich, 'filthy' rich, as Mr. Chandler called it."[91] Lutie cannot aspire to such a position in relationship to property or wealth because that position depends on her exclusion and exploitation. The "filthiness" of their wealth—its intertwinement with exclusive and exploitative values and practices—is washed clean by the very people whom it excludes and exploits.

---

85. Jenkins, *Private Lives, Proper Relations*, 48.
86. Petry, "Ann Petry Talks about First Novel," 49.
87. Lipsitz, "Racialization of Space," 10.
88. Lipsitz, "Racialization of Space," 12.
89. Petry, *The Street*, 37. For more on this signage, see Barrett, "(Further) Figures of Violence," 207–8.
90. Petry, *The Street*, 41, 43.
91. Petry, *The Street*, 311, 65, 43.

Lutie fails, then, in part because she internalizes the values of a system designed to exclude and exploit her instead of embracing alternative value systems forged by Black communities. As Lipsitz explains, many Black communities, recognizing their exclusion from white value systems organized around exchange value, have developed alternative social and spatial organizations that emphasize "use value over exchange value, sociality over selfishness, and inclusion over exclusion."[92] In Lutie's case, her desire to replicate the normative façade of the Chandlers, made possible by their private property and privilege, leads her to desire a nuclear family home and "respectable" work, even though the real estate and employment options available to her make those goals virtually impossible. As she acknowledges, "if they hadn't been so damn poor she and Jim might have stayed married" and "if you were black and you lived in New York and you could only pay so much rent, why, you had to live in a house like this one."[93] Hardison notes that Lutie's internalization of the Chandlers' "capitalist spirit" ultimately "devastates" her "aspirations for middle-class respectability."[94] It is at least in part Lutie's investment in white middle-class norms—both property and propriety—that destroys her life.

Both *The Street* and Petry's later novel, *The Narrows*, feature Black female protagonists who are betrayed by their own commitment to property and propriety—Lutie in *The Street* and Abbie Crunch in *The Narrows*. But both novels also feature Black female characters who model alternative value systems and modes of survival, most notably Lutie's neighbor Min in *The Street,* who lives with men out of wedlock to get by economically, and Abbie Crunch's tenant Mamie in *The Narrows,* who has affairs with men out of wedlock for her own personal pleasure. Whereas Lutie and Abbie follow a politics of respectability, both Min and Mamie respond differently to their exclusion from the twin ladders of property and propriety, recognizing the need to develop alternative strategies for survival, and pursuing those strategies without the shame internalized by Lutie and Abbie. Importantly, both characters also have a narrative voice, emphasizing their role in voicing alternative strategies for survival. Kimberly Drake points out that "the reader might be taken aback when Petry gives [Min] a narrative point of view, particularly when it reveals her strength, common sense, and ambition."[95] However, "Min is not ignorant of middle-class moral standards. . . . Rather she is aware that her own moral standards are derived from a different culture and class. Min's ability to resist some of the aspects of bourgeois ideology that could interfere with her physical and emotional survival eventually prepares her to criticize and even

---

92. Lipsitz, "Racialization of Space," 10.
93. Petry, *The Street*, 183, 407.
94. Hardison, *Writing through Jane Crow*, 74.
95. Drake, "Women on the Go," 76.

reject that ideology."⁹⁶ Significantly, both characters also survive despite their total disregard for bourgeois respectability. Mary Helen Washington notes that "Mamie . . . suffers no punishment, no tragic end, no fatal repercussions. . . . The last voice we hear is Mamie's—and she is singing the blues."⁹⁷ Their nonnormative Black female behavior becomes a model for survival and even satisfaction.

Lutie, in modeling herself after the false idols of Franklin and the Chandlers instead, misses the opportunity to develop alternative networks of support and care. This failure is largely because, as Hardison argues, Lutie consistently "undervalues" the Black community.⁹⁸ Lutie's moral disapproval of Lil and her goal of individual uplift causes her to leave the support structure of her father's home.⁹⁹ Drake writes that she similarly "refuses to see herself reflected in Min" and thus loses "the chance to develop a friendship that could have saved Lutie's life from destruction; Min is aware that the Super is planning to harm Lutie and her son, and although she contemplates exposing him, she never does so, primarily because of the distance Lutie has placed between them."¹⁰⁰ Min, without any sense of connection or solidarity to Lutie, only sees her as competition for male attention.¹⁰¹ As a result, Drake argues, "Petry forces the reader to see that it is precisely Lutie's middle class ambitions which cost her a valuable ally and, as a result, her own happiness."¹⁰² Lutie's aspiration to align herself with privilege-based models of individual uplift and respectability prevent her from recognizing or contributing to alternative networks of Black resilience, community, and care.

By emphasizing such missed opportunities for care, Petry's novel articulates a move away from an individualist ethics of eye-for-an-eye justice toward what later feminist scholars would call an ethics of care. Whereas an ethics of justice is typically characterized by "fairness and equality and a rational-objective decision-making based on universal rules and principles," an ethics of care is "relational-emotional, need-centered, holistic, and contextual in nature."¹⁰³ As Bethany Nowviskie explains, the ethics of justice valorized "an impartial stance," positing that "as a man grew in judgment and developed

---

96. Drake, "Women on the Go," 76.
97. Washington, *Invented Lives*, 302–3. For more on the figure of the Black female blues singer, see duCille, *Coupling Convention*, 66–85; and Hardison, *Writing through Jane Crow*, 54–84.
98. Hardison, *Writing through Jane Crow*, 78.
99. See Jenkins, *Private Lives, Proper Relations*, 50–51.
100. Drake, "Women on the Go," 75.
101. See Petry, *The Street*, 23–26, 114.
102. Drake, "Women on the Go," 75.
103. Hagen, "Relational Principles," 99. See also Botes, "Comparison," 1071.

ethical understanding, he separated himself from others. The mark of a fully developed (implicitly masculine) self was its ability to stand apart from and reason outside of familial systems and social bonds."[104] A feminist ethic of care, in contrast, as it was formulated by feminist scholars such as Carol Gilligan, Nel Noddings, and Joan Tronto, turned away from privilege-driven investments in objectivity, individuality, and universality and toward "a humanistic appreciation of *context, interdependence, and vulnerability*" and "personal, worldly *action and response*."[105] In Petry's work, this means moving away from the fantasy that individualist modes of economic success, propriety, and justice are equally and objectively available to all, and valuing instead context-specific needs, vulnerabilities, and modes of care.

The tragic end of *The Street* finds Lutie acting on the principle of justice: she kills Boots in retaliation for his attempt to rape her and for his complicity in his boss Jubine's attempt to use his money to do the same. Where Bigger murders out of fear, Lutie murders out of rage brought on by her frustrated desire for agency, autonomy, and uplift. But while there may be a righteous justice to her response—an eye for an eye—that act does not liberate Lutie from the trap Jubine, Boots, Super, and the street have set for her. *Native Son* ends with Bigger claiming murder as an act of retaliation against his entrapment and as an expression of his male-coded agency. Lutie sees it as the ultimate destruction of all her false hopes and dreams. With language that recalls her first recoiling sight of Min, the woman she looks down on as a "shapeless small dark woman" who could "sit in a chair and melt into it," Lutie now looks at the dead body of Boots as evidence of her failed strategy of individual uplift: "She would never get out of this room. She would never, never get out of here. For the rest of her life she would be here with this awful faceless thing on the sofa."[106] The benefits of the ethics of justice are as foreclosed to her as are the benefits of property and propriety. In this way, *The Street* reveals the exclusivity and violence of three interlocking models of individualism: the economic individualism of Benjamin Franklin; the "salvic" individualism of the politics of respectability; and the eye-for-an-eye individualism of the ethic of justice. Common to all three of these ideologies is the idea of the individual standing apart from her community, or rising above, rather than connecting with that community in acts of mutual aid, interdependence, and care. *The Street*, then, is as much about the "filth" of these three models of individual uplift and exceptionalism as it is about Lutie's failure to invest in an alternative network

---

104. Nowviskie, "Capacity through Care," 425.
105. Nowviskie, "Capacity through Care," 425, emphasis in original.
106. Petry, *The Street*, 23, 431.

of care—in fact, her active sacrifice of the very possibility of such networks because of her "investment" in individual uplift.

At brief moments in *The Street,* Lutie seems to sense the possibility of alternative networks of care that might have helped her survive the street. The circles she traces on the window in the final moments of the novel—a "series of circles that flowed into each other"—do signal her overwhelming sense of the street as a trap, but they also signal those glimmers of moments when Lutie responds to the street quite differently.[107] While she is still together with her husband Jim, they make frequent journeys into Harlem to enjoy the "flow of talk," a pleasure she briefly rediscovers when she decides, against the doctrine of respectability, to go to the local bar, drink, and sing.[108] As Hardison puts it, "In singing the blues, as in her dreams, Lutie leaves the oppressions of the street and she bonds with the black community," whom she otherwise "undervalues."[109] In only seeing the street as a cage that prevents her individual exceptional rise, Lutie misses the very real possibilities for mutual support, connection, and "flow" within that space. Her investment in individualism is concomitant with her undervaluing of the Black community, a replication of white normative values and their violence against Black people. It is fitting that in the final moments of the novel, she is completely alone, tracing on the window not only the cage she has placed around herself, but also those missed opportunities for connection.

Rather than being part of Wright's "school," Petry's *The Street* is a critical response to Wright's work that is just as sharp as those of her male peers, though importantly different in focus. Henry Louis Gates Jr. has argued that *Invisible Man* (1952) Signifies on *Native Son* in several ways:

> Wright's re-acting protagonist, voiceless to the last, Ellison Signifies upon with a nameless protagonist . . . [who] is nothing *but* voice, since it is he who shapes, edits, and narrates his own tale. . . . Bigger's voicelessness and powerlessness to act (as opposed to react) signify an absence, despite the metaphor of presence found in the novel's title; the reverse obtains in *Invisible Man,* where the absence implied by invisibility is undermined by the presence of the narrator as the author of his own text.[110]

---

107. Petry, *The Street,* 435. For a similar reading of this scene, see Lowney, *Jazz Internationalism,* 108.

108. Petry, *The Street,* 175, 145. See also the people who "flowed and spilled through the gates like water running over a dam" as Lutie makes her escape to Chicago (Petry, *The Street,* 434).

109. Hardison, *Writing through Jane Crow,* 78.

110. Gates, *Signifying Monkey,* 106, emphasis in original.

But where Ellison's critique of *Native Son* emphasized individual consciousness, agency, and voice, Petry's also questions that individualism's problematic associations with respectability politics, capitalism, and eye-for-an-eye justice. In other words, if Ellison's novel critiques Bigger's lack of consciousness, Petry's novel critiques Bigger's lack of both consciousness and caring. And while the political possibilities of care remain an untapped resource in *The Street*, in *The Narrows* they take center stage.

The Narrows, Communal Responsibility, and a Network of Care

As much as Petry's *The Street* acts a critical rejoinder to Wright's *Native Son*, her lesser-known novel, *The Narrows,* can be understood as a critical rejoinder to Ellison's *Invisible Man*, which came out one year prior. In Ellison's novel, the only sentence that approaches the fame of its first—"I am an invisible man"— is probably its last: "Who knows but that, on the lower frequencies, I speak for you?"[111] However, what Ellison would describe as the invisible man's "universal" resonance is complicated by the fact that his experiences of degradation and dehumanization are so often aligned with being made to feel equivalent to white women in the eyes of white men.[112] This pattern repeats itself, including in the invisible man's objectification at the Battle Royale alongside a naked white woman; Mr. Norton's view of him as a stand-in for his dead daughter; Emerson's sexual desire for him; the Brotherhood's apparently humiliating decision to assign him to the "Woman Question"; his attempt to access white male power by sexually possessing white women only to find himself invisible even then; and his closing dream of castration. As Catherine Saunders argues, "Ellison's understanding of the mechanisms of invisibility stopped short of his recognizing men's projection of their own desires and fears onto women."[113] Likewise, Carolyn Sylvander writes that in Ellison's novel, "women . . . operate as nothing more than symbol. . . . They are not, in Ellison's own analysis of stereotyping, fully human."[114] For all of Ellison's critiques of Wright, Wright's dehumanizing treatment of women was not one of them.

Like *Invisible Man, The Narrows* is similarly preoccupied with what Ellison would call "the taboos built around the fear of the white woman and the black

---

111. Ellison, *Invisible Man*, 3, 581.
112. Ellison, "Art of Fiction," 212. See also Kim, "Invisible Desires," 309–12.
113. Saunders, "Makers or Bearers of Meaning?," 4.
114. Sylvander, "Ralph Ellison's *Invisible Man*," 79.

man getting together."[115] However, where *Invisible Man* equates the social and political denial of its protagonist's humanity with his invisibility *as a man*—constituted again and again by his humiliating similarity to white women—and thus assumes that Black men must reject their identification with women, Petry's novel does not take that "solution" for granted. If male-female identification is a source of emasculation in *Invisible Man*, in *The Narrows* it is a source of hope. Rather than being dehumanized by identifying with other dehumanized people, characters in *The Narrows* show their humanity most precisely when they identify with others across the lines of race, gender, and power. Conversely, they show their inhumanity when they dehumanize others in their attempts to empower themselves. As a result, *The Narrows* acknowledges the same conflict between race and gender that *Invisible Man* exposes, but it resolves these conflicts by formulating an intraracial network of care—one that is grounded in the very processes of empathy and identification about which Wright and later Ellison were so dismissive.

Featuring a large cast of characters made up of white and Black residents of the fictional town of Monmouth, Connecticut, *The Narrows* revolves around a doomed romance between a Black man named Link Williams and a white heiress named Camilo Sheffield, whose extended families become intertwined in a series of misunderstandings and acts of revenge that lead to Link's tragic death. Link and Camilo first meet by chance when she comes to the Black part of town out of curiosity after reading "a series of articles on the relationship between bad housing and crime in this section."[116] Link is a former Dartmouth student with academic ambitions, currently working as bartender at the Last Chance, which is owned by his father figure, Bill Hod. Link's adopted mother, Abbie Crunch, does not approve of Link's relationship with Bill, but she has lost the right to complain because she temporarily abandoned Link after the death of her husband, and Bill stepped in to fill her place. Now, Abbie shares a house with Link, renting the other rooms to Malcolm Powther, the butler at Camilo's mansion, Powther's wife Mamie, who is having an affair with Bill, and their three children, the youngest of whom, J.C., is really Bill's son. Abbie eventually learns of Link's affair and humiliates Camilo by throwing her out of the house, naked. Camilo responds to this humiliation by calling Link a "black bastard," and Link responds by ending the relationship, letting her believe that it is because he has been having an affair with Mamie and not because of his wounded pride. Camilo tries to "get even" by accusing Link of rape, and Link is murdered by Camilo's husband, out for revenge.[117]

---

115. Ellison, "On Initiation Rites and Power," 543–44.
116. Petry, *The Narrows*, 62.
117. Petry, *The Narrows*, 257, 319.

Like *The Street*, which was told through the points of view of the various residents of Lutie's building, *The Narrows* is told primarily from the point of view of Link, Abbie, Powther, and Mamie, the residents of Abbie's house. But the novel briefly breaks with this formula to focalize the point of view of the local newspaper editor, Peter Bullock. Alex Lubin argues that this choice foregrounds "Petry's fascination with tabloid news and the ways various popular cultural forms represent" and shape "interracial intimacy."[118] Just as Wright carefully tracked and took inspiration from newspaper representations of the Robert Nixon case in preparation for writing *Native Son*, Petry's private papers reveal that she was carefully tracking the 1949 press coverage of Paul Robeson's son's interracial marriage.[119] Wright uses these media representations to expose the press's complicity in the environmental entrapment of Black men. In Petry's novel, the focus is on the press's complicity with longer threads of historical violence. As Lubin writes, in *The Narrows*, "the interracial sex plot" becomes "a means for Petry to explore historical legacies of slavery, interracial violence, and postwar American popular representations of African Americans."[120] Link, a Dartmouth-educated student of Black history, emphasizes this shift from sociological to historical paradigms of racial injustice. By moving away from the urban landscape of *The Street*, *The Narrows* also explores the ways in which small-town Black communities are entrapped by the historical legacies of slavery encoded not only in the spatial and economic organization of the city but also in the popular press and in every aspect of daily life, including intimate and interpersonal relations.

Both Bullock and the leftwing white photographer Jubine play central roles in Link and Camilo's tragedy because both publish photographs about the affair that have profound effects on public opinion and the novel's outcome. In many ways, Bullock and Jubine couldn't be more different: Bullock is a conservative and Jubine is a "Communist," and whereas Bullock lies to get the story he wants, Jubine merely selects and distorts.[121] But while some critics have seen Jubine as a stand-in for Petry, the novel draws uncomfortable parallels between Bullock's and Jubine's approaches to representation, as the photographs they publish have similar motives and effects. In Bullock's record of Link and Camilo's affair, he follows a familiar path in representing Camilo as "The Victim" by representing Link as "The Criminal," which he does by printing a picture that shows a Black convict "not as a man but as a black

---

118. Lubin, introduction to *Revising the Blueprint*, 3.
119. See Rabinowitz, "Pulping Ann Petry," 56.
120. Lubin, introduction to *Revising the Blueprint*, 8.
121. Petry, *The Narrows*, 47.

animal, teeth barred in a snarl, eyes crazy, long razor scar like a mouth."[122] Jubine redeems Link, but he does so by distorting the image of Camilo. In his photographs of the affair, she becomes "Toulouse-Lautrec's Harlot" and Link becomes an "Apollo."[123] Thus, where Bullock exploits racist stereotypes to criminalize Link, Jubine exploits sexist stereotypes to redeem him. Much like St. Clair Drake's article, "Why Men Leave Home," the "truthlie" of Jubine's photographs redeems Black male humanity via dehumanizing stereotypes about women, rendering Jubine ill-equipped to protest the racism and sexism that plague Link and Camilo simultaneously.[124]

In the novel, the press's polarized sense of black-and-white justice is complicated by the far more nuanced and circular relationships that the novel draws among its interracial cast of characters. Michael Berry shows that *The Narrows* is structured around a "repetition and resemblance between events and characters across the lines of race, gender, class, and generation."[125] All of these characters are both oppressed and complicit in each other's oppression. Link, the primary organizing consciousness of the novel, puts it this way: "I executioner. You executioner," where the trope of "execution" consists of one person establishing their power over another person by the terms set by historic systems of domination, be they racial, sexual, or economic.[126] Like the invisible man, Link describes himself as repeatedly executed by attacks on his masculinity: Bill emasculates him by beating him for seeking the service of a prostitute; Abbie seemingly emasculates him by sending him into the hands of a sexually predatory rich white man when she demands that he get used to working for white people; and Camilo appears to buy him like a "plantation buck," treating him like a "kept man" and a "mechanical toy."[127] As Yoon Young Choi explains, "the novel calls attention to the ways in which Camilo's race and class conspire to de-legitimize Link's claims to 'proper'"—or normative—"masculine gender," and further connects that experience to that of other Black men, such as Powther, who is repeatedly "executed" by Mamie's infidelity.[128]

Unlike the invisible man, however, Link not only identifies with others who have been "executed"—or, in Ellison's terminology, castrated—but he also identifies with those who do the "executing." For example, in the chain of

---

122. Petry, *The Narrows*, 372, 377.
123. Petry, *The Narrows*, 398, 365.
124. Petry, *The Narrows*, 373.
125. Barry, "'Same Train Be Back Tomorrer,'" 154.
126. Petry, *The Narrows*, 321.
127. Petry, *The Narrows*, 399–400, 391–96, 150, 280, 291.
128. Choi, "Failing Face of a Nation," 22; and Petry, *The Narrows*, 260.

events that ends Link and Camilo's relationship, Abbie executes Camilo by calling her a "whore" and casting her out into the street, Link executes Camilo by belittling their relationship, Bullock executes Link with his newspaper coverage of the case, and Jubine executes Camilo by having "tried the case, handed in a verdict, with his goddamn pictures."[129] As a result, both when Camilo accuses him of rape and when he is about to be killed by Camilo's family, Link recognizes these two forms of violence as revenge-based forms of "justice" for his own "execution" of their white privilege and power. He also connects these acts of revenge with his own past acts of revenge, such as when he tried to kill Bill for "executing" his masculinity. As Barrett argues, in *The Narrows*, "any attempt to reduce this skewed, looping multiplicity to a simple binarism is an impossible and disingenuous task."[130] For the appropriately named Link, every character at one point or another plays the role of executioner ("executioners, all"), and they are all, at one point or another, "hung . . . from the sour apple tree."[131] As Abbie realizes at the novel's end, execution is "an eye for an eye, and a tooth for a tooth" ethical response to the experience of being executed that fails to achieve the justice it seeks, instead only continuing the cycle of execution.[132]

Although these circular chains of execution risk flattening the historical operation of power and privilege, in the novel they serve to reveal the ways in which characters occupying a range of subject positions are implicated in the perpetuation of patriarchal, heteronormative, and white supremacist power structures. Hardison explains that "Petry's promotion of interracial and cross-class female bonds does not refute the specificity of black women's disenfranchisement" but "instead highlights racist society's sexism, which includes black men's participation in black women's Jane Crow oppression."[133] Petry's exploration of her characters' complicity with existing power structures also extends beyond Black men's participation in Black women's oppression to Black women's participation in these power structures as well. Indeed, much like Lutie, Abbie's "respectable" wish to redeem herself is only possible if she puts herself above women like Camilo and Mamie, sacrificing other women to "save" herself. For Nellie McKay, Abbie's "flaws do not come from evil within her, but instead from her uncritical acceptance of certain white patriarchal values that demean black people and black culture, and keep all

---

129. Petry, *The Narrows*, 365, 399.
130. Barrett, "Signs of the Visible," 241.
131. Petry, *The Narrows*, 260.
132. Petry, *The Narrows*, 424.
133. Hardison, *Writing through Jane Crow*, 112.

women enslaved to oppressive ideas of the meaning of womanhood."[134] By representing Camilo, Abbie, and Mamie as "distorted mirrors for each other," the novel emphasizes "the importance of interracial cross-class homosocial bonds," contrasting an eye-for-an-eye ethic of justice that pits people against each other with an intraracial ethic of care that draws them together.[135]

In this way, *The Narrows* turns away from oversimplified, binary explanations of the operations of power toward complex, historical ones, "shatter[ing] binary racial codifications into a multiplicity of terms."[136] In contrast to Jubine's protest photographs, which are always done in sharp "contrasts," Petry's more nuanced novel examines intraracial complicity and accountability.[137] In this way, her approach echoes Link's refrain throughout the novel—a quote from Elizabethan writer John Heywood that Link ironically notes was also once voiced by Benjamin Franklin—"When all candles bee out, all cats bee gray."[138] Although the characters' fates often feel overdetermined by the novel's emphasis on the ways in which these complex histories repeat themselves, the novel also emphasizes the choices that individual characters make to ensure that these overdetermined fates come to pass, as well as the occasional choices or opportunities that they have to resist those fates. As McKay notes, "unlike the purely naturalistic novel, [Petry's] characters do not automatically perceive these factors as agents of their doom. Rather they envision options, choices, and some control of their destiny. And while racism triggers the major conflict in this novel, it neither explains nor determines their fates."[139] In *The Street*, Lutie thinks, "It was that street. It was that god-damned street."[140] In *The Narrows*, Link attributes "three-quarters" of the blame to "that Dutch man of warre that landed in Jamestown in 1619," but Abbie attributes the rest to human agency: "It was all of us. . . . We all had a hand in it."[141] In this way, Choi claims, Petry pushes beyond "the conventions of black masculinist protest novels and naturalism of the mid-twentieth century" to insist on both "a historicized accounting for contemporary race politics" and a "more radical consideration" of "accountability."[142] In "The Novel as Social Criticism," Petry argued that she saw the fictional emphasis on social problems as grounded

---

134. McKay, introduction to *The Narrows*, xv.
135. Hardison, *Writing through Jane Crow*, 102.
136. Barrett, "Signs of the Visible," 241.
137. Petry, *The Narrows*, 48.
138. Petry, *The Narrows*, 71, 79, 94, 148, 257, 319. See also Petry's nuanced account of racism, complicity, and accountability in the novel in Petry, "Ann Petry," interview by John O'Brien, 162.
139. McKay, introduction to *The Narrows*, xiii.
140. Petry, *The Street*, 436.
141. Petry, *The Narrows*, 399, 419.
142. Choi, "Failing Face of a Nation," 27–28.

not in Marxism or sociology, but in the ethical "idea that man is his brother's keeper."[143] "In encouraging women to be their sisters' keepers," Hardison argues, "*The Narrows* envisions rewriting history through Abbie's acts of reconciliation," effectively making room for powerful acts of Black agency within larger sociological and historical systems of oppression.[144]

The residents of Abbie's household not only represent the novel's focal centers, but they also represent a range of ethical actions. Powther chooses eye-for-an-eye justice, turning on Link because he mistakenly believes that Link has slept with his wife, with this mistake emphasizing the potential for injustice that the ethic of "justice" enables. Mamie chooses to do nothing, a choice that is different from eye-for-an-eye justice and yet similarly motivated by the idea that she does not owe Camilo anything. Mamie has an opportunity to correct Camilo's assumption that she and Link are having an affair, but she opts not to reach out to Camilo because "she's white."[145] Both choices are rooted in the characters' sense of historical injustice, as is Bill's plan to have Camilo killed to avenge Link's murder. Abbie, by contrast, moves away from the ethic of justice and toward an ethic of care by deciding to try to save Camilo, an act that is motivated, in part, by her recognition of her ground for solidarity with Camilo: "Link walking down Dumble Street with her [Abbie]. . . . Adoration, devotion in the young face, in the eyes. . . . He was in love with that girl. In love with her [Camilo]."[146] There is still a limited quality to this formulation of resistance, as it is too late to save Link (and because the only place Abbie can think to turn is the questionable protection of the police). Nevertheless, the novel sees hope in Abbie's ability to think beyond her immediate sense of personal injustice and see herself as her sister's keeper, both rejecting naturalism's denial of human agency and rejecting the vision of human agency that is aligned with a narrow ethic of justice.

The novel's investment in a nonnormative intraracial network of care is also signaled by its loving representation of adoptive familial bonds, including Link's adoptive relationship to both Abbie and Bill. As Cynthia Callahan notes, in the mid-twentieth century, "the standards of the largely white middle-class nuclear norm became the measure by which all other groups were judged. Regardless of its actual attainability for many citizens, the mythical biological nuclear family did tremendous cultural work in the mid-twentieth century for all Americans as an aspirational image serving the project of national unity."[147]

---

143. Petry, "Novel as Social Criticism," 34.
144. Hardison, *Writing through Jane Crow*, 110.
145. Petry, *The Narrows*, 303.
146. Petry, *The Narrows*, 427.
147. Callahan, "Adopted or Married," 107.

But while Callahan sees Petry placing "adoption on a continuum with marriage and other forms of kinship bonds constructed through affiliation," I would argue that the novel pushes further than this.[148] Unlike Lutie, whose deference to bourgeois respectability leads her to refuse bonds outside of the normative nuclear family, families in *The Narrows* are almost entirely non-normative. Abbie's legal adoption of Link is placed on a continuum with Bill's informal adoption of Link, just as Powther's and Abbie's respective marriages are placed on a continuum with Mamie's and Link's respective affairs. In this way, the novel disrupts the normative image of the white nuclear family and insists on the bonds of love and care that exist beyond biological and legally acknowledged bonds. As Link says near the end of the novel, to the "shock" of Camilo's husband, "the truth is . . . we were in love."[149] Lutie, seduced by the image of the private white home, misses available opportunities to form supportive bonds with Lil and Mim. Abbie begins *The Narrows* on a similar path, losing her husband to a stroke because she dismissively assumes he is drunk and losing opportunities to connect with Camilo. It is only in the novel's final pages that she embraces a way of thinking beyond middle-class respectability and an ethic of individual justice, and toward an intraracial network of care.

Ironically, while Petry's seemingly more naturalistic *The Street* was well received, *The Narrows*' reception has been decidedly mixed, sometimes hailed as her masterpiece, but often dismissed, especially by early reviewers, as melodrama.[150] As Linda Williams explains, melodrama is popularly condemned as an "excess of sensation and sentiment," a genre that, with its "virtuous victims and leering villains," simply "exceeds the bounds of good taste" of more "sophisticated realists and moderns."[151] A significant chunk of Petry's reviewers condemned *The Narrows* on these grounds, describing it as "a disappointment after *The Street*" because it was "implausibl[e,]" "improbable," "impossible," "sensational," "synthetic," "unrealistic," "almost totally unconvincing," and—repeatedly—"foolishly melodramatic."[152] In many cases, these reviewers are explicit that the novel's interracial romance is the thing they

---

148. Callahan, "Adopted or Married," 104.
149. Petry, *The Narrows*, 407.
150. For those who consider *The Narrows* Petry's best work, see Bell, "Ann Petry's Demythologizing," 105; Clark, *Radical Fiction of Ann Petry*, 2; Griffin, "Hunting Communists," 137; and Sehgal, "May's Book Club Pick."
151. Williams, *Playing the Race Card*, 11–12. See also Sollors, foreword to *Race and the Rhetoric of Resistance*, x.
152. Govan, "Of Books and Writers," 20; Morris, "Complexity of Evil," 4; Lewis, "*The Narrows*," 22; Ragan, "Melodrama of the Racial Angle," sec. 4, p. 5; Scott, "In the Narrows," sec. 6, p. 8; Fuller, "Validity Lacking," sec. E, p. 2; A.P.W., "Story Unrealistic in 'The Narrows,'" 54; V.P.H., "New England Novel Fine," sec. G, p. 20; and "Books," 78, among others.

find impossible to believe. Even those who express admiration for the novel still describe the interracial romance plot as "explosive" and "controversial."[153] Screenwriters at Fox, Metro, and Paramount declared it "as utterly impossible" for film adaptation "as any book they've ever seen."[154] But perhaps it was also Petry's turn to a feminist network of care that lay beneath this masculinist dismissal of *The Narrows* as the worst kind of "women's writing."[155] By moving further away from the "hard and deep" truths of the sociological protest tradition, *The Narrows* invited comparison with the very sentimental mode that Wright had earlier rejected. To classify *The Narrows* as melodrama, however—a genre defined not just by its emotional excess but by its vision of the world as populated by victims, villains, and heroes—is to miss both the novel's refusal of sentiment without action and its insistence on a complex, historicized understanding of intraracial complicity, accountability, and care. Petry's work refuses the victim/villain model of respectability and individual justice that typifies racial melodramas such as *Uncle Tom's Cabin*. In its place, Petry centers the transformative possibilities of Black female resistance to—*not* their sociological conformity with—the normative pressures of white, patriarchal, bourgeois America.

As Petry's career continued, she turned to a genre even less privileged by the white literary establishment, and even more neglected in subsequent accounts of Black literary history: children's literature. She had one prior foray into the genre with an illustrated book called *The Drugstore Cat* (1949), which she wrote immediately after her "white life" novel, *Country Place* (1947). In 1955 Petry published the nonfiction children's book *Harriet Tubman: Conductor on the Underground Railroad,* which she followed with a historical novel for children, *Tituba of Salem Village* (1964) and an illustrated book of religious stories for children, *Legends of the Saints* (1970), before returning to adult fiction with *Miss Muriel and Other Stories* (1971). In her 1969 essay, "The Common Ground," Petry wrote that her children's literature was devoted to recovering Black women's contributions to history, a goal that also motivated later authors of neo–slave narratives such as Margaret Walker, Octavia Butler, and Toni Morrison.[156] As Petry put it: "Over and over again, I have said: These are people. Look at them, listen to them; watch Harriet Tubman in the nineteenth

---

153. Barkham, "Brief Review of Books," sec. 3, p. 2; and Petry, "Ann Petry Startled," 20.
154. Henry Volkening to Ann Petry, 24 April 1953, Ann Petry Collection.
155. Kaplan, *Motherhood and Representation,* 59.
156. See, for example, Walker's *Jubilee* (1966), Butler's *Kindred* (1979), and Morrison's *Beloved* (1987).

century, a heroic woman, a rescuer of other slaves. . . . Look at them and remember them."[157] Of these books, *Harriet Tubman* sold especially well and, according to Petry's daughter, led to Tubman's inclusion in American history textbooks.[158] And yet, the literary and critical establishment became less and less interested in Petry's work as she turned toward this less "elite" genre.[159]

In many ways, Petry's turn toward children's literature was a turn away from the expectations of a white literary and critical establishment that was not yet ready to value Black women's history but was all too ready to place narrow limits on the appropriate form and content of Black writing. When asked in 1973 whether she considered herself a "naturalist" writer—the form expected of Black writers of her generation—she bristled: "To be absolutely honest about it, it really doesn't interest me. . . . If I belong to a certain tradition, I don't want to belong, because my writing would be very boring if I always wrote in a particular style."[160] Her frustration with the expectations and interests of white audiences was also on display when she turned down an invitation to speak at an institute on the "Young Adult in Conflict" in 1970: "I can't talk any more about what 'being black in white America means.' In a few more years I will have done with writing about it, too."[161] Although Petry is often connected with Black authors' post–World War II interest in the "white life" genre, her later turn to children's literature is perhaps more indicative of the direction that subsequent Black women writers would take in refusing the white literary establishment's privileging of white, male, and elite audiences, interests, and perspectives. As Petry's prior novels also indicated, her vision of the possibility of "common ground" among humans was not grounded in the narrow interests of those already-privileged identities. Rather, when she thought of the "capacity of that thing called a man," she thought of "a capacity for friendship"—what later Black feminist writers might call coalitions—and which, Petry said, "is really a capacity for love."[162]

---

157. Petry, "Common Ground," 71.

158. Petry, *At Home Inside*, 88, 86.

159. Wesseling, Wu, and Nelson, introduction to *Routledge Companion to Children's Literature*, 1. Major studies of Petry's work mention her children's literature only in passing (see Lubin, introduction to *Revising the Blueprint*, 8; Holladay, *Ann Petry*, 16–17; and Clark, *Radical Fiction of Ann Petry*, 19–20).

160. Petry, "Ann Petry," interview by John O'Brien, 160.

161. Ann Petry to Dorothy Broderick, 26 February 1970, Ann Petry Collection.

162. Petry, "Common Ground," 72, quoting American poet Archibald MacLeish, in Bush, *Dialogues*, 267.

CHAPTER 5

Renaissance Women

Vision and Vulnerability in the Black Chicago Renaissance

In 1966 Gwendolyn Brooks was invited to write the foreword to a new volume of poetry by young Black writers, many of whom would come to define the Black Arts Movement and Black Women's Literary Renaissance of the 1960s and '70s. Edited by Langston Hughes, *New Negro Poets: USA* (1966) included works by LeRoi Jones (Amiri Baraka), Dudley Randall, Mari Evans, Margaret Danner, and Audre Lorde, among others. In her foreword, Brooks wrote:

> At the present time, poets who happen also to be Negroes are twice-tried. They have to write poetry, and they have to remember that they are Negroes. Often they wish that they could solve the Negro question once and for all, and go on from such success to the composition of textured sonnets or buoyant villanelles about the transience of a raindrop, or the gold-stuff of the sun. *They* are likely to find significances in those subjects not instantly obvious to their fairer fellows. The raindrop may seem to them to represent racial tears—and those might seem, indeed, other than transient. The golden sun might remind them that they are burning.[1]

Brooks's doubts about the "universal" transience of the raindrop, coupled with her opening reference to "poets who happen also to be Negroes," are direct

---

1. Brooks, foreword to *New Negro Poets*, 13, emphasis in original.

critiques of the tendency within the mid-twentieth-century white literary establishment to congratulate Black writers for emphasizing "universal" concerns over "racial" ones, or for being writers who only "happen to be" Black. "Finest of all," reviewer Paul Engle had written of Brooks's first book, *A Street in Bronzeville* (1945), her poems "can be read for what they are and not, as the publishers want us to believe, as Negro poems."[2] Brooks's historic Pulitzer Prize for *Annie Allen* (1949) cemented her "exception[al]" status among such readers. As poet Haki Madhubuti later summarized, "in the eyes of white poetry lovers and white book promoters, the publicity was to read 'she is a poet who happens to be black.'"[3]

Although Brooks's 1966 foreword turns this presumption on its head—arguing that Black experiences are not incidental but full of meaning and historical heft—the attitude that Black experiences must be avoided for Black art to be considered "universal" was pervasive within the mid-twentieth-century white literary establishment, which in the Cold War era became increasingly invested in American liberalism and the idea that "universal" or "classic" literature would help "create well-rounded human beings fit for democracy."[4] As writer John Oliver Killens would reflect in his essay for *The Black Aesthetic* (1971): "From Hollywood to Broadway to Madison Avenue, I hear variations of the same refrain: 'John, why do you insist upon writing about Negroes? Why don't you write about people?' . . . Another goes like this: 'The thing I liked about your story, John, it was universal. It could have been about anybody.'"[5] For the white literary establishment that controlled the production of film, theater, and literature, the highest "compliment" they could offer was to tell Black writers that their Black identities were inconsequential to their writing; they were writers who only "happened" to be Black. It was for this reason that Killens would say, in a refrain common among Black artists of the 1960s and '70s, that "when Western man speaks of universality, he is referring to an Anglo-Saxon universality."[6]

Numerous scholars of the Black Chicago Renaissance—named for the cultural activity centered in Chicago from the late 1930s to the late 1950s—have argued that Black artists of Brooks's generation were caught up in this fantasy of participating in "unlabeled" universalism.[7] Lawrence Jackson argues that the Cold War drove "ex-communists and ex-leftists" to "redeem . . . their

---

2. Engle, "Chicago Can Take Pride," E11.
3. Madhubuti, "Gwendolyn Brooks," 83–84.
4. Schneider, "Remaking the Renaissance Man," 53.
5. Killens, "Black Writer," 380–81.
6. Killens, "Black Writer," 381.
7. Hill and Holman, preface to "Negro in Literature," 296.

radical pasts by making" a "conservative turn," one that Barbara Christian associates with an increasing "interest in the universal" and tendency to "emphasize those qualities blacks shared with all other human beings."[8] Many scholars see this as a turn away from the proletarian and social realist impulses of the 1930s and '40s, in favor of what Stacy Morgan describes as "a heightened engagement with American high modernism and 'universalist' impulses."[9] Bill Mullen similarly argues that in Chicago, where so much cultural activity was centered, "the coming cold war, the appearance of McCarthyism, and the increasing economic and political power of Chicago's black middle class and anti-communists . . . conspired to force the silencing or evacuation from the city of its most progressive individuals and to permanently 'liberalize' its leading institutions."[10] Not only did this institutional liberalization supposedly result in a generation of Black writers caught up in liberal fantasies of "unlabeled" universalism, but, according to Penny Von Eschen, it created a "deep fissure" between activist and mainstream Black political culture that led "young activists" in the 1960s to be "cut off from an older generation" of Black activism "and compelled to reinvent the wheel."[11]

On the other hand, a few scholars have shown that despite the pressures of Cold War liberalism, many Black writers of the postwar period continued to create important spaces for Black-centered political and artistic community.[12] In fact, quite a few of the writers who came of age in the 1930s and '40s continued to write prolifically in the 1950s and '60s, and some of them, including Brooks, Danner, and Margaret Walker, not only continued to write, but wrote books directly associated with the Black Arts Movement.[13] Several Black organizations and spaces that had nurtured Black writers in the 1930s and '40s also remained active in the 1950s, and new ones arose. For example, the Chicago Public Library's Hall Branch in Bronzeville—which served as a "salon for the masses," a gathering-space for "political radicals," and "a hub for Bronzeville's literati"—ran from 1933 all the way through 1955.[14] The Harlem Writers Guild,

---

8. Jackson, *Indignant Generation*, 5; and Christian, "Nuance and the Novella," 242. The "conservative turn" is a phrase Jackson borrows from historian Michael Kimmage's *The Conservative Turn*. See also Bone, "Richard Wright and the Chicago Renaissance," 467.

9. Morgan, *Rethinking Social Realism*, 303.

10. Mullen, *Popular Fronts*, 17.

11. Von Eschen, *Race Against Empire*, 187.

12. See Washington, *Other Blacklist*, 11; and Wald, *Exiles from a Future Time*, 267.

13. See Danner and Randall's *Poem Counterpoem* (1969), Walker's *Prophets for a New Day* (1970), and numerous publications by Brooks, from *Riot* (1969) to *Beckonings* (1975), all published by Broadside Press. Many writers of Brooks's generation, including Walker, also participated in the first Fisk University Conference in 1966 (see Llorens, "Writers Converge").

14. Goldsby, "Salon for the Masses"; and Olson, *Chicago Renaissance*, 252.

started by John Oliver Killens "as a storefront workshop for young black writers seeking to express their creativity and promote social change" operated throughout the 1950s and '60s and beyond, nurturing in its early years writers who would make their marks in later decades, including Maya Angelou, Paule Marshall, and Audre Lorde.[15] Melba Joyce Boyd has shown that, in these ways, the Black Arts Movement "stood on the shoulders of writers"—many of them Black women—"whose expertise and experience were grounded in the preceding decades."[16] Mary Helen Washington argues that far from being "cut off," these mid-twentieth-century Black writers "carried the resistant traditions of the Black Popular Front of the 1930s and 1940s into the 1950s and became a link to the militant politics and aesthetics of the 1960s and 1970s."[17]

Gwendolyn Brooks's work lies at the heart of these contradictory accounts of 1950s Black literature—on one hand, a poster child for Black writers' acceptance by the white literary establishment; on the other hand, a bridge to the Black Arts Movement of the 1960s, with which she, more than any other Black writer of the period, was closely involved. For years, these contradictory threads of Brooks's career have been explained as shifts in her politics brought about by her exposure to radical young poets at the 1967 Fisk University Conference.[18] One such poet, Madhubuti—himself an early proponent of the idea that authors of "the late 1950s and early 1960s" had spent too much of their time and energy addressing "the conscience of [white] America"—would argue that while he admired many things about Brooks's early work, he also felt that in it there was "too much 'grant me that I am human, that I hurt, that I can cry,'" too much "art for art's sake," too much of a sense that it was "written for whites."[19] Brooks occasionally endorsed these characterizations—saying in a 1986 interview that "before [1967] . . . I, too, had liked the sound of the word 'universal'"—but she also occasionally pushed back on this narrative.[20] Speaking to Claudia Tate in 1983, she bristled at Tate's assertion that her "earlier works, *A Street in Bronzeville* and *Annie Allen*, don't seem to focus directly on heightened political awareness" and that it was only after the Black Arts Movement that she and other writers began to infuse their writing

---

15. De Veaux, *Warrior Poet*, 38–39.
16. Boyd, "'Prophets for a New Day,'" 56.
17. Von Eschen, *Race Against Empire*, 187; and Washington, *Other Blacklist*, 12.
18. See, for example, Bloch, "'Shut Your Rhetorics in a Box,'" 447; and Boyd, *Wrestling with the Muse*, 168, among many others. See also Erkkila, *Wicked Sisters*, 185–234, which critiques this narrative.
19. Madhubuti, "Gwendolyn Brooks," 84, 86.
20. Brooks, "Life Distilled," 120. See her endorsements of this narrative in Brooks, *Report from Part One*, 84–86; Brooks, "My People Are Black People," 62; and Brooks, "*Black Books Bulletin*," 74.

with "positive race images and heightened political consciousness."[21] Brooks replied, "Many of the poems, in my new and old books, are 'politically aware'; I suggest you reread them. . . . I've been talking about blackness and black people all along."[22]

This chapter proposes to take seriously Brooks's claim that she "had liked the sound of the word 'universal,'" while also taking seriously her insistence that she had "been talking about blackness and black people all along."[23] After all, while it may be true that when the white literary establishment spoke of the universal they were "referring to an Anglo-Saxon universality," that did not mean that this was true for Black authors.[24] In contrast to the argument that Black writers turned to liberal universalism and the mastery of Western aesthetic forms to appeal to white readers, this chapter argues that many Black writers were far more interested in challenging public fantasies about "universal" literature and "the universal man"—including those concepts' intentional "elision of any reference to race, ethnicity, or peoplehood."[25] Black writers' appeals to the human were based not on dominant white American fantasies of unlabeled universalism or unfettered liberty, but rather on uniquely Black visions of and for the world, grounded in their own experiences of material vulnerability. Black writers' interest in vision and vulnerability also helps to explain what Liesl Olson has observed to be the "defining feature" of the Black Chicago Renaissance—a push and pull between "a modernist birth-right that revels in stylistic experiment" and the "documentary impulse" associated with leftwing social realism—as complementary components of mid-twentieth-century Black critiques of "unlabeled" universalism.[26] Unlike those who describe the "stylistic experiment[s]" of the period as a turn to Western aesthetic forms intended to win approval from white audiences, this chapter shifts our attention to the material conditions—or vulnerabilities—that forced Black writers to continue working within the white literary establishment in the first place, and which have given that establishment outsized power in shaping the reception and understanding of their work. With this context in mind, I explore the strategies Black authors used to defy the expectations of the white literary establishment, to develop new philosophical and aesthetic frameworks, and to begin reaching new audiences both within Black communities and around the world.

---

21. Brooks, "Interview with Gwendolyn Brooks," 106, 108.
22. Brooks, "Interview with Gwendolyn Brooks," 106, 108.
23. Brooks, "Life Distilled," 120; and Brooks, "Interview with Gwendolyn Brooks," 106–8.
24. Killens, "Black Writer," 381.
25. Schneider, "Remaking the Renaissance Man," 54, 59.
26. Olson, *Chicago Renaissance*, 243.

In focusing on the work of Gwendolyn Brooks, this chapter also aims to recover the integral work Black women writers played in these efforts: first, because Black women writers give us important ways to think about how one might claim one's rights to vision and vulnerability without the privileges that whiteness, maleness, and wealth provide; and second, because of the undervalued but extraordinary work Black women were doing to build radical Black literary communities during these years. Reading Brooks's only novel, *Maud Martha* (1953), as a critique of the European image of the Renaissance Man—an image of "unlabeled" universality associated with the concepts of unfettered individual sovereignty, liberty, and ability—this chapter shows that far from retreating from the global radicalism of the 1930s and '40s, the Renaissance women of the Black Chicago Renaissance were foundational in building the groundwork for the political and aesthetic possibilities that would come to fruition in the following decade. Taking seriously Brooks's indignation with "unlabeled" universalism not only demands that we reattend to the characterization of mid-twentieth-century Black literature as invested in an appeal to "Anglo-Saxon universality," but also that we reattend to the especially important but underappreciated role played by Black women writers in this period.

The Cold War Meets the Black Chicago Renaissance

Brooks's 1966 foreword was not the first time she had addressed the ubiquitous claim that she was a poet who only "happened to be black." In 1950 she contributed a similar essay to *Phylon*'s special issue on "The Negro in Literature: The Current Scene." Bearing the title of "Poets Who Are Negroes," Brooks's 1950 essay refuses the idea that Black poets must treat their Blackness as secondary or incidental. She writes: "Every Negro poet has 'something to say.' Simply because he is a Negro; he cannot escape having important things to say. His mere body, for that matter, is an eloquence. His quiet walk down the street is a speech to the people. Is a rebuke, is a plea, is a school."[27] For Brooks, Black poets have "important things to say" not despite but because they are Black. Years later, Brooks would admit that around the time she wrote this essay for the *Phylon* special issue, she still felt she had "to prove" that she "could write well," and indeed the essay argues that "the Negro poet's most urgent duty, at present, is to polish his technique, his way of presenting his truths and his beauties."[28] But while the essay in this way confirms the pressure Brooks must have felt from the white literary establishment to "prove" she

---

27. Brooks, "Poets Who Are Negroes," 312.
28. Brooks, "Update on Part One," 96; and Brooks, "Poets Who Are Negroes," 312.

could "write well," it also showcases her defiance of their assumptions about what "writing well" means by associating it not with the erasure of Black "truths and . . . beauties" but with their articulation.[29] She would reaffirm this argument about the value of Black "truths and . . . beauties" in her 1966 foreword by quoting her earlier *Phylon* essay at length and adding: "This is as true today—when we, white and black, are a collective pregnancy that is going to proceed to its inevitability, getting worse before it gets better—as it was before the major flower of the volcano."[30] Together, the two essays show that Brooks's investment in the unique value that Black artists bring to their work spanned the early decades of her career.

The sentiment of these two essays runs counter to the Cold War's push toward "unlabeled" universalism in mainstream American discourse. As Mary Helen Washington and Penny Von Eschen have shown, in the aftermath of World War II, it was in the United States' interest to depict US racism as "disconnected from the struggles of other colonized peoples" and rooted in individual prejudice, rather than historical and institutional inequities.[31] Swedish economist Gunnar Myrdal's book *The American Dilemma* (1944) offered a key framework for these interests by defining "the country's racial dilemma as a moral problem, a failure to live up to" the country's own liberal principles.[32] For Myrdal, the only question was "whether or not whites would permit complete assimilation."[33] At the same time, liberal cultural critics such as Lionel Trilling, I. A. Richards, and others began advocating for an "American universalist rhetoric of open-ended, nonethnic citizenship" organized around the cultural development of the "good man and the citizen."[34] Drawing on the idea of the "*uomo universale*," or the "Renaissance Man"—a supposedly "unlabeled" figure who embodied the idea that "a man can do all things if he will" and is thus "limitless in his capacities for development"—they presented the development of this citizen's "liberal imagination" "as a universal solution to political struggles around class and race," but one that carefully avoided "any question of the redistribution of power and wealth."[35] In this context, Jodi Melamed argues, Black literary "excellence" was understood in terms of Black

---

29. Brooks, "Update on Part One," 96; and Brooks, foreword to *New Negro Poets*, 13. See also Mootry, "'Down the Whirlwind of Good Rage,'" 9.
30. Brooks, foreword to *New Negro Poets*, 13.
31. Washington, *Other Blacklist*, 20. See also Van Eschen, *Race Against Empire*, 167–84.
32. Jackson, *Indignant Generation*, 5. See also Myrdal, *American Dilemma*, lxxix.
33. Jackson, *Indignant Generation*, 5. See also Myrdal, *American Dilemma*, 53–57.
34. Schneider, "Remaking the Renaissance Man," 66, 55. See also Harvard Committee, *General Education*, 73–78.
35. Hill and Holman, preface to "The Negro in Literature," 296; Britannica, "Renaissance Man"; Trilling, *Liberal Imagination*, xxi; and Schneider, "Remaking the Renaissance Man," 55–56. See also Davies, *Humanism*, 15–20.

assimilation into this "unlabeled" universalism, and that "excellence" could be used "to prove that America was making strides in freeing itself from the corrosive effects of white supremacy."[36]

The pressure placed on Black authors by the white literary establishment's investment in "unlabeled" universalism is visible across every contribution to the *Phylon* special issue. Often compared to earlier works such as Alain Locke's *The New Negro* (1925) or W. E. B. Du Bois's series in *The Crisis* on "The Negro in Art: How Shall He Be Portrayed" (1926), the *Phylon* special issue is typically seen as reflecting the "conservative integrationist narratives" and paternalistic notions of "black artistic maturity" that were aligned with the "conservative turn" of the 1950s.[37] It is notable, however, that while the *Phylon* editors were certainly aware of these narratives, they presented them not as critical mandates, but as opportunities for a Black critical response. In fact, in gathering "a congress of those . . . most competent to assess" Black literature, the editors broke with the tradition set by their Harlem Renaissance predecessors and selected an entirely Black list of writers and scholars.[38] Their call to this all-Black cast of contributors was an invitation to weigh in on the central claims of the "conservative turn," asking contributors, "Would you agree with those who feel that the Negro writer, the Negro as subject, and the Negro critic and scholar are moving toward an 'unlabeled' future in which they will be measured without regard to racial origin and conditioning?"[39] The editors' reference to "those who feel" offers evidence of the pressure coming from outside this all-Black congress to conform to "unlabeled" universalism, and to describe Black literary "maturity" as an ongoing problem with Black writers. But the *Phylon* issue also offered a space, a forum, and an authorized outlet for Black artists and scholars to trouble this narrative.

Although many scholars have seen the *Phylon* issue as indicative of postwar Black writers' conformity with the narrative of "unlabeled" universalism, the majority of the issue's contributors refuse both what they describe as the white literary establishment's "perverted" definition of universality and that establishment's controlling arm.[40] First, they argue that like any writer, Black writers should be able to write about their own experience (not to have to

---

36. Melamed, *Represent and Destroy*, 21.
37. Washington, *Other Blacklist*, 19; Jenkins, *Private Lives, Proper Relations*, 38; and Jackson, *Indignant Generation*, 5.
38. Hill and Holman, preface to "The Negro in Literature," 296.
39. Hill and Holman, preface to "The Negro in Literature," 296.
40. Ford, "Blueprint for Negro Authors," 375. See, for example, Washington, *Other Blacklist*, 20; Jackson, *Indignant Generation*, 330–31; and Kent, "Aesthetic Values," 38, which describes the *Phylon* contributors' positions as "paradoxical."

be "nonracial" to be considered "universal").[41] Second, they argue that Black writers should be able to write whatever they want (not to have "appropriate" topics, genres, or aesthetic forms dictated to them by the white literary establishment).[42] And third, while a small few praise Black writers for demonstrating an increased "cultural maturity," the majority argue that it is not writers but rather audiences who need to become more "competent."[43] Whereas one contributor locates his optimism in this respect in his perception that America is finally moving "toward national maturity," others do so by looking beyond white American audiences: for Langston Hughes, Margaret Walker, and Era Bell Thompson, Black authors' "increased activity" and "widening audience" can be explained by the rise of Black bookshops, the growth of the Black press, and "a growing global perspective" in Black writing that is matched by "greater interest" in that writing "abroad."[44] Far from conforming to the demands of the white literary establishment, these contributors place their hope in factors that would become pivotal for the Black Arts Movement: Black writers' turn to and cultivation of global networks, Black audiences, and the Black press.

The volume's *indignation*—to use Lawrence Jackson's term—with white publishers and audiences can also be identified more broadly in Black writing of the period.[45] Black writers' repudiation of strictures on Black writing is visible not only in their use of Western aesthetic forms, but also in their turn to Black vernacular, blues, jazz, and gospel influences. It is visible not only in their turn to "literary" genres and "white life" novels, but also to thrillers, romances, humorous serials for the Black press, and books for Black children. As social protest novelist William Gardner Smith noted in his contribution to the *Phylon* special issue, Black writers were also actively cultivating new audiences in the Black community and abroad. Repelled by both communism

---

41. See, for example, Ford, "Blueprint for Negro Authors," 375; and Lee, "Criticism at Mid-Century," 329.

42. See, for example, Gloster, "Race and the Negro Writer," 370–71; and Redding, "Negro Writer," 373. For more on the contributors' discussion of what scholars now call "white life" novels as an example of their artistic freedom, see Charles, *Abandoning the Black Hero*, 11–13; and Li, *Playing in the White*, 21–23.

43. See, for example, Locke, "Self-Criticism," 391, versus Jackson, "Essay in Criticism," 338; Tillman, "Threshold of Maturity," 387–88; Hughes, "Some Practical Observations," 308; and Walker, "New Poets," 349. See also Jenkins's critique of Locke's argument in *Private Lives, Proper Relations*, 37–43.

44. Tillman, "Threshold of Maturity," 387–88; Hughes, "Some Practical Observations," 308; Thompson, "Negro Publications and the Writer," 305; Walker, "New Poets," 349; and Hughes, "Some Practical Observations," 308.

45. Jackson, *Indignant Generation*, 3. See, for example, Zora Neale Hurston's 1950 essay, "White Publishers Won't Print."

and capitalism, he argued, "the Negro writer of strength and courage stands firmly as a champion of the basic human issues—dignity, relative security, freedom and the end of savagery between one human being and another. And in this stand he is supported by the mass of human beings the world over."[46] Indeed, many successful writers—Richard Wright, Chester Himes, and James Baldwin—left the country in this period, and Paul Robeson and Du Bois continued to work in support of global anticolonial movements even at the loss of their own rights as US citizens.[47] At home, Robeson's Harlem-based radical newspaper *Freedom* (1950–55), Killens's Harlem Writers Guild (1950–), and Du Bois's *Freedomways* (1961–85) became new spaces for Black progressive writers to build community.[48] Together, these varied acts of literary and political world-making reflect not an appeal to but a refusal of Cold War liberalism and the narrow expectations of America's mainstream literary establishment.

Nevertheless, many of the Black writing groups and communities of the 1950s continued to be male-dominated. As Jenkins notes, Black literary and political development in those groups was often also "assumed to be a matter of black *masculine* empowerment."[49] For example, although numerous cutting-edge Black women writers participated in the Harlem Writers Guild, Audre Lorde later observed that she "felt tolerated but never really accepted. . . . For the most part the men were the core."[50] In the *Phylon* special issue, of the twenty-three contributors, only three are women—Gwendolyn Brooks, Margaret Walker, and Era Bell Thompson—and while many of the contributors acknowledge the significance of Brooks's Pulitzer Prize and Walker's prize-winning *For My People* (1942), the significance of Black women's fiction is generally underplayed, and the issue's male-centered language—speaking of "the Negro" in terms of "his work" and "his writing"—goes unquestioned.[51] Most significantly, of the many questions that the editors pose to their contributors, none have to do with gender, and their questions about the position of "the Negro writer, the Negro as subject, and the Negro critic and scholar" do not take into account the possibility that Black female writers, subjects, critics, and scholars might have unique perspectives to share.[52]

Behind the scenes, however, Black women were centrally involved in the local community-building work that was sustaining Black writers during the

---

46. Smith, "Negro Writer," 303.
47. See Fabre, *From Harlem to Paris*, 4–6; and Washington, *Other Blacklist*, 11.
48. See Washington, *Other Blacklist*, 15–17.
49. Jenkins, *Private Lives, Proper Relations*, 39, emphasis in original.
50. Lorde, "Interview with Audre Lorde," 54–55.
51. Jackson, "Essay in Criticism," 338. See also Jenkins, *Private Lives, Proper Relations*, 39.
52. Hill and Holman, preface to "The Negro in Literature," 296.

Black Chicago Renaissance. Alice Browning's *Negro Story* magazine (1944–46), run out of her home in Chicago, offered a platform for important midcentury writers such as Richard Wright, Chester Himes, Gwendolyn Brooks, Ralph Ellison, and Langston Hughes, and "provided a springboard" for postwar Black writing.[53] Vivian Harsh's Book Review and Lecture Forum at the Hall Branch of the Chicago Public Library in Bronzeville also hosted community events with such notable writers as Richard Wright, Langston Hughes, Zora Neale Hurston, Arna Bontemps, and Gwendolyn Brooks.[54] And it was Brooks and her close friend Margaret Burroughs who provided regular spaces for writers, intellectuals, and artists to gather by hosting parties and gatherings in their homes throughout the 1950s.[55] Burroughs went on to become one of the founders of the National Conference of Artists (NCA) in 1959, and was the primary force behind the founding of the DuSable Museum of African American History and Art in 1961. As Melba Joyce Boyd notes, by the late 1950s and early 1960s, Burroughs had "assumed the responsibility of institution building, a major tenet of the Black Arts philosophy" that emerged in 1965.[56] Writing in 1969, Heritage Press publisher Paul Breman similarly observed that "the cultural life of the black community" in Chicago was "dominated by [these] two women," and that Gwendolyn Brooks had developed "into a major influence," especially on "young . . . mainly female" poets.[57] Likewise, Margaret Danner, who had been a member of the South Side Writers Group alongside Wright, Brooks, and Margaret Walker, moved to Detroit in 1961 and founded a poetry and cultural center called Boone House in 1962. Boone House became an important home for such writers as Dudley Randall, Robert Hayden, Hoyt Fuller, Owen Dodson, and Naomi Long Madgett, several of whom went on to be major figures in the Black Arts Movement, and who found in Danner's Boone House "a poetry community to inspire each other."[58] And Margaret Walker, winner of the 1942 Yale Younger Poets prize, went on to become a foundational figure in the Black Women's Literary Renaissance because of the groundbreaking 1973 conference for Black women writers that she organized for the bicentennial of Phillis Wheatley's *Poems on Various Subjects,* at which Alice Walker shared her landmark remarks, "In Search of Our Mothers' Gardens" (1974). The work of these women of Brooks's generation—and in particular their efforts to sustain Black literary communities—has been largely left

---

53. Mullen, "Popular Fronts," 945.
54. See Olson, *Chicago Renaissance,* 252; and Goldsby, "Salon for the Masses."
55. See Brooks, *Report from Part One,* 69–70.
56. Boyd, *Wrestling with the Muse,* 161.
57. Breman, "Poetry into the Sixties," 102.
58. Randall, quoted in Boyd, *Wrestling with the Muse,* 105.

out of dominant accounts of Black literary history in the 1950s and '60s. How might our picture of the Black Chicago Renaissance and the literary periods that followed it change if we refocused our attention on the literature and the labor of these Black women?

The World of Gwendolyn Brooks and the Rise of Maud Martha

Considered in the male-dominated context of mid-twentieth-century American letters, Gwendolyn Brooks's choice to center working-class Black women in her earliest works, and to write with such intimacy about their inner lives, is a powerful one. As Mary Helen Washington, Candice Jenkins, and others have argued, many prior Black female writers felt constrained "by the need to defend black women and men against the vicious and prevailing stereotypes that mark nineteenth-century American cultural thought."[59] By the mid-twentieth century, Jenkins argues, these stereotypes about Black biological inferiority had transformed into allegations of social "pathology" aimed largely "at the black woman's role within the household," which, John Charles explains, was associated with a "a systematic violation of black privacy."[60] As Jenkins maintains, some Black authors turned to "respectability politics" to protect the Black community from this threatening white gaze; others, Charles contends, turned to "white life" literature as "a strategy for critically engaging with a key discursive source of racial (and sexual) oppression without having to reinforce notions of black abjection as a necessary part of that engagement."[61] But these protective gestures also cut Black writers, and especially Black female writers, off from the expression of intimacy. Jenkins writes that "the vulnerability that African Americans have been subject to at the hands of white racism often *is* the vulnerability of intimacy."[62] In order words, to avoid putting Black vulnerability on display for the pathologizing white gaze of the white literary establishment was also to limit available venues for the expression of Black intimacy.

Brooks, by interweaving throughout her work a range of small, taboo-shattering moments of vulnerability—such as her Black female characters' feelings about infidelity, sex, abortion, and childbirth—must be considered a forerunner to the later Black feminist writers who Erica Edwards argues

---

59. Washington, *Invented Lives*, 73.
60. Jenkins, *Private Lives, Proper Relations*, 9; and Charles, *Abandoning the Black Hero*, 9.
61. Charles, *Abandoning the Black Hero*, 10.
62. Jenkins, *Private Lives, Proper Relations*, 19, emphasis in original.

"work against the respectability-based tactics of protecting Black life" to create "a kind of hyper-private black space within which the vulnerability of intimacy is once again possible."[63] Brooks's expressions in her early work of what she called "woman rage" is especially relevant here.[64] As Lorde would later write, Black women's anger is a natural response to their vulnerability in the face of the violence of a racist, sexist America: "Women of Color in america [sic] have grown up within a symphony of anger, at being silenced, at being unchosen, at knowing that when we survive, it is in spite of a world that takes for granted our lack of humanness, and which hates our very existence outside of its service."[65] Caught within a social structure that also stereotypes or pathologizes Black anger, and that demands "respectability" from Black women to protect not just themselves but the entire Black family, all while prioritizing, authorizing, and institutionalizing white feelings, Black women are triply prevented from expressing that righteous rage.[66] As a result, the expression of anger exposes Black women to vulnerability. But for these reasons and more, Lorde sees the expression of that anger as a form of resistance and power: "Anger expressed and translated into action in the service of our vision and our future is a liberating and strengthening act of clarification, for it is in this painful process of this translation that we identify who are our allies with whom we have grave differences, and who are our genuine enemies."[67] Brooks's expression of Black female vulnerability and rage claims literary space for these new forms of intimacy, solidarity, and resistance.

As with Lorde's reformulation of vulnerability as strength, Brooks's characters are not only vulnerable; they are also visionaries. Koritha Mitchell argues that the domestic focus of so much mid-twentieth-century Black women's writing was not a mere reaction to anti-Black stereotypes about dysfunctional homes but was a positive embrace of the act of Black homemaking, "place-making," and "meaning-making."[68] Such acts of Black female meaning-making stand as counter-discourses to those structures of meaning-making associated with the Western conception of the *uomo universale* or the Renaissance Man, who is represented as white, male, sovereign, and limitless in his capacities. Brooks's creation of Black female characters who possess *both* vulnerability *and* vision challenges the surveillance of the white literary establishment and the Western concept of the "universal man." For Brooks, the

---

63. Edwards, *Other Side of Terror*, 30, quoting Jenkins, *Private Lives, Proper Relations*, 20.
64. Brooks, "Interview with Gwendolyn Brooks," 107.
65. Lorde, "Uses of Anger," 129.
66. See Jenkins, *Private Lives, Proper Relations*, 8–10, 13–14; and Anderson, *White Rage*, 3–4.
67. Lorde, "Uses of Anger," 127.
68. Mitchell, *From Slave Cabins*, 21.

Renaissance Woman is one who sees her vulnerability not as antithetical to her vision (because, as for the Renaissance Man, it is a sign of nonsovereignty or limitation), but rather one who sees her vulnerability as intertwined with her vision at their very core. In her early work, we see a visionary response to the limited worldview of the white literary establishment, and an expression of vulnerability that signals her growing address to and care for readers capable of something more.

Brooks's first and only novella, *Maud Martha*, came on the heels of two successful books of poetry, *A Street in Bronzeville* and the Pulitzer Prize–winning *Annie Allen*, which together cemented Brooks's position as the darling of the white literary establishment.[69] However, the critical focus on how her work was received by the white literary establishment has overshadowed the work she was doing to challenge their constraints and expectations. In fact, although early reviews of *A Street in Bronzeville* claimed that she was "the first Negro poet to write . . . without relying on the fact of color to draw sympathy and interest," it was also the white publishing industry that believed her "Negro poems" would be more marketable.[70] When Brooks first approached Emily Morison from Knopf with her collection of "love poems, war poems, nature poems, patriotism poems," and "'prejudice' poems," Morison replied that she liked the "Negro poems" and "hoped that" when Brooks "had a full collection of these," she "would try Knopf again."[71] Brooks followed Morison's "wisdom" but rejected her company, taking her collection of "Negro poems," which would become *A Street in Bronzeville*, to Elizabeth Lawrence at Harper.[72] Perhaps in a quiet rebuke of Morison's advice, however, this collection of "Negro poems" intentionally included "love poems" and "war poems" such as "When You Have Forgotten Sunday: A Love Story" and "Gay Chaps at the Bar," now tied together by the geographic location of that segregated Bronzeville street.

In addition to ensuring that the range of poems included in her first volume was not constrained by a white publisher's narrow expectations regarding appropriate themes for Black literature, Brooks also took a great deal of care with how the press packaged and presented her work. Early letters with Lawrence signal Brooks's wariness over how a book of "Negro poems" might be packaged by a white publisher, with her initial submission even including a suggestion of a Bronzeville-based illustrator for the book. As Kinohi

---

69. See Addington, "Toward Crossroads Confluence," 115; and Bloch, "'Shut Your Rhetorics in a Box,'" 443.
70. Engle, "Chicago Can Take Pride," E11.
71. Brooks, *Report from Part One*, 71. See also Brooks, "Gwendolyn Brooks," 32.
72. Brooks, *Report from Part One*, 71.

Nishikawa argues, Brooks's efforts to shape the design of even her earliest books demonstrate that even before she left Harper for Black presses in the late 1960s, she "was always trying to find ways of making her poetic voice look more like home."[73] When Lawrence sent her a preview of the cover for *A Street in Bronzeville*—the title of her book against a brick wall background—Brooks expressed relief that the cover was "dignified." She wrote: "How happy I am that there are no funny little figures, with patches, open collars, and so on!"[74] Despite her excitement to have found a publisher, Brooks was worried about how the white literary establishment might choose to package her poems and attentive to all the power she had at her disposal to redirect those efforts.

Indeed, although Richard Wright famously articulated the desire to decenter the interests of white audiences in his essay "Blueprint for Negro Writing" (1937), in their respective dealings with the white editors of their early works, Brooks arguably did more than Wright to challenge white audiences' interests.[75] After all, whereas Wright agreed to censor the more provocative moments in *Native Son* (1940) to ensure the book's inclusion as a Book-of-the-Month-Club selection, Brooks resisted her publisher's efforts to make her book more palatable to white readers.[76] In fact, when Elizabeth Lawrence first received Brooks's submission, she turned to Wright to review the manuscript, and he expressed concern that various elements of Brooks's book might be too jarring for a mainstream audience. One concern was that the title "was conceived out of a local frame of reference and most people would not know what it meant."[77] His other concern was the poem "the mother." He wrote: "Maybe I'm just simply prejudiced, but I don't think that poems can be made about abortions; or perhaps the poet has not yet been born who can lift abortions to the poetic plane."[78] Harper editor Edward Aswell agreed with Wright "at every point," but Brooks pushed back on both of these efforts to modify her work, and—with Lawrence's strategic support for her defiance of "the masculinist culture and politics of the mid-twentieth-century literary marketplace"—she won.[79] On the title, Brooks also insisted that she had

---

73. Nishikawa, "From Poet to Publisher," 50.
74. Gwendolyn Brooks to Elizabeth Lawrence, 30 June 1945, Selected Records of Harper & Brothers.
75. See Wright, "Blueprint for Negro Writing," 99.
76. See Raynaud, "Changing Texts," 173.
77. Richard Wright to Edward Aswell, 18 September 1944, Selected Records of Harper & Brothers.
78. Richard Wright to Edward Aswell, 18 September 1944, Selected Records of Harper & Brothers.
79. Edward Aswell to Richard Wright, 22 September 1944, Selected Records of Harper & Brothers; and Goldsby, "'Something Is Said,'" 245.

"thought of the title first and wrote most of the poems especially for it" and that the book "might suffer if the 'stitching' that the heading . . . gives it were taken out."[80] Explaining to Lawrence that Bronzeville was a neighborhood on Chicago's South Side, Brooks implied that readers should do the work to find this out before she should be asked to change her central concept just to accommodate their ignorance. On "the mother," she replied that "the stressed thing . . . was not the matter of abortions but the fact that the woman wanted many children but knew that all she could guarantee them was poverty."[81] She responded not by offering to remove the poem but by sending an additional poem about a Black woman's taboo feelings, "Ballad of Pearl May Lee," this one about a dark-skinned woman's complicated rage in response to her cheating lover's lynching, which raised further eyebrows in the Harper office but was nevertheless included in the book.[82] In these instances, Brooks demonstrated the centrality of Black places, perspectives, and voices—and especially Black women's voices—to her aesthetic vision, a resolve only later acknowledged as ahead of its time.[83]

Harper's effort to align Brooks with Wright, to the extent that they considered excluding her most complicated representations of Black female experience, also needs to be considered alongside reviewers' efforts to efface Brooks's Blackness to align her with the "universal."[84] Both efforts deny the specificity of the Black female experience upon which Brooks's early poems insist. *Annie Allen* and *Maud Martha*, two book-length works focused on the interior lives of Black women from childhood to adulthood, including their growing awareness of racism, colorism, poverty, sexism, and self-love, similarly frustrate critical efforts to not see the specificity of Black women's experience. *Annie Allen* also represented an additional challenge to the white literary establishment because it refused establishment pressure to make Black life legible and marketable to white audiences. As Lawrence's first letter to Brooks indicated, Harper very much hoped Brooks would turn her considerable literary talent

---

80. Gwendolyn Brooks to Elizabeth Lawrence, 28 September 1944 and 25 February 1945, Selected Records of Harper & Brothers. See also Goldsby, "'Something Is Said,'" 254.

81. Gwendolyn Brooks to Elizabeth Lawrence, 28 September 1944, Selected Records of Harper & Brothers.

82. Gwendolyn Brooks to Elizabeth Lawrence, 28 September 1944, Selected Records of Harper & Brothers. On "the feeling against" including "Ballad of Pearl May Lee," see Elizabeth Lawrence to Gwendolyn Brooks, 2 April 1945, Selected Records of Harper & Brothers.

83. See Brooks, "Update on Part One," 98; Brooks, "Interview with Gwendolyn Brooks," 107; and Brooks, "Conversation with Gwendolyn Brooks," 5.

84. See Gwendolyn Brooks to Elizabeth Lawrence, 25 March 1945, Selected Records of Harper & Brothers; Elizabeth Lawrence to Gwendolyn Brooks, 2 April 1945, Selected Records of Harper & Brothers; and Engle, "Chicago Can Take Pride," E11.

to the more profitable genre of fiction. Enquiring whether Brooks might have a novel in mind, Lawrence wrote: "There is so much of narrative interest in your poetry that we feel you will turn eventually to writing fiction. And fiction of course, is more profitable than poetry for both author and publisher."[85] However, Harper rejected Brooks's first attempt at prose—a set of vignettes titled "American Family Brown"—because they did not "add up to a strongly unified and dramatic whole," and Brooks put that more profitable genre aside to write *Annie Allen*.[86]

In this new collection, Lawrence and several early readers were further surprised to find that Brooks had abandoned altogether the "narrative interest" that they had so appreciated in her first book.[87] Although Lawrence was always careful to emphasize her admiration, she also wrote:

> I am disturbed by a feeling that recently you have been escaping from life itself into a world of words and sounds. . . . *A Street in Bronzeville* was clear, decisive writing with the emphasis on content rather than form. In many of these new poems, on the contrary, the form, the mannerisms, tend to intrude and obscure the content. There is a preciousness, an artificiality, about some of it that is foreign to you as I know you. . . . You are too good a poet to have to resort to trick and shock devices.[88]

Brooks, in turn, expressed surprise that her "reaching toward a more careful language should strike anyone as 'a trick and shock device,'" but she continued with the book as planned, carefully pushing back on many of the publisher's suggestions for cuts.[89] Still, even when *Annie Allen* was accepted, Lawrence warned: "I can offer you an advance of one hundred dollars, which is half the advance we gave on *A Street in Bronzeville*."[90] Among the factors influencing this drop in investment was their sense that "it would be surprising if this book did as well in sales. The other book had the advantage of appealing to

---

85. Elizabeth Lawrence to Gwendolyn Brooks, 22 September 1944, Selected Records of Harper & Brothers.
86. Elizabeth Lawrence to Gwendolyn Brooks, 26 September 1947, Selected Records of Harper & Brothers.
87. Elizabeth Lawrence to Gwendolyn Brooks, 22 September 1944, Selected Records of Harper & Brothers.
88. Elizabeth Lawrence to Gwendolyn Brooks, 14 July 1948, Selected Records of Harper & Brothers.
89. Gwendolyn Brooks to Elizabeth Lawrence, 17 July 1948, Selected Records of Harper & Brothers.
90. Elizabeth Lawrence to Gwendolyn Brooks, 11 August 1948, Selected Records of Harper & Brothers.

an audience that extended beyond the ranks of poetry lovers. It had a certain news value."[91] In other words, obscured by Brooks's later "legitimizing" win of the Pulitzer Prize is the fact that the aestheticism of *Annie Allen*—the book's supposed interest in form over the "narrative interest" and "news value" that publishers expected of Black authors in the wake of the success of novels like *Native Son*—was not an effort to prove to the white literary establishment that she could appeal to their expectations, but more likely an effort to prove that she could not be kept in the small box they had made for Black writers.[92]

Maud Martha, Brooks's next work—an adaptation of her earlier "American Family Brown"—continued to frustrate her editor's early hopes for a big bestseller. Lawrence continued to encourage Brooks to work on her novel, and she had made several efforts to connect Brooks with Wright as a potential mentor and model, not only by asking Wright to read *A Street in Bronzeville* but also by sending Brooks a copy of Wright's *Black Boy* (1945).[93] Lawrence had also gushed to other members of the literary world and to Brooks herself that she was "essentially a novelist," and that the positive reception of her poetry was sure to "bear fruit" once her novel came along.[94] But where Lawrence might have hoped for the "news value" of *Native Son,* Brooks delivered a manuscript to which Lawrence could find no comparison, and which she doubted would sell. To Brooks, she said: "Your book is in all likelihood special fare for a discriminating minority. It is possible—but it will be surprising—if it proves a money-maker. Still, greater miracles have happened, and I shall keep all my fingers crossed."[95] Privately, she told Brooks's early mentor Inez Cunningham Stark that it "has not the full stature Gwen could give it."[96] Certainly, it was no *Native Son*. As Brooks put it in a 1984 interview, her main character, unlike

---

91. Elizabeth Lawrence to Gwendolyn Brooks, 11 August 1948, Selected Records of Harper & Brothers.

92. See, for example, Bloch, "'Shut Your Rhetorics in a Box,'" 443; and Shockley, *Renegade Poetics,* 27–28.

93. See Elizabeth Lawrence to Gwendolyn Brooks, 22 September 1944 and 16 February 1945, Selected Records of Harper & Brothers.

94. Elizabeth Lawrence, Fellowship Letter of Recommendation for Gwendolyn Brooks, undated (circa 1945), Selected Records of Harper & Brothers; and Elizabeth Lawrence to Gwendolyn Brooks, 14 September 1945, Selected Records of Harper & Brothers. See also Elizabeth Lawrence to Gwendolyn Brooks, 30 October 1944, Selected Records of Harper & Brothers; and Elizabeth Lawrence to Edward Aswell, 8 November 1944, Selected Records of Harper & Brothers.

95. Elizabeth Lawrence to Gwendolyn Brooks, 2 March 1953, Selected Records of Harper & Brothers. See also Elizabeth Lawrence to Gwendolyn Brooks, 5 November 1953, Selected Records of Harper & Brothers.

96. Elizabeth Lawrence to Inez [Cunningham Stark] Boulton, 5 November 1953, Selected Records of Harper & Brothers.

Wright's Bigger Thomas, was "a lovely little person, wrestling with the threads of her milieu."[97] She continued: "The novel is very funny, very often!—and not at all disappointing, even *though* my heroine was never raped, did not become a lady of the evening, did not enter the world of welfare mothers" and, again unlike Bigger Thomas, "did not murder the woman who stepped on her toe on the bus."[98]

Brooks's sardonic defense of *Maud Martha* references both her defiance of the white literary establishment's narrow expectations for Black writing and her feelings about their lukewarm response to her book. Indeed, Brooks's focus on the everyday experience of a Black female protagonist led early reviewers to regard the book as feminine and slight. As Washington summarizes, they saw "the young black woman heroine" of *Maud Martha* as

> a "spunky Negro girl" as though the novel were a piece of juvenile fiction. Reviewers, in brief notices of the novel, insisted on its optimism and faith: Maud's life is made up of "moments she loved," she has "disturbances," but she "struggles against jealousy" for the sake of her marriage; there is, of course, "the delicate pressure of the color line," but Maud has the remarkable "ability to turn unhappiness and anger into a joke."[99]

For Washington, none of these reviewers recognized *Maud Martha* "as dealing with the very sexism and racism" that their own "reviews enshrined."[100] As Brooks would later say when asked about her early work: "A lot of women are now observing that a good many of my poems are about women. . . . I hope you sense some real rage in 'The [sic] Ballad of Pearl May Lee.' . . . That's *all* political."[101] In other words, her early work could only be seen as lacking a "heightened political awareness" because it appeared in a critical context that did not take Black women's politics seriously.[102]

Maud Martha's reception among critics and audiences also indicates the degree to which the novel defied the literary establishment's critical expectations, both because her novel refused to align with the social realist genre of her predecessors and because it claimed space within the highly stylized, modernist-influenced form that was typically reserved for male "heroes." Brooks defied both expectations by writing in lyric prose about an ordinary

---

97. Brooks, "Interview," 114.
98. Brooks, "Interview," 114, emphasis in original.
99. Washington, "'Taming All That Anger Down,'" 453.
100. Washington, "'Taming All That Anger Down,'" 453.
101. Brooks, "Interview with Gwendolyn Brooks," 107, emphasis in original.
102. Brooks, "Interview with Gwendolyn Brooks," 106.

Black woman to whom very little happens, and who does very little. As a result, the novel was lightly praised for its "charm" and its "impressionist style," but few reviewers knew what else to make of it.[103] Washington and Christian both note that whereas highly stylized coming-of-age novels by Black men such as Ralph Ellison's *Invisible Man* (1952) and James Baldwin's *Go Tell It on the Mountain* (1953) were heralded as major Black novels, Brook's "lovely little novel" came and "quietly went out of print."[104] As Christian argues, *Maud Martha* "ran counter to the tone of 'the Negro Novel' that both blacks and whites would have expected in 1953" because it "replaced intense drama with a careful rendering of the rituals, the patterns, of the ordinary life," one "where racism is experienced in sharp nibbles rather than screams."[105] Just as Maud Martha the character develops "her own standards, her own concept of the valuable," so *Maud Martha* the novel attaches to an "unheroic ordinary black girl from Chicago, a value that is almost always celebrated in the heroic, the extraordinary, the male."[106] Maud Martha knows her own value, and she develops her sense of that value through her experience of the "sharp nibbles" of racism, poverty, and sexism. Unlike the liberal humanist ideal of the Renaissance Man, she is conscious of the limits that surround her, but knows she has value and vision nonetheless.[107] Much as Evie Shockley argues of *Annie Allen*, *Maud Martha* "change[s] the subject" of the Western aesthetic forms with which it plays, claiming space within them for the subject position of the ordinary Black woman and, in so doing, changing the very subject—the topic or meaning—of that genre.[108] Rather than merely claiming space for Black women within Western frameworks, Brooks insists that making room for Black female experience requires that the framework change.

Maud Martha Meets the World

Originally imagined as "almost another book of poems," *Maud Martha* reads like a series of vignettes of poetic prose, overlapping often with the themes and even language of *A Street in Bronzeville*, but unfolding as a series of moments

---

103. On the novel's "charm," see Kogan, "Two Chicagoans Charm, Shock," 6; Winslow, "Soft Meditations," 114; and Review of *Maud Martha*, 458. On the novel's "impressionistic style," see "Briefly Noted," 153; E.C., "Book of the Week," 50; Martin, "Book Reviews," 11; and Jackson, "Poet's First Novel," 436.

104. Brooks, "Interview," 114; and Christian, "Nuance and the Novella," 239. See also Washington, "'Taming All That Anger Down,'" 464–65.

105. Christian, "Nuance and the Novella," 241.

106. Christian, "Nuance and the Novella," 252.

107. Christian, "Nuance and the Novella," 241.

108. Shockley, *Renegade Poetics*, 18.

in one woman's life, rather than as a series of lives occupying connected spaces.[109] Christian argues that "the critical aspects of Maud Martha's sensibility are her ability to see beneath the mundane surface of things and to transform that little that is allowed her into so much more than it originally was."[110] For writer Paule Marshall, who would credit *Maud Martha* as "a model that would guide [her] as a novelist over the years," Maud Martha "possess[es] a rich and complex inner life that makes her an extraordinary creation."[111] As Marshall would tell Mary Helen Washington, "In her daily life, Maud Martha functions an artist" whose perceptions of the world transform "the ordinary rituals of daily life . . . into art."[112] In this way, the novel mirrors another modernist text, James Joyce's *A Portrait of the Artist as a Young Man* (1916), also a semi-autobiographical novel told in a series of disjointed, poetic chapters.[113] But where Joyce's *Portrait* chronicles the development of a young man into an artist, leaving home to "forge in the smithy of his soul the uncreated conscience of his race," Brooks's novel denies her protagonist this explicitly heroic and seemingly unfettered trajectory.[114] The only thing Maud Martha imagines having the power to "forge" is herself: "To create—a role, a poem, picture, music, a rapture in stone: great. But not for her. What she wanted was to donate to the world a good Maud Martha. That was the offering, the bit of art, that could not come from any other. She would polish and hone that."[115]

---

109. Gwendolyn Brooks to Elizabeth Lawrence, 21 January 1952, Selected Records of Harper & Brothers. On the novel's similarity to *A Street in Bronzeville*, see Maud Martha's "dream" and the "grayness" of her kitchenette, like the "grayed in, and gray" residents of "kitchenette building" and their "dreams" (Brooks, *Maud Martha*, 193, 206; and Brooks, *Street in Bronzeville*, 20); the chapter on "kitchenette folks," mirroring the overall structure of *A Street in Bronzeville* (Brooks, *Maud Martha*, 250–68); and the men at the 011 Club who "knew how to dance, how to smoke, how much stress to put on love," like the men in "gay chaps at the bar" who "knew how to order . . . / how to give women / the summer spread . . . of our love" (Brooks, *Maud Martha*, 290; and Brooks, *Street in Bronzeville*, 64). Before deciding to "make the story that of the development of one individual," she had also tentatively titled the manuscript "Bronzevillians" (Gwendolyn Brooks to Elizabeth Lawrence, 15 September 1952 and 21 January 1952, Selected Records of Harper & Brothers).

110. Christian, "Nuance and the Novella," 252.

111. Marshall, "Gwendolyn Brooks—An Appreciation," 53. Since Marshall's *Brown Girl, Brownstones* (1959) is often credited as "the forerunner of the Afro-American woman's literary explosion of the 1970s," it is notable that she saw *Maud Martha* as her own inspiration (Christian, "Nuance and the Novella," 239).

112. Marshall, quoted in Washington, Book Review of *Black Women Novelists*, 179.

113. Brooks was also working on a book of poems modeled after modernist writer Lytton Strachey's *Eminent Victorians* (1918), even proposing the title "Eminent Bronzevillians" to her editor (Gwendolyn Brooks to Elizabeth Lawrence, 17 October 1950, Selected Records of Harper & Brothers).

114. Joyce, *Portrait of the Artist*, 262.

115. Brooks, *Maud Martha*, 164.

The novel's presentation of Maud Martha's artistic worldview on her ordinary life distinguishes her not only from dominant images of the unfettered white, male artist but also from dominant images of Black women that were in circulation in the Black press and other fiction at the time. Whereas middle-class Black magazines such as *Ebony* and *Jet* often presented glamorous or respectable images of Black women and housewives as a rejoinder to the pathologizing surveillance of Black homes, Maud Martha's home fails to live up to these aspirational images. Of her home, she thinks: "*The Defender* would never come here with cameras."[116] The novel also resists the patterns set by documentary and social realist texts like Wright's *12 Million Black Voices* (1941) and Ann Petry's *The Street* (1946), insofar as Maud Martha never sees her home as what Wright would call "our death sentence" or what Petry would call "that god-damned street."[117] And while Brooks would later insist that her "works express rage and focus on *rage*," that rage is expressed very differently in her novel than in the work of these other authors.[118] For example, in "Maud Martha spares the mouse," Maud Martha's act of empathy toward the mouse in her kitchenette acts as a rejoinder to the opening scene of *Native Son,* in which Bigger brutally kills a rat in his. Scholars often focus on Maud Martha's act of empathy in this scene, arguing that here Brooks "depart[s] from Wright's naturalistic cycle of destruction" to affirm a worldview that is "nurturing," "life-centered," and "creativ[e]."[119] Importantly, though, the rat and the mouse are not just the *objects* of Bigger's and Maud Martha's respective acts of rage and empathy, or "figure[s]" for their "living conditions"; they are also figures for Bigger and Maud Martha themselves—*subjects* who find themselves trapped in their kitchenettes and in the larger traps of poverty and racism.[120] Bigger's rat emits "a long thin song of defiance, its black beady eyes glittering," much like Bigger himself.[121] In contrast, the "bright black eyes" of Maud Martha's mouse contain "no appeal—the little creature seemed to understand that there was no hope of mercy from the eternal enemy, no hope of reprieve or postponement—but a fine small dignity. It waited."[122] It is this assertion of dignity in the face of absolute vulnerability, and this refusal to appeal to the conscience of "the eternal enemy," that stops Maud Martha in her tracks. She

---

116. Brooks, *Maud Martha*, 203.
117. Wright, *12 Million Black Voices*, 106; and Petry, *The Street*, 436.
118. Brooks, "Interview with Gwendolyn Brooks," 106, emphasis in original.
119. Walther, "Re-Wrighting *Native Son*," 144. See also Ahern, "Creative Multivalence," 318–20; and Frazier, "Domestic Epic Warfare," 137.
120. Walther, "Re-Wrighting *Native Son*," 143.
121. Wright, *Native Son*, 6.
122. Brooks, *Maud Martha*, 211–12.

"could not bear the little look."[123] Maud Martha may offer the mouse empathy rather than rage, but the more powerful image is the mouse's refusal to give her—"the eternal enemy"—either the righteous rage or the pitiful pleading that she expects. In this way, the scene signals Brooks's refusal of what Simone Browne calls the "racializing surveillance" of Black individuals and homes, refusing to provide that enemy's powerful gaze with either one of the reifying images of Black subjection that they have come to expect.[124]

By affirming the power of the mouse's dignity in the face of vulnerability, the mouse scene also offers a critique of Renaissance and Enlightenment conceptions of individual sovereignty and unfettered liberty. Although some scholars note Maud Martha's "power" in this scene to "take life or let live," Eve Dunbar cautions against being too invested in any concept of "sovereignty" that depends on dominance over the "nonsovereign mouse."[125] She argues:

> I push against readings extolling Maud Martha's sovereignty as expressed by her decision to "let live" because it binds her to nonradical notions of humanist subjectivity. In a sovereign subject–nonsovereign object binary system, there is little room for decentering white supremacy because sovereignty itself requires exclusion of the nonsovereign from its ranks. Black subject making that centers sovereignty, then, is climbing on the backs of those thought to lack access to sovereignty.[126]

I would add that the scene also troubles Western humanist conceptions of sovereignty by making it impossible to separate a "sovereign" Maud Martha from the nonsovereign mouse. After all, to whatever degree Maud Martha saves the mouse, she also *is* the mouse, projecting onto the mouse's "bright black eyes" the very "fine small dignity" in the face of "the eternal enemy" that she elsewhere insists upon for herself.[127] From any perspective on sovereignty that demands the exclusion of the nonsovereign, this moment would seem like a paradox, but Maud Martha has no difficulty seeing "dignity" in the mouse despite its lack of "limitless capacity," and she has no difficulty seeing "power" in herself even if the only power she has is to save a mouse. In this way, the scene functions as a refusal of the white pitying or pathologizing gaze, and an assertion of the dignity and creative power experienced and articulated

---

123. Brooks, *Maud Martha*, 212.
124. Browne, *Dark Matters*, 16–17.
125. Ahern, "Creative Multivalence," 319; Frazier, "Domestic Epic Warfare," 137; and Dunbar, "Loving Gorillas," 138.
126. Dunbar, "Loving Gorillas," 138.
127. Brooks, *Maud Martha*, 211–12.

through Maud Martha's consciousness of her own (and the mouse's) vulnerability. In other words, the power that she takes from this moment comes not from a feeling of sovereignty or dominance over the mouse but from her appreciation of the mouse's dignity, which is itself informed by her recognition of the vulnerability that she and the mouse clearly share.

The chapter called "a birth" similarly explores Maud Martha's location of her own power not in sovereignty but in vulnerability. The scene is remarkable, not least for having few literary predecessors in its graphic depiction of childbirth.[128] Much like "the mother" in *A Street in Bronzeville*, "a birth" refuses to shy away from Black women's most intimate experiences. In the scene, the child comes so quickly that there is no time to bring Maud Martha to a "respectable" place such as a hospital, and she ends up having the baby at home in her kitchenette. The space is so crowded together with her neighbors' space, so lacking in privacy, that many of the women on her floor—women "she had never said more than 'Hello'" to—end up "troop[ing] in."[129] Here, however, the lack of privacy Maud experiences in the cramped quarters of the kitchenette are not a trap, nor a death sentence, nor even an indignity, as in Wright's work, but a surprising and unexpected space for female community: "Weren't they sweet," Maud Martha thinks. "People are sweet."[130] These neighbors also act as a necessary supplement to the lack of support she receives from within the nuclear family, with a husband "in fright" and "glad of an excuse to escape."[131] Their presence—and her appreciation of their presence—makes her feel stronger.[132]

In addition to highlighting Maud Martha's nonsovereign dependence on her neighbors, the chapter also highlights her lack of sovereignty in the face of the uncontrollable suffering of childbirth: "She screamed longer and louder, explaining breathlessly in between times, 'I just can't help it. Excuse me.'"[133] Paul's response is to recognize how lucky he is to never have to face such suffering himself. He thinks: "He had had no idea that she could scream that kind of screaming. It was awful. How lucky he was that he had been born a man.

---

128. Anaïs Nin's short story "Birth" (1938) preceded *Maud Martha* by over a decade, but Doris Lessing's *A Proper Marriage* (1954) and Sylvia Plath's *The Bell Jar* (1963) were published later, and writing about childbirth didn't become common until the 1970 and '80s. See Poston, "Childbirth in Literature"; Chester, *Cradle and All*; and Cosslett, *Women Writing Childbirth*, though notably none mention *Maud Martha*.
129. Brooks, *Maud Martha*, 241.
130. Brooks, *Maud Martha*, 241.
131. Brooks, *Maud Martha*, 233, 236.
132. Notably, Brooks would return to childbirth as a metaphor for the pain and promise of the civil rights movement, arguing in *New Negro Poets* that "we, white and black, are a collective pregnancy that is going to proceed to its inevitability, getting worse before it gets better" (Brooks, foreword to *New Negro Poets*, 13).
133. Brooks, *Maud Martha*, 237.

How lucky he was that he had been born a man!"[134] But while Maud Martha's suffering is enormous, it is also an ordinary and ubiquitous experience among women. Her mother says, "Why there's nothing to make a fuss *about*. You're just going to have a baby, like millions of other women. Why should I make a fuss?"[135] Later, Maud Martha scoffs when her mother demands praise for not fainting. She thinks: "Was it, she suddenly wondered, as hard to watch suffering as it was to bear it?"[136] But despite all this suffering, or rather, because of it, she again feels her own power: "She preferred to think, now, about how well she felt. Had she ever in her life felt so well? . . . 'I just had a baby, and I feel strong enough to go out and shovel coal!' . . . Oh she felt fine."[137] Taken together, the scene draws our attention both to Maud Martha's utter lack of privacy and her experience of pain so great that it disrupts her sovereign sense of self. But the scene also ends with Maud's feeling of power, a feeling she associates not with independence, sovereignty, and liberty, but with community, vulnerability, and survival.

Like "a birth," much of *Maud Martha* decenters direct experiences of racism in favor of time spent in the private spaces of the Black community. White characters tend only to emerge when they frustrate Maud Martha's cultural or economic engagement with the world—for example, when she wishes to see a movie, have her hair done, take her child to see Santa Claus, or buy a hat.[138] Like the mouse, when her sense of self-worth is challenged by white characters, she does not look to them for affirmation or recognition. Rather, as when she decides to leave her white employer after just one day of insults, she looks inward to the everyday pleasures of her ordinary life for affirmation of her human dignity: "Why, one was a human being. One wore clean nightgowns. One loved one's baby. One drank cocoa, by the fire—or the gas range—come evening, in the wintertime."[139] In walking away from that paid work to protect and affirm her own dignity, she also feels no need to explain herself to her offender: "I'll never come back, Maud Martha assured herself. . . . She knew Mrs. Burns-Cooper would be puzzled," but "what difference did it make whether the firing squad understood or did not understand the manner of one's retaliation."[140] Like the mouse, she sees no need to appeal to this woman's conscience.

---

134. Brooks, *Maud Martha*, 236.
135. Brooks, *Maud Martha*, 237, emphasis in original.
136. Brooks, *Maud Martha*, 239.
137. Brooks, *Maud Martha*, 240–41.
138. Brooks, *Maud Martha*, 220, 281, 316, 297.
139. Brooks, *Maud Martha*, 305.
140. Brooks, *Maud Martha*, 305.

And yet, although Maud Martha refuses to give her "eternal enemy" the satisfaction of surveilling her pain, the novel quietly reveals to its readers her complicated interiority. Observing her husband's interest in a lighter-skinned woman, for example, she thinks: "I could . . . scratch . . . spit . . . scream."[141] But she doesn't act on these thoughts: "If the root was sour what business did she have up there hacking at a leaf?"[142] Likewise, when a white man in a Santa Claus costume insults her daughter, she recognizes the "scraps of baffled hate in her, hate with no eyes, no smile and—this she especially regretted, called her hungriest lack—not much voice."[143] Much like the protagonists in "the mother" and "Ballad of Pearl May Lee," Maud Martha experiences a mix of vulnerability and rage in the face of racial, economic, and gendered obstacles that are beyond her control. And although she finds herself unable to express these feelings more outwardly to the world, Brooks's *narrative world* makes the creative space necessary to explore them. Prefiguring Toni Morrison's later exploration of the most terrible act of motherly love in *Beloved* (1987), Brooks's female characters explore what it means to speak, to choose, to feel, when those acts are always already circumscribed. As Joanne Gabbin argues, her work "represents both beauty and fury" and in this way "anticipates black writers like Sonia Sanchez, Alice Walker, and Audre Lorde who have also successfully explored the triple consciousness of women confronting race, gender, and caste."[144] She makes space for Black intimacy, creativity, and community not by denying Black women's vulnerability, but by creating the space to express it.

In the novel's final moments, Maud Martha also looks beyond American borders for new spaces and sources of community and creativity, as many of Brooks's male peers were doing in the postwar period. However, as a poor Black woman in Chicago, Maud Martha's access to this global terrain is far more limited. She cannot afford to travel, but she latches on to the idea of it through her brother's return home from the war: "The sun was shining, and some of the people in the world had been left alive, and it was doubtful whether the ridiculousness of man would ever completely succeed in destroying the world—or, in fact, the basic equanimity of the least and commonest flower."[145] In this glimpse of her life and the lives of her loved ones in relation to the greater world and the long stretch of history, Maud Martha feels hopeful that the "ridiculousness of man"—or "Man"—will never completely destroy

---

141. Brooks, *Maud Martha*, 230. See also Brooks, *Maud Martha*, 177, 197.
142. Brooks, *Maud Martha*, 230.
143. Brooks, *Maud Martha*, 318.
144. Gabbin, "Blooming in the Whirlwind," 252.
145. Brooks, *Maud Martha*, 321.

the dignity of the "least and commonest flower," another vulnerable image for herself. As with the "Gay Chaps at the Bar" sonnet series that concludes *A Street in Bronzeville,* poor Black women's access to this global space is limited; the sonnet series enters the larger collection via the epigraph of a soldier's letter home.[146] But Maud Martha finds in her brother's return from the global stage a small invitation into a world beyond the confines of segregation-era America. In the novel's final words, she thinks: "The weather was bidding her bon voyage."[147] Having refused to accommodate the ignorance of its white audience and instead centered a poor Black woman's most inward-looking feelings of intimacy, creativity, and community, *Maud Martha* concludes with its protagonist's blossoming interest in a worldview that both sees and sees beyond America's participation in the "ridiculousness of man."

Brooks continued to play around with ideas about Maud Martha's trajectory over the next several decades as she worked on a sequel for *Maud Martha* that never quite came to fruition. As it appears in her notes, interviews, and a chapter published in 1955, "The Rise of Maud Martha" would have focused on the growth of Maud Martha's sexual, economic, philosophical, and artistic independence. Summarizing her planned "theme" in a notebook, Brooks writes:

> Maud Martha's struggle to "stand herself up," to secure for herself height and fibre, and to discover what she is "meant for." Her husband—who has not really loved her, who has devoted his life to chasing surfaces, and who, via this indifference and neglect, has made her feel small and almost nonexistent—dies in the 1950 Chicago streetcar and oil-truck collision. It is up to her to sustain herself and three children. She has a love affair, bouts with the "social" world, with poverty, with loneliness and disillusion. She has problems with her children. However, it is in and through them that she finally (in this narrative) finds her height and her meaning in life.[148]

In keeping with this theme, Brooks's published chapter followed Maud Martha after the death of her husband and ended with her realization that his death does not bring unhappiness—he has made her feel like a "pumpkin" far too long for that—but rather brings a surprising sense of possibility and belonging in the world: "She could actually feel herself rising. She felt higher and more like a citizen of—what?"[149] Like her experience of suffering in "a birth,"

---

146. See Brooks, *Street in Bronzeville,* 64.
147. Brooks, *Maud Martha,* 322.
148. Brooks, "Clippings and Miscellaneous Notes," circa 1954, Gwendolyn Brooks Collection.
149. Brooks, "Rise of Maud Martha," 432.

the new burden of being a single mother only reminds her of her strength: "A road was again clean before her. She held the destinies of herself and of her children in her individual power—all was up to her."[150]

Likewise, a sketch from Brooks's papers dated 1985 describes Maud Martha's rejection of a second marriage proposal years after Paul's death as a kind of rejuvenation. Mirroring her courtship with Paul—during which she had thought, "He is thinking that . . . I will do"—the new suitor tells her that she is "old," "dark," and "not pretty," but that he has decided that he "would want [her] for [his] wife" nonetheless.[151] Instead of being pleased to have "hook[ed] him" as she was with Paul, this time she offers a righteous retort. "Of course you would," she tells him. "You are a broken-down old hulk. What you [need] is a nurse."[152] Making it clear that her willingness to be used by men is long in the past, she concludes, "This is no country for old men. . . . It is for me."[153] Brooks's discussions of her plans for the sequel in interviews also reveal that she saw her heroine claiming her rightful place not only in this country but also in the Pan-African community. "I want her to go to Africa," Brooks told Akasha Hull in 1977.[154] "I haven't figured out how she's going to get there. . . . Her resources are going to be slender," but "something will come along that will give her that opportunity."[155] "The Rise of Maud Martha" would have rejected the economic, racist, and sexist, silencing of poor Black women while also expanding on the global turn of the ending of *Maud Martha* to imagine how a poor Black woman—face-to-face with racial, sexual, and economic constraints on her "sovereignty"—might nonetheless make space for her vision and her vulnerability in the world.

In 1971 Harper published *The World of Gwendolyn Brooks*, a collection that—apart from Brooks's understudied children's book, *Bronzeville Boys and Girls* (1956)—brings together all of Brooks's work with Harper, including *A Street in Bronzeville* (1945), *Annie Allen* (1949), *Maud Martha* (1953), and two more volumes of poetry, *The Bean Eaters* (1960) and *In the Mecca* (1968). It would be her last collection with Harper. Many critics have identified Brooks's

---

150. Brooks, "Rise of Maud Martha," 432.
151. Brooks, *Maud Martha*, 194; and Brooks, "on amtrak," 18 February 1985, Gwendolyn Brooks Collection.
152. Brooks, *Maud Martha*, 197; and Brooks, "on amtrak," 18 February 1985, Gwendolyn Brooks Collection.
153. Brooks, "on amtrak," 18 February 1985, Gwendolyn Brooks Collection.
154. Brooks, "Update on Part One," 92.
155. Brooks, "Update on Part One," 92.

subsequent move to Black publishers as the result of her "radicalization" at the 1967 Fisk Conference, even though numerous factors complicate the idea of a single decisive shift in her work. For one, her move to Broadside Press occurred gradually, beginning before 1967 with the reprinting of "We Real Cool" (1960) as a broadside in 1966, continuing with Broadside's publication of her three-poem series *Riot* in 1969, and culminating in their publication of *Report from Part One* in 1972, after which she determined to "never, ever go back to those major publishing houses," despite "offers."[156] Depending on when she was asked, Brooks also pointed to different moments as "turning point[s]" in her career.[157] When Harper tried to exclude her latest book, *In the Mecca*, from *The World of Gwendolyn Brooks*, she angrily wrote to her agent: "My work is changing and is going to continue to change, and the first hints of the change are in the Mecca book. The 'Omnibus' as they [Harper] are planning it would NOT stamp me as part of this eruptive time, which I AM!"[158] Ten years later, however, she told Claudia Tate that if there was a "turning point, 'politically,'" in her career, it was *The Bean Eaters* (1960), so much so that it "had a hard time getting reviewed. . . . Frederick Bock, who was a reviewer for *Poetry Magazine*, gave us to understand that he was very upset by what he thought was a revolutionary tendency in my work. . . . He thought I was bitter."[159] And, although Harper insisted on marketing *Bronzeville Boys and Girls* (1956) by emphasizing its "universality," writing on the front flap that even though "the poems are set in Chicago . . . there are countless children like" these, the book serves as an important precursor to the numerous Black Arts–era books for young people written by such poets as Sonia Sanchez, Nikki Giovanni, and Lucille Clifton.[160] Finally, in her interview with Claudia Tate, Brooks would say that it only "takes a little patience to sit down and find out that in 1945 I was saying what many of the young folks said in the sixties."[161]

Although, for a time, Brooks did participate in the narrative that her work and her politics had been dramatically transformed by her experience at Fisk, that narrative has had the unfortunate effect of diminishing her place in Black literary history and its periodization, such that she is typically portrayed as a follower, rather than a leader; a student, rather than a teacher.[162] Less than a

---

156. Brooks, "Evening with Gwendolyn Brooks," 21. On the influence of Lawrence's 1964 retirement on Brooks's departure from Harper, see Goldsby, "'Something Is Said,'" 262–63.

157. Brooks, "Interview with Gwendolyn Brooks," 107.

158. Brooks, quoted in letter from agent Roslyn Targ to editor Ann Harris, 1 February 1971, quoted in Kent, *Life of Gwendolyn Brooks*, 233.

159. Brooks, "Interview with Gwendolyn Brooks," 107. See Bock, "Prize Winning Poet."

160. Dust jacket, *Bronzeville Boys and Girls*, 1956, Gwendolyn Brooks Papers.

161. Brooks, "Interview with Gwendolyn Brooks," 106.

162. See Brooks, *Report from Part One*, 84–85.

major change in her writing or her politics, Brooks's move to Black publishers indicated her rejection of the white literary establishment's misrepresentation and misuse of her earlier work. Zofia Burr writes, "What [Brooks] was seeking to repudiate in talking of a 'turn' in her career (away from the white elite audience and toward the black masses) was not so much her own earlier work but the critical tradition that had accumulated around it, which spoke of her as a 'true,' 'universal,' and 'genuine' poet in an effort to discipline other black poets who placed politics ahead of art."[163] By moving to Black presses, Brooks was able to offer tangible support to the work they were doing and thereby to younger Black artists. As Dudley Randall later explained: "She saw the need to help a Black publisher. I remonstrated with her, warned her that she'd lose money, told her that Broadside Press could give her neither the advances nor the promotion that Harper could, but she insisted."[164] She was also able to speak more directly to Black audiences without the white literary establishment serving as intermediary. "That's the glorious thing about today," she would say in 1971: "We aren't . . . concerned about what whites think of our work. . . . My people are black people; it is to them that I appeal for understanding."[165] Brooks's move to Black publishers showed that what she and other postwar Black artists needed was not to prove their own "maturity" to the white literary establishment, but to have access to audiences mature enough to value their work, in all its "beauty and fury," in all its vision and vulnerability.

Brooks is only one among several Black women writers of the mid-twentieth century whose work troubles dominant accounts of the period. The careers of Margaret Walker, Margaret Danner, and Margaret Burroughs also spanned the Black Chicago Renaissance, the Black Arts Movement, and the Black Women's Literary Renaissance, but their labor to build Black literary communities has been rendered all but invisible, and their art and intellectual work has been treated as hard to categorize, easy to marginalize, or simplest to forget. Other writers like Paule Marshall and Audre Lorde, whose careers also span these periods, are typically aligned with the 1970s and '80s. But as Lorde would explain in a letter to Akasha Hull, the poems in her first mainstream publication, *Coal* (1976), were really written in the "50s and early 60s." She wrote:

> It is not that the poems were not being written, but that they were not being printed nor read. . . . I was writing . . . black women's poems, long before the

---

163. Burr, *Of Women, Poetry, and Power*, 142.
164. Randall, "Black Publisher, Black Writer," 35.
165. Brooks, "My People Are Black People," 61–62.

feminist movement in this country—the second wave, that is[—]began to be aware of me.... It was for this reason I wanted the poems in *Coal* dated, and I am sorry I allowed Norton to talk me out of the idea. I think it's important for us to realize the distortions of perceptions that can be created by what the media chooses to print, and when.[166]

Dominant frameworks for understanding Black literary history, so often dictated by manifestos and debates by and between Black men, have made it difficult to understand both these women's careers and their contributions to the development of Black literature and Black intellectual thought. Too often, the manifestos that declare major breaks with the past have also depended on the misrepresentation of earlier writers, as when James Baldwin admitted that his attack on Richard Wright had "used his work as a kind of springboard into my own," or when Larry Neal admitted that his criticism of Ralph Ellison had been "one stage in a long series of attempts . . . to deal with the fantastic impression that Ellison's work has had on my life."[167] Instead of misrepresenting or breaking with prior writers to make space for themselves, Brooks, Walker, and the other Black women writers of their generation tried to "coax us into the habit of listening," offering their creativity, their thought, and their labor as a bridge to the next generation of Black women artists, activists, and intellectuals.[168]

---

166. Audre Lorde to Akasha Hull, 11 January 1978, Audre Lorde Collection, referring to Hull's characterization of Lorde as one of several "important new names" (Hull, "Black Women Poets from Wheatley to Walker," 96).
167. Baldwin, "Alas, Poor Richard," 197; and Neal, "Black Writer's Role, II," 36.
168. Bambara, foreword to *This Bridge Called My Back*, vii.

CODA

Bravery and the Backlash

Lorraine Hansberry at the Forum

In June of 1964, acclaimed Black playwright Lorraine Hansberry took part in a forum held in New York City that was sponsored by John Oliver Killens's Association of Artists for Freedom, an association of Black artists who began to organize together in the aftermath of the Birmingham church bombing that killed four young Black girls in 1963. Advertised as "The Black Revolution and the White Backlash," the forum promised to provide a space for Black and white artists, writers, and critics to "discuss where the Black Revolt is going and whether or not the white liberal has [a] place in it."[1] "Who speaks for the Negro," the forum's advertisements asked, "and who listens?"[2] Alongside Killens, the Black panelists included writers Paule Marshall, Amiri Baraka (LeRoi Jones), and Lorraine Hansberry, as well as actors Ruby Dee and Ossie Davis. Representing white liberals were *Fortune* magazine writer Charles E. Silberman, also the author of the recently published book *Crisis in Black and White* (1964); James Wechsler, editor of the *New York Post*; and the event's moderator, TV talk show host David Susskind. As the discussion unfolded, Silberman positioned himself as more or less in agreement with his Black co-panelists, but Wechsler and Susskind grew increasingly combative. Afterward, Wechsler would write a follow-up for the *New York Post* that blamed

---

1. "Black Revolution and the White Backlash" advertisement, 24.
2. "Black Revolution and the White Backlash" advertisement, 24. Robert Penn Warren's well-known collection, *Who Speaks for the Negro?* (1965), was published the following year.

the forum's atmosphere on the panel's Black participants, accusing them of a "feverish assault" on white liberals that represented a "repudiat[ion]" of "the spirit and strategy of the non-violence movement."[3] Three years later, Harold Cruse wrote in his polemical critique of pre-1960s Black intellectualism that the Black panelists' "ambush" of "captive white liberals" had been purely performative.[4] For Cruse, the forum represented the last stand of a group of "Left-tinged" Black intellectuals who "would have the public believe" that they were "prepared to play a unique role" in the new Black radicalism then emerging, but whose time had come and gone.[5]

In reality, many of the Black writers who appeared on the stage for this forum were figures whose work, politics, and influence would outlast both Wechsler's complaints and Cruse's predictions. Amiri Baraka, though active in the avant-garde Beat scene in the 1950s, is best known for his leadership of the Black Arts Movement, which he founded in 1965 and continued to advocate for and defend up until his death in 2014.[6] John Oliver Killens would go on to organize the first major Black writers conference that was held at Fisk University in 1966; the second, held in 1967, was the historic event that encouraged Gwendolyn Brooks to officially align herself with the Black Arts Movement.[7] And Paule Marshall, whose debut novel *Brown Girl, Brownstones* was published in 1959, went on to become a major figure in Caribbean American writing and the Black Women's Literary Renaissance, with her later novels often read and taught alongside the works of Toni Morrison, Alice Walker, Toni Cade Bambara, and Jamaica Kinkaid.[8] For Lorraine Hansberry, however, the 1964 forum ended up being her last public appearance. She died of cancer six months later, two months before Baraka purchased a space for the Black Arts Repertory Theatre/School that led to the Black Arts Movement, two years before Killens's historic Black writers' conference, and five years before the Black Women's Literary Renaissance got its start with Bambara's *The Black Woman: An Anthology* (1970).[9] As a result, unlike that of the other Black writers on the stage who would become central figures in the coming

---

3. Wechsler, "Sound Barrier," 26.
4. Cruse offers this rephrasing of Wechsler's argument in *Crisis of the Negro Intellectual*, 206.
5. Cruse, *Crisis of the Negro Intellectual*, 206–7. For Cruse, Baraka was "the only one in the . . . group who really deserved the title of Literary Radical" (Cruse, *Crisis of the Negro Intellectual*, 207).
6. See, for example, Baraka, "Post-Racial Anthology?," 173.
7. See Gilyard, *John Oliver Killens*, 212, 217, 227.
8. See Marshall, "Talk with Mary Helen Washington," 54; Marshall, "*PW* Interviews Paule Marshall," 75; Marshall, "Interview with Paule Marshall," 77; and Marshall, "Art and Politics of Paule Marshall," 171.
9. See Kotin, "Funding the Black Arts Repertory Theatre/School," 1358.

Black Arts and Black feminist literary and political movements, Hansberry's work and her legacy were seemingly frozen in time. Indeed, Cruse saw Hansberry as particularly emblematic of the Black literary past. "Far from being the *beginning* of anything," he wrote, Hansberry's work "was the end of a trend" in Black writing—the "culmination of the efforts of the Harlem leftwing literary and cultural in-group to achieve integration of the Negro in the arts."[10] Her work, he argued, represented the last gasp of the old idea that Black writers must conform to Western humanism and universalism to be received as artists, or the end of the idea that for Black art to be called "human and universal," it must be "universally white."[11] This was an idea, Cruse said, for which the next generation of Black artists would no longer stand.

Cruse's dismissal of Hansberry's work was based largely on the mainstream reception of her popular and prize-winning 1959 Broadway debut, *A Raisin in the Sun,* which had made Hansberry, at the age of twenty-nine, the youngest Black female playwright on Broadway and the first to win the New York Drama Critics' Circle Award, and a recognized spokesperson for civil rights. The play, the title of which is taken from a Langston Hughes poem, explores a poor Black family's struggle to agree on how to use their father's life insurance money after his death. Despite losing a significant amount of the money in the oldest son's investment scheme, the Younger family comes together in their refusal to accept a bribe from a white housing covenant that wants to stop them from moving into their neighborhood. With its Black author, Black director, and almost all-Black cast, the play broke ground in its insistence on Black artistic control over stage representations, and its refusal of the minstrel stereotypes that dominated prior white-authored and white-directed productions. White critics, however, latched on to the play's themes of domesticity, middle-class aspiration, and integration, and Hansberry quickly became the new darling of the white literary establishment. In this role, she was treated much as Gwendolyn Brooks had been the decade prior, as a Black writer who was worthy of her "exceptional" status because her characters only "happened" to be Black. Over and over, white reviewers praised Hansberry for her "treatment of her people as whole human beings in wholly human dilemmas," a demonstration of universality that they equated with the play's supposed "lack of racial emphasis."[12] As the *Saturday Review* put it, "the fact that they are colored people, with all the special problems of their race, seems less important than that they are people with exactly the same problems everyone else has.

---

10. Cruse, *Crisis of the Negro Intellectual,* 278–79, emphasis in original.
11. Cruse, *Crisis of the Negro Intellectual,* 282.
12. Mannes, "Sour Bird, Sweet Raisin," 34.

... Their interfamily joys and anxieties are universal ones."[13] Nan Robertson, writing for the *New York Times,* even falsely attributed this idea to Hansberry herself, incorrectly quoting her as saying that *Raisin* "wasn't a 'Negro' play" at all, but a play about "people who happen to be Negroes."[14] Blackness, for these reviewers, was antithetical to their white-centered conception of the universal and the human.

The white literary establishment's reception and framing of Hansberry's work no doubt helped shape the negative perception among the rising generation of Black radical critics and artists such as Cruse and also Baraka, who similarly dismissed *Raisin* as being out of step with the radical Black art of the younger generation because, he believed, it spoke "for the American middle-class [sic]."[15] In fact, Hansberry had a deep background working with leftwing organizations, including her time writing for Paul Robeson's radical *Freedom* newspaper, as well as her later writing for the Student Nonviolent Coordinating Committee and *Freedomways,* both of which would become important bridges to Baraka's Black Arts Movement.[16] Hansberry also had little patience for those who characterized her work as assimilationist, apolitical, or exceptional. When critics tried to describe *Raisin* as exceptional because it supposedly rose above the "protest" genre that they associated with Black artists, she replied that her "play is actively a protest play, actively so. There is no contradiction between protest and art and good art. You know, that's an artificial argument."[17] And when asked over and over how she felt when *Raisin* was described as "not a Negro play" at all, "but a play about people," she replied that this was a "misstatement" because "to create the universal you must pay very great attention to the specific."[18] Her ex-husband and literary executor Robert Nemiroff would later rephrase her reply in more biting terms: "Well,

---

13. Hewes, "Plant Grows in Chicago," 28.

14. Hansberry, "Dramatist Against Odds," X3.

15. Amiri Baraka to Lorraine Hansberry, 23 June 1961, Lorraine Hansberry Papers. Baraka elsewhere disparaged the "Negro middle class" as "a group that has always gone out of its way ... to prove to America ... that they were not really who they were, i.e., Negroes" (Baraka, "Myth of a 'Negro Literature,'" 294).

16. See Hansberry's "Women Voice Demands in Capital Sojourn" (1951) for *Freedom*; *The Movement* (1964) for SNCC; and "Legacy of W. E. B. Du Bois" (1965) for *Freedomways.* While at *Freedom,* Hansberry shared an office with leftwing playwright Alice Childress, wrote stories about the women-run protest group, Sojourners for Truth and Justice (STJ), and drew inspiration from other influential women on the left such as Shirley Graham Du Bois and Claudia Jones (see Higashida, *Black Internationalist Feminism,* 57–66; Leshinsky, "Power of Mentorship," 129–36; and Washington, "Alice Childress, Lorraine Hansberry, and Claudia Jones," 193–94).

17. Hansberry, "Unaired Interview," 66.

18. See Hansberry, "Protest, Part I," 60; and Hansberry, "Interview with Lorraine Hansberry," 74.

I hadn't noticed the contradiction because I'd always been under the impression that Negroes are people."[19] All human experience, Hansberry argued, was historically constructed: "Virtually all of us are what our circumstances allow us to be."[20] Hansberry saw her play as actively insisting on the complexity of Black perspectives and experiences, which included radical, anticolonial, atheist, Marxist, and feminist positions, and which refuted the one-dimensional stereotypes that had dominated the stage up until that moment. Her characters, she argued, were "ordinary" but also "complicated and large."[21] Even Baraka eventually came to agree, writing in 1986 that "we missed the essence of the work—that Hansberry had created a family on the cutting edge of the same class and ideological struggles as existed in the movement itself and among the people."[22]

Such misconceptions of Hansberry's work may have been in part because her many efforts to refute the exclusionary humanism through which her work was read were still unpublished or unfinished at the time of her death. Hansberry's personal scrapbook, for example, contains a copy of Nan Robertson's *New York Times* review of *Raisin* with the words "never said *no* such thing" scrawled in the margins, and her papers contain a series of letters back and forth with the *New York Times* editor demanding a retraction that she would never receive; the editor only expressed "regret" at Hansberry's "bitterness."[23] In several interviews, Hansberry's discussions of her Nigerian character, whom both she and the FBI considered *Raisin*'s most radical figure, were cut before the interviews aired.[24] Her interview with Mike Wallace, in which she refused to cooperate with his caricatures of Black nationalism, never aired at all.[25] Her commissioned screenplay about slavery for NBC, *The Drinking Gourd* (1972), was deemed too controversial by the network and went unproduced.[26] And it wasn't until 1970, fifteen years after her death, that Hansberry was revealed to have been the author of two anonymous letters to the lesbian

---

19. Hansberry, *To Be Young Gifted and Black*, 113. See Hansberry, "Interview with Lorraine Hansberry," 73–74, 91n2. Killens echoes this response in his later contribution to *The Black Aesthetic*, saying that such questions "never fail . . . to jar me, laboring, as I always have, under the illusion that Negroes *are* people (Killens, "Black Writer," 381, emphasis in original).

20. Hansberry and Richards, "Interview," 159.

21. Hansberry and Richards, "Interview," 156.

22. Baraka, "Critical Reevaluation," 19.

23. L.H. Scrapbook, Lorraine Hansberry Papers, emphasis in original; and Lewis Funke, *New York Times* Drama Editor, to Lorraine Hansberry, 6 April 1959, Lorraine Hansberry Papers.

24. See Hansberry, "Interview with Lorraine Hansberry," 83–85; and Federal Bureau of Investigations, "Memorandum," 3.

25. See Hansberry, "Unaired Interview," 71–72.

26. See Colbert, *Radical Vision*, 107.

journal *The Ladder* published in 1957.[27] As Lisbeth Lipari argues, "considering her peers—she was one year older than Toni Morrison, four years older than Audre Lorde, two years younger than Maya Angelou, and one year younger than Adrienne Rich—one can only imagine the contribution Hansberry might have made had she lived longer."[28]

Based on the full spectrum of Hansberry's published and unpublished work, scholars are increasingly arguing that Hansberry was, in many ways, ahead of her time.[29] Soyica Diggs Colbert argues not only that Hansberry understood the struggle for Black freedom to be both global and intersectional, but that she insisted that "women's desires and roles" were "central to Black freedom movements."[30] In interviews, for example, she quickly moved questions about the stereotypical "strength" of Black women away from essentialist stereotypes and toward sociohistorical constructions—drawing together her reading of Simone de Beauvoir and Frantz Fanon to argue that Black women were "twice militant" because they were "twice oppressed."[31] Moreover, she claimed that it was this experience that led to their "assumption of leadership" in the fight for Black liberation, and for their own.[32] Hansberry also anticipated later Black feminist calls for the need for solidarity across these differentiated positionalities, as well as later Black feminist interest in the political power of Black women's imaginative work. It was for this reason that Hansberry loved the dramatic form: "I am particularly attracted to a medium where . . . [you can] treat character in the most absolute relief—one against the other—so that everything, sympathy and conflict, is played so sharply, you know—even a little more than a novel."[33] For Hansberry, narrative genres such as novels and drama allowed artists to expose the sociohistorical construction of power and identity, to explore intersectional positionalities and modes of resistance, and to imagine moments of solidarity across difference.

In these ways, Hansberry's work looks forward to the Black feminist theorists who would insist on Black women's right to articulate their existence and imagine worlds in which they would be free. But Hansberry's work not only foreshadowed the theoretical interventions that would follow her; it was also grounded in the Black female writing that came before her. Like Pauline

---

27. See Grier, "Lesbiana," 33.
28. Lipari, "Rhetoric of Intersectionality," 221–22.
29. See, for example, Strain's *Sighted Eyes / Feeling Heart*; Perry's *Looking for Lorraine*; and Colbert's *Radical Vision*.
30. Colbert, *Radical Vision*, 71.
31. Hansberry, "Interview with Lorraine Hansberry," 77–78.
32. Hansberry, "Interview with Lorraine Hansberry," 78.
33. Hansberry and Richards, "Interview," 155.

Hopkins, she understood African American political struggles to be part of a global, anticolonial struggle for Pan-African liberation. Like Nella Larsen, she was interested in adapting white literary templates to explore the intersection of class with race and gender—adapting, in the case of *Raisin,* from Arthur Miller's *Death of a Salesman* (1949).[34] Like Hurston, she worked within a genre previously associated with the primitivist stereotypes of blackface minstrelsy, reclaiming the genre for Black female authors and insisting on her characters' right to embody their emotional complexity—their pains and their pleasures—on that stage. Like Petry, she was drawn to narrative forms that made it possible to imagine the possibility of solidarity and care across racialized, gendered, and economic differences. And, like Brooks, she fought the white, male-dominated literary establishment to insist on Black artists' right to tell Black people's and Black women's stories without catering to white desires, stereotypes, or misconceptions. In these ways, and more, Hansberry's radical consciousness was grounded in the work of the Black women writers who came before her—women who never consented to be represented by narrative structures that would erase their humanity, and who devoted their imaginative and intellectual lives to their own brave rearticulations of human experience, solidarity, and possibility.

The 1964 forum became Hansberry's final opportunity to voice her critique of white efforts to equate "humanism" with whiteness while diminishing or dismissing Black articulations of humanity, human community, and the world. The forum's promised topic—to "discuss where the Black Revolt is going and whether or not the white liberal has [a] place in it"—aimed to address two issues: first, the urgent need for systemic change to address racism and violence against Black people; and second, the degree to which white liberals would commit to a reconfigured model of interracial solidarity to achieve that goal.[35] As Hansberry put it in a follow-up piece on the forum published in the *Village Voice*: "For generations it has been assumed that what Negroes wanted more desperately than anything else was simply to be absorbed into 'this house'; perhaps it seems an affront to some that the most thoughtful elements of the Negro people would like to see this house rebuilt."[36] Paule Marshall expressed the same sentiment at the forum, arguing that "in order for the Negro to participate fully in the American life . . . the system which has permitted [the white man] a privileged place at the expense of the Negro will have to undergo fundamental changes."[37] Both writers also understood their work to be part of a larger movement for human freedom. In Marshall's

---

34. See Hansberry, "Willie Loman, Walter Younger," 7.
35. "Black Revolution and the White Backlash" advertisement, 24.
36. Hansberry, "Miss Hansberry on 'Backlash,'" 16.
37. Association of Artists for Freedom, "Black Revolution and the White Backlash," 180.

words, Black people's "demand for complete equality is part of the larger demand for human dignity and fundamental freedom being sounded all over the world.... We are part of a huge world community and our struggle here part of the world-wide struggle for human rights."[38] Much like the later writers of the Combahee River Collective Statement (1977), the editors of the women of color feminist anthology, *This Bridge Called My Back* (1981), and the editors of *But Some of Us Are Brave* (1982), they understood their goal not to be mere inclusion within existing systems, but a reorganization of those systems around oppressed people's definitions of humanity.

The forum was organized around asking white liberals if they would join Black activists in calling for systemic changes, even when those changes would necessarily and inevitably decenter white liberal perspectives and diminish white power and privilege. Although Baraka's more cynical position that this question was not worth asking would come to be seen as more representative of 1960s "literary radicalism," Hansberry's desire for a dialogue in which Black women have a powerful voice would resonate with later Black and Third World feminist calls for coalition-building.[39] She also demonstrated a deep awareness that white liberal calls for patience and moderation act to silence nonwhite perspectives on the goal of human freedom. Echoing Martin Luther King's "A Letter from Birmingham Jail" (1963), which critiqued the white moderate for "paternalistically" believing "he can set the time-table for another man's freedom," Hansberry argued: "The charge of impatience is simply unbearable.... We have to find some way with these dialogues to show and to encourage the white liberal to stop being a liberal and become an American radical."[40] To James Wechsler's defensive argument "that separatism was disastrous to any human cause" and his refusal to be reduced to "role of waterboy in the freedom movement," Hansberry reminded him that he was failing to see things from their perspective. She said: "The point is that we have a different viewpoint because... we have been kicked in the face so often.... The vantage point of Negroes is entirely different" from that of the white liberal, she argued, and white liberals needed to listen to "the things we are trying to say."[41] If there was going to be a true "merger," she continued, "it

---

38. Association of Artists for Freedom, "Black Revolution and the White Backlash," 180.

39. Cruse, *Crisis of the Negro Intellectual*, 207. On later calls for coalition-building, see Reagon, "Coalition Politics," 346; Bambara, foreword to *This Bridge Called My Back*, vii; and Anzaldúa, "La Prieta," 209.

40. King, "Letter from Birmingham Jail," 26; and Association of Artists for Freedom, "Black Revolution and the White Backlash," 184.

41. Association of Artists for Freedom, "Black Revolution and the White Backlash," 182. Hansberry's comments were edited out of the printed transcript of the forum that appeared in the *National Guardian* but are preserved in the Lorraine Hansberry Audio and Moving Image Collection and on Ellis and Smith's *Say It Plain, Say It Loud* website.

has to be a merger on the basis of true and genuine equality and if we think that it isn't going to be painful, we're mistaken."[42] As Black feminist theorists would later argue, solidarity and coalitions are not about "comfort"; they require hard work and are only possible if peoples' differences are expressed and acknowledged, not silenced and denied.[43]

Unfortunately, with the exception of Silberman, the white liberals at the forum were not able to hear that they were not the final authority on the "human cause."[44] As white jazz critic Nat Hentoff wrote in a follow-up piece in the *Village Voice*, the white liberals onstage lacked "the capacity to really listen to what was being said."[45] Instead, they insisted on centering themselves as authorities on civil rights, accusing their Black co-panelists of betraying white-liberal-approved civil rights leaders, and trying to delegitimate their call for systemic change by describing their words as "criminally irresponsible," "carefully couched calls for violence and bloodshed," and "dangerous, irresponsible, and ineffective talk."[46] After the forum, *Village Voice* writer Jack Newfield continued in this vein by describing the forum as a "mugging": "Imagine three goldfish dropped into a fish tank filled with sharks. Or imagine Billy Budd mugged by the Emperor Jones," he argued, deploying—just as Wechsler and Susskind had—the segregation era's worst stereotypes about Black criminality and savagery to silence the panelists' critiques of white liberal complacency toward racism in the US and colonialism around the world.[47] By using sub-human stereotypes to denigrate Black perspectives on "the world-wide struggle for human rights," "human dignity," and "freedom for . . . humankind," these white voices demonstrated their deep desire to paint Black articulations of the human as insular, divisive, and dangerous, while retaining authority over the discourse of the human for themselves.[48]

If the Association of Artists for Freedom's 1964 forum was something of a failed attempt to get white Americans to listen, it was nevertheless an important declaration of Black artists' bravery to speak from a position and point of view that they knew many white Americans did not want to see or hear—to

---

42. Association of Artists for Freedom, "Black Revolution and the White Backlash," 192.
43. Reagon, "Coalition Politics," 346.
44. Association of Artists for Freedom, "Black Revolution and the White Backlash," 178.
45. Hentoff, "Town Hall Mugging," 4.
46. Association of Artists for Freedom, "Black Revolution and the White Backlash," 188–89.
47. Newfield, "Mugging the White Liberal," 5.
48. Association of Artists for Freedom, "Black Revolution and the White Backlash," 180. Ruby Dee's comment about "freedom for . . . humankind" was edited out of the *National Guardian* transcript but appears in the original audio preserved in the Lorraine Hansberry Audio and Moving Image Collection.

assert their right and power to speak for the human community. With the publication of *But Some of Us Are Brave* two decades later, Black feminist theorists would give bravery a defining place in their work, demonstrating what Brittney Cooper calls the "intellectual courage" to redefine liberation, solidarity, and the human not by subsuming Black women's experience within Western definitions of "the universal," but by insisting on "naming the distinct oppressive conditions under which many Black women lived their lives."[49] As bell hooks argues, solidarity should not be based on the violent and exclusionary "notion of unity" or sameness but on the "notion of communion" or being "willing and able to communicate with one another."[50] Near the end of the forum, when Susskind asked with performative exasperation what it is a "decent human being" is supposed to do, John Oliver Killens response was "listen": "I want to say, as a decent human being, that I think the white liberal should be more ready to listen."[51] Susskind refused the kind of bravery that this listening would demand of him, insisting instead that Black Americans needed to decide whether they are with white Americans or against them, and on white Americans' terms. Do they "really want the merger which . . . Miss Hansberry spoke about," Susskind asked, or do they "want to bring down the whole structure."[52] It was Hansberry who once again refused that false opposition, responding: "The latter may be necessary to make the first possible."[53]

The backlash that Black writers faced at this forum was not unlike the later conservative backlash against Black feminist critiques of the white- and male-dominated academic canon, or the still later backlashes against Black-female-led movements and critical frameworks such as Black Lives Matter and critical race theory. At each moment, Black women's insistence that their lives, their needs, and their narratives matter have been characterized as "divisive" by a public discourse that continues to invest in the exclusionary assumptions of Western humanism. Hansberry's refusal of homogeneity, her insistence on listening, and her bravery to speak demonstrated her commitment to a long counter-discourse of brave humanism. Like many Black women writers before her, she was invested in a more capacious understanding of the human than Western humanism could offer—one capable of acknowledging human diversity and vulnerability, and of appreciating the liberatory potential of human creativity and care. Indeed, in Akasha Hull and Barbara Smith's introduction to *But Some of Us Are Brave,* they looked to Hansberry and one of her 1957

---

49. Cooper, afterword to *But Some of Us Are Brave,* 381–82.
50. hooks, interview in *Black Is . . . Black Ain't.*
51. Association of Artists for Freedom, "Black Revolution and the White Backlash," 194.
52. Association of Artists for Freedom, "Black Revolution and the White Backlash," 199.
53. Association of Artists for Freedom, "Black Revolution and the White Backlash," 199.

letters to *The Ladder* as a key source of inspiration. Quoting at length both Hansberry's argument and her call for "equipped women . . . to take some of the ethical questions which a male-dominated culture has produced" and "dissect and analyze them to pieces," Hull and Smith described Hansberry's letter as "an amazingly prescient anticipation of current accomplishments of lesbian-feminist political analysis."[54] More than this, they also recognized her letter as a sign of their place in a much longer lineage of Black women's intellectual work of critique, creation, and communion. As they put it, "most amazing of all is that Hansberry was speaking, without knowing it, directly to us."[55] Taken together, this long lineage of Black women's intellectual thought invites us to imagine what it would take to create a world—a liberatory politics, a literary history, a genealogy of critical thought—built around Black women writers' brave humanism.

54. Hansberry, "Letter to Editor," 30, quoted in Hull and Smith, "Politics of Black Women's Studies," xxiii; and Hull and Smith, "Politics of Black Women's Studies," xxiii.
55. Hull and Smith, "Politics of Black Women's Studies," xxiii.

BIBLIOGRAPHY

Archival Sources

Am I Not a Woman and a Sister? Manuscripts, Archives and Rare Books Division, Schomburg Center for Research in Black Culture, New York Public Library Digital Collections. https://digitalcollections.nypl.org/items/510d47da-75bb-a3d9-e040-e00a18064a99.

Ann Petry Collection, 1908–1997, #1391. Howard Gotlieb Archival Research Center, Boston University.

Ann Petry Papers, Sc MG 954, Manuscripts, Archives and Rare Books Division, Schomburg Center for Research in Black Culture, New York Public Library.

Audre Lorde Collection, 1950–2002. Spelman College Archives.

Federal Bureau of Investigation, "Memorandum: Lorraine Vivian Hansberry Nemiroff," document no. 100-44090, February 5, 1959. FBI Files on Lorraine Hansberry, F. B. Eyes Digital Archive. https://fbeyes.wustl.edu/items/fbeyes_050.html.

Flag, Announcing Lynching, Flown from the Window of the NAACP Headquarters on 69 Fifth Ave., New York City, 1936. Visual Materials from the National Association for the Advancement of Colored People Records, Library of Congress. https://www.loc.gov/item/95517117/.

Gwendolyn Brooks Collection, 1909–2003, 01/01/MSS00086. Rare Book and Manuscript Library, University of Illinois at Urbana-Champaign.

Gwendolyn Brooks Papers, BANC MSS 2001/83 z. Bancroft Library, University of California, Berkeley.

James Weldon Johnson Memorial Collection (JWJ). Beinecke Rare Book and Manuscript Library, Yale University.

Levy, Builder. *I AM A (WO)MAN*, 1968. Collection of the Smithsonian National Museum of African American History and Culture, Gift of Arnika Dawkins and the Arnika Dawkins Gallery.

Ligon, Glenn. *Condition Report*, 2000. Tate Gallery. https://www.tate.org.uk/art/artworks/ligon-condition-report-l02822.

Lorraine Hansberry Audio and Moving Image Collection. Moving Image and Recorded Sound Division, Schomburg Center for Research in Black Culture, New York Public Library.

Lorraine Hansberry Papers, Sc MG 680. Manuscripts, Archives and Rare Books Division, Schomburg Center for Research in Black Culture, New York Public Library.

National Association of Colored Women. Minutes of the Second Convention of the National Association of Colored Women: Held at Quinn Chapel, 24th Street and Wabash Avenue, Chicago, Ill., August 14th, 15th, and 16th, 1899. Daniel Murray Pamphlet Collection, Library of Congress. https://www.loc.gov/item/91898212/.

Selected Records of Harper & Brothers, 1909–1960 (bulk 1939–1955), C0103. Manuscripts Division, Department of Special Collections, Princeton University Library.

Terry, Roderick, *I Am a Man,* 1995. Collection of the Smithsonian National Museum of African American History and Culture, Gift of Roderick Terry. https://nmaahc.si.edu/object/nmaahc_2013.99.44.

Whittier, John Greenleaf. "Our Countrymen in Chains," 1837. Printed Ephemera: Three Centuries of Broadsides and Other Printed Ephemera, Digital Collections, Library of Congress. https://www.loc.gov/item/2021767295/.

Withers, Ernest C. *"I Am a Man": Sanitation Workers' Strike, Memphis, Tennessee,* 1968. Photographs and Prints Division, Schomburg Center for Research in Black Culture, New York Public Library.

Published Sources

A.P.W. "Story Unrealistic in *The Narrows.*" Review of *The Narrows,* by Ann Petry. *Rocky Mountain News* (Denver, CO), December 13, 1953, 54.

Addington, Thom C. "Toward Crossroads Confluence: *Annie Allen* and African American Literary Periodization." *Journal of Ethnic American Literature* 7 (2017): 107–55.

Ahad-Legardy, Badia. *Afro-Nostalgia: Feeling Good in Contemporary Black Culture.* University of Illinois Press, 2021.

Ahern, Megan K. "Creative Multivalence: Social Engagement beyond Naturalism in Gwendolyn Brooks's *Maud Martha.*" *African American Review* 47, no. 2/3 (2014): 313–26.

Alkalimat, Abdul. *The History of Black Studies.* Pluto Press, 2021.

Allen, Amy. "Rethinking Power." *Hypatia* 13, no. 1 (1998): 21–40.

Allen, Norm R. *African-American Humanism: An Anthology.* Prometheus, 1991.

Ammons, Elizabeth. Introduction to *Short Fiction by Black Women, 1900–1920,* edited by Elizabeth Ammons, 3–20. Oxford University Press, 1991.

Anderson, Carol Elaine. *White Rage: The Unspoken Truth of Our Racial Divide.* Bloomsbury, 2016.

Antieau, Chester James. "Natural Rights and the Founding Fathers—The Virginians." *Washington and Lee Law Review* 17 (1960): 43–79.

Anzaldúa, Gloria. "La Prieta." 1981. In *This Bridge Called My Back: Writings by Radical Women of Color,* edited by Cherríe Moraga and Gloria Anzaldúa, 198–209. Kitchen Table: Women of Color Press, 1983.

Armstrong, Nancy. *How Novels Think: The Limits of Individualism from 1719-1900.* Columbia University Press, 2005.

Association of Artists for Freedom. "The Black Revolution and the White Backlash." 1964. In *Conversations with Lorraine Hansberry,* edited by Mollie Godfrey, 176–99. University Press of Mississippi, 2021. Reprinted from "Black Revolution and White Backlash," *National Guardian,* July 6, 1964, 5–9.

Bacon, Mary Hope. "'One Great Bundle of Humanity': Frances Ellen Watkins Harper (1825–1911)." *The Pennsylvania Magazine of History and Biography* 113, no. 1 (January 1989): 21–43.

Badmington, Neil. *Posthumanism.* Bloomsbury Publishing, 2000.

Baker, Houston A., Jr. *Blues, Ideology, and Afro-American Literature: A Vernacular Theory.* University of Chicago Press, 1984.

———. *Workings of the Spirit: The Poetics of Afro-American Women's Writing.* University of Chicago Press, 1991.

Baker, Lee D. *From Savage to Negro: Anthropology and the Construction of Race, 1896–1954.* University of California Press, 1998.

Baldwin, James. "Alas, Poor Richard." 1961. In *Nobody Knows My Name: More Notes of a Native Son,* 181–215. Delta, 1962.

———. "Everybody's Protest Novel." 1949. In *Notes of a Native Son,* 13–23. Beacon, 1984.

———. "Many Thousands Gone." 1951. In *Notes of a Native Son,* 24–45. Beacon, 1984.

Balshaw, Maria. "Harlem—From Lenox to Seventh Avenue: Mapping the Negro Capital of the World." In *City Sites: Multimedia Essays on New York and Chicago, 1870s–1930s,* edited by Maria Balshaw, Anna Notaro, Liam Kennedy, and Douglas Tallack. University of Birmingham Press, 2000. https://artsweb.cal.bham.ac.uk/citysites/harlem/section03.htm.

Bambara, Toni Cade. Foreword to *This Bridge Called My Back: Writings by Radical Women of Color,* edited by Cherríe Moraga and Gloria Anzaldúa, vi–viii. 1981. Kitchen Table: Women of Color Press, 1983.

———. Preface to *The Black Woman: An Anthology,* edited by Toni Cade Bambara, 1–7. 1970. Washington Square Press, 2005.

Banks, Kimberly J. "Jessie Redmon Fauset (1882–1961)." In *Kindred Hands: Letters on Writing by British and American Women Authors, 1865–1935,* edited by Jennifer Cognard-Black and Elizabeth MacLeod Walls, 217–34. University of Iowa Press, 2006.

Baraka, Amiri (LeRoi Jones). "A Critical Reevaluation: *A Raisin in the Sun*'s Enduring Passion." 1986. In *"A Raisin in the Sun" and "The Sign in Sidney Brustein's Window,"* edited by Robert Nemiroff, 9–20. Vintage Books, 1995.

———. "The Myth of a 'Negro Literature.'" 1966. In *On Being Black: Writings by Afro-Americans from Frederick Douglass to the Present,* edited by Charles T. Davis and Daniel Walden, 293–301. Fawcett Publications, 1970.

———. "A Post-Racial Anthology?" Review of *Angles of Ascent: A Norton Anthology of Contemporary African American Poetry,* edited by Charles Henry Rowell. *Poetry Magazine* (May 2013): 166–73.

Barkham, John. "Brief Review of Books." Review of *The Narrows,* by Ann Petry. *Toledo Blade,* August 16, 1953, sec. 3, p. 2.

Barnes, Albert C. "Negro Art and America." 1925. In *The New Negro,* edited by Alain Locke, 19–25. Macmillan, 1992.

Barrett, Lindon. "(Further) Figures of Violence: *The Street* in the American Landscape." *Cultural Critique* 25 (Fall 1993): 205–37.

———. "Signs of the Visible: (Re)Moving Pictures in the Narrows." In *Blackness and Value: Seeing Double*, by Lindon Barrett, 214–42. Cambridge University Press, 1999.

Barry, Michael. "'Same Train Be Back Tomorrer': Ann Petry's *The Narrows* and the Repetition of History." *MELUS: Multi-Ethnic Literature of the United States* 24, no. 1 (1999): 141–59.

Bell, Bernard. "Ann Petry's Demythologizing of American Culture and Afro-American Character." In *Conjuring: Black Women, Fiction, and Literary Tradition*, edited by Marjorie Pryse and Hortense J. Spillers, 105–15. Indiana University Press, 1985.

Biondi, Martha. *The Black Revolution on Campus*. University of California Press, 2012.

"The Black Revolution and the White Backlash," advertisement. *New York Amsterdam News*, June 6, 1964, 24.

Blackmon, Douglas A. *Slavery by Another Name: The Re-Enslavement of Black Americans from the Civil War to World War II*. Anchor Books, 2009.

Bloch, Julia. "'Shut Your Rhetorics in a Box': Gwendolyn Brooks and Lyric Dilemma." *Tulsa Studies in Women's Literature* 35, no. 2 (Fall 2016): 439–62.

Boas, Franz. *Anthropology and Modern Life*. 1928. Routledge, 2021.

———. *The Mind of Primitive Man: A Course of Lectures Delivered Before the Lowell Institute, Boston, Mass., and the National University of Mexico, 1910–1911*. Macmillan, 1911.

Bock, Frederick. "A Prize Winning Poet Fails to Measure Up." Review of *The Bean Eaters*, by Gwendolyn Brooks. *Chicago Daily Tribune*, June 5, 1960, C12.

Bone, Robert. *The Negro Novel in America*. 1958. Yale University Press, 1965.

———. "Richard Wright and the Chicago Renaissance." *Callaloo* 9, no. 3 (Summer 1986): 446–68.

Bone, Robert, and Richard A. Courage. *The Muse in Bronzeville: African American Creative Expression in Chicago, 1932–1950*. Rutgers University Press, 2011.

Bonner, Marita. "On Being Young—a Woman—and Colored." 1925. In *The Crisis Reader: Stories, Poetry, and Essays from the NAACP's Crisis Magazine*, edited by Sondra Kathryn Wilson, 227–31. Random House, 1999.

"Books: Briefly Noted." Review of *The Narrows*, by Ann Petry. *New Yorker*, August 29, 1953, 78–80.

Borges de Campos, Bárbara. "Marks in the Margins: How Glenn Ligon's Paintings Describe the Historic Erasure of Black Americans." *Sleek Magazine*, June 5, 2020. https://www.sleek-mag.com/article/how-glenn-ligons-paintings-describe-the-historic-erasure-of-black-americans/.

Botes, Annatjie. "A Comparison Between the Ethics of Justice and the Ethics of Care." *Journal of Advanced Nursing* 32, no. 5 (December 2000): 1071–75.

Bourne, George. *Slavery Illustrated in Its Effects upon Woman and Domestic Society*. Isaac Knapp, 1837.

Boyd, Marion. "Nella Larsen's Story." *Forum* 83, no. 4 (April 1930): 41.

Boyd, Melba Joyce. "'Prophets for a New Day': The Cultural Activism of Margaret Danner, Margaret Burroughs, Gwendolyn Brooks and Margaret Walker During the Black Arts Movement." *Revista Canaria de Estudios Ingleses* 37 (November 1998): 55–67.

———. *Wrestling with the Muse: Dudley Randall and the Broadside Press*. Columbia University Press, 2004.

Braithwaite, William Stanley. "The Negro in American Literature." 1925. In *The New Negro: Voices of the Harlem Renaissance*, edited by Alain Locke, 29–44. Atheneum, 1992.

Breman, Paul, "Poetry into the Sixties." In *The Black American Writer,* vol. 2, edited by C. W. E. Bigsby, 99–109. Everett/Edwards, 1969.

"Briefly Noted: Fiction." Review of *Maud Martha,* by Gwendolyn Brooks. *New Yorker,* October 10, 1953, 153–60.

Britannica, The Editors of Encyclopaedia. "Renaissance Man." *Encyclopedia Britannica,* September 13, 2020. https://www.britannica.com/topic/Renaissance-man.

Brooks, David. "From Western Lit to Westerns as Lit." *Wall Street Journal,* February 2, 1988, 36.

Brooks, Gwendolyn. *Annie Allen.* 1949. In *Blacks,* by Gwendolyn Brooks, 77–140. Third World Press, 1987.

———. "*Black Books Bulletin* Interviews Gwen Brooks." Interview by Haki Madhubuti. 1974. In *Conversations with Gwendolyn Brooks,* edited by Gloria Wade Gayles, 74–84. University Press of Mississippi, 2003.

———. "A Conversation with Gwendolyn Brooks." Interview by Studs Terkel. 1961. In *Conversations with Gwendolyn Brooks,* edited by Gloria Wade Gayles, 3–12. University Press of Mississippi, 2003.

———. "An Evening with Gwendolyn Brooks: The Pulitzer Prize-Winner and Poet Laureate Shuns Pretense, Invites Challenges." Interview by B. Denise Hawkins. *Black Issues in Higher Education* 11, no. 18 (1994): 16–17, 20–21.

———. Foreword to *New Negro Poets: USA,* edited by Langston Hughes, 13–14. Indiana University Press, 1966.

———. "Gwendolyn Brooks." Interview by Roy Newquist. 1967. In *Conversations with Gwendolyn Brooks,* edited by Gloria Wade Gayles, 26–36. University Press of Mississippi, 2003.

———. "Interview." Interview by Gwendolyn Brooks. 1984. In *Conversations with Gwendolyn Brooks,* edited by Gloria Wade Gayles, 111–16. University Press of Mississippi, 2003.

———. "Interview with Gwendolyn Brooks." Interview by Claudia Tate. 1983. In *Conversations with Gwendolyn Brooks,* edited by Gloria Wade Gayles, 104–10. University Press of Mississippi, 2003.

———. "A Life Distilled: An Interview with Gwendolyn Brooks." Interview by Kevin Bezner. 1986. In *Conversations with Gwendolyn Brooks,* edited by Gloria Wade Gayles, 117–24. University Press of Mississippi, 2003.

———. *Maud Martha.* 1953. In *Blacks,* by Gwendolyn Brooks, 141–322. Third World Press, 1987.

———. "My People Are Black People: Interview with Gwendolyn Brooks." Interview by Ida Lewis. 1971. In *Conversations with Gwendolyn Brooks,* edited by Gloria Wade Gayles, 54–66. University Press of Mississippi, 2003.

———. "Poets Who Are Negroes." *Phylon* 11, no. 4 (4th Quarter, 1950): 312.

———. *Report from Part One.* 1972. Broadside Press, 1991.

———. "The Rise of Maud Martha." 1955. In *Invented Lives: Narratives of Black Women, 1860–1960,* edited by Mary Helen Washington, 429–32. Anchor Books, 1987.

———. *A Street in Bronzeville.* 1945. In *Blacks,* by Gwendolyn Brooks, 17–75. Third World Press, 1987.

———. "Update on Part One: An Interview with Gwendolyn Brooks." 1977. Interview by Akasha (Gloria T.) Hull and Posey Gallagher. In *Conversations with Gwendolyn Brooks,* edited by Gloria Wade Gayles, 85–103. University Press of Mississippi, 2003.

———. "Why Negro Women Leave Home." *Negro Digest* 9, no. 3 (March 1951): 26–28.

Brown, Carolyn J. *Song of My Life: A Biography of Margaret Walker.* University Press of Mississippi, 2014.

Browne, Simone. *Dark Matters: On the Surveillance of Blackness.* Duke University Press, 2015.

Bryant, Jerry H. "Wright, Ellison, Baldwin—Exorcising the Demon." *Phylon* 37, no. 2 (1976): 174–88.

Burgess, Ernest W. Preface to *The Negro Family in Chicago,* by E. Franklin Frazier, ix–xii. University of Chicago Press, 1932.

Burr, Zofia. *Of Women, Poetry, and Power: Strategies of Address in Dickenson, Miles, Brooks, Lorde, and Angelou.* University of Illinois Press, 2002.

Bush, Warren V., ed. *The Dialogues of Archibald MacLeish and Mark Van Doren.* E. P. Dutton, 1964.

Callahan, Cynthia. "Adopted or Married: Families of Choice in Ann Petry's *The Narrows.*" *MELUS: Multi-Ethnic Literature of the United States* 43, no. 3 (2018): 103–23.

Camus, Jean Pierre. "Upon Forgiving Our Enemies." 1639. In *The Spirit of St. Francis de Sales,* translated by J.S., 101–3. Burns Oates & Washbourne, 1925.

Carby, Hazel V. Introduction to *The Magazine Novels of Pauline Hopkins,* edited by Henry Louis Gates Jr., xxix–l. Oxford University Press, 1988.

———. "The Politics of Fiction, Anthropology and the Folk: Zora Neale Hurston." In *New Essays on "Their Eyes Were Watching God,"* edited by Michael Awkward, 71–93. Cambridge University Press, 1990.

———. *Race Men.* Harvard University Press, 1998.

———. *Reconstructing Womanhood: The Emergence of the Afro-American Woman Novelist.* Oxford University Press, 1987.

Carroll, Rebecca. "Meaning, Without the White Gaze." *Atlantic,* August 7, 2019. https://www.theatlantic.com/ideas/archive/2019/08/toni-morrison-free-white-gaze/595675/.

Cassidy, Thomas. "Contending Contexts: Pauline Hopkins's *Contending Forces.*" *African American Review* 32, no. 4 (1998): 661–72.

Césaire, Aimé. *Discourse on Colonialism.* 1955. Monthly Review Press, 2000.

Charles, John C. *Abandoning the Black Hero: Sympathy and Privacy in the Postwar African American White-Life Novel.* Rutgers University Press, 2019.

Chesnutt, Charles. "The Courts and the Negro." 1908. In *Stories, Novels, and Essays,* 895–905. Library of America, 2002.

Chester, Laura, ed. *Cradle and All: Women Writers on Pregnancy and Birth.* Faber & Faber, 1989.

Choi, Yoon Young. "Failing Face of a Nation: The Anxiety of Miscegenation in Ann Petry's *The Narrows.*" *Feminist Studies in English Literature* 22, no. 3 (2014): 5–32.

Christian, Barbara. *Black Women Novelists: The Development of a Tradition, 1892–1976.* Greenwood Press, 1980.

———. "Nuance and the Novella: A Study of Gwendolyn Brooks's *Maud Martha.*" In *A Life Distilled: Gwendolyn Brooks, Her Poetry and Fiction,* edited by Maria K. Mootry and Gary Smith, 239–53. University of Illinois Press, 1987.

Clark, Keith. "A Distaff Dream Deferred? Ann Petry and the Art of Subversion." *African American Review* 26, no. 3 (1992): 495–505.

———. *The Radical Fiction of Ann Petry.* Louisiana State University Press, 2013.

Clark, Suzanne. "Narrative Fitness: Science, Nature, and Zora Neale Hurston's Folk Culture." In *Restoring the Connection to the Natural World: Essays on the African American Environmental Imagination,* edited by Sylvia Mayer, 45–71. LIT Verlag, 2003.

Clausen, Christopher. "It Is Not Elitist to Place Major Literature at the Center of the English Curriculum." *Chronicle of Higher Education,* January 13, 1988, A52.

Colbert, Soyica Diggs. *Black Movements: Performance and Cultural Politics.* Rutgers University Press, 2017.

———. *Radical Vision: A Biography of Lorraine Hansberry.* Yale University Press, 2021.

Combahee River Collective. "A Black Feminist Statement." 1977. In *But Some of Us Are Brave: Black Women's Studies,* edited by Akasha (Gloria T.) Hull, Patricia Bell-Scott, and Barbara Smith, 13–22. Feminist Press, 2015.

Cooper, Anna Julia. *A Voice from the South.* Aldine Printing House, 1892. https://docsouth.unc.edu/church/cooper/cooper.html.

Cooper, Brittney C. Afterword to *But Some of Us Are Brave: Black Women's Studies,* edited by Akasha (Gloria T.) Hull, Patricia Bell-Scott, and Barbara Smith, 379–85. Feminist Press, 2015.

———. *Beyond Respectability: The Intellectual Thought of Race Women.* University of Illinois Press, 2017.

———. "Love No Limit: Towards a Black Feminist Future (in Theory)." *The Black Scholar* 45, no. 4 (Winter 2015): 7–21.

Cosslett, Tess. *Women Writing Childbirth: Modern Discourses of Motherhood.* Manchester University Press, 1994.

Crenshaw, Kimberlé W. "Demarginalizing the Intersection of Race and Sex: A Black Feminist Critique of Anti-Discrimination Doctrine, Feminist Theory and Anti-Racist Politics." *The University of Chicago Legal Forum* 1989, no. 1 (1989): 139–67.

Cruse, Harold. *The Crisis of the Negro Intellectual.* 1967. New York Review of Books, 2005.

Daniels, Melissa Asher [Melissa Daniels-Rauterkus]. "The Limits of Literary Realism: *Of One Blood*'s Post-Racial Fantasy by Pauline Hopkins." *Callaloo* 36, no. 1 (2013): 158–77.

Davie, Sharon. "Free Mules, Talking Buzzards, and Cracked Plates: The Politics of Dislocation in *Their Eyes Were Watching God." PMLA* 108, no. 3 (1993): 446–59.

Davies, Tony. *Humanism.* Routledge, 2008.

Davis, Allison. "Our Negro 'Intellectuals.'" 1928. In *The Crisis Reader: Stories, Poetry, and Essays from the NAACP's Crisis Magazine,* edited by Sondra Kathryn Wilson, 326–33. Random House, 1999.

Davis, Jane. "More Force than Human: Richard Wright's Female Characters." *Obsidian II* 1, no. 3 (1986): 68–83.

Davis, Kimberly Chabot. *Beyond the White Negro: Empathy and Anti-Racist Reading.* University of Illinois Press, 2014.

Davis, Thadious. *Nella Larsen: Novelist of the Harlem Renaissance.* Louisiana State University Press, 1994.

De Veaux, Alexis. *Warrior Poet: A Biography of Audre Lorde.* Norton, 2004.

Delany, Martin R. *Principia of Ethnology: The Origin of Races and Color, with an Archeological Compendium of Ethiopian and Egyptian Civilization, from Years of Careful Examination and Enquiry.* 1879. 2nd and rev. ed. Harper & Brother, 1880.

Denning, Michael. *The Cultural Front: The Laboring of American Culture in the Twentieth Century.* Verso Books, 1998.

Dingledine, Don. "'It Could Have Been Any Street': Ann Petry, Stephen Crane, and the Fate of Naturalism." *Studies in American Fiction* 34, no. 1 (Spring 2006): 87–106.

Dolamo, Ramathate TH. "Botho/Ubuntu: Perspectives of Black Consciousness and Black Theology." *Studia Historiae Ecclesiasticae* 40 (2014): 215–29.

Drake, Kimberly. "Women on the Go: Blues, Conjure, and Other Alternatives to Domesticity in Ann Petry's *The Street* and *The Narrows*." *Arizona Quarterly: A Journal of American Literature, Culture, and Theory* 54, no. 1 (1998): 65–95.

Drake, St Clair. "Why Men Leave Home." *Negro Digest* 8, no. 6 (April 1950): 25–27.

Du Bois, W. E. B. "The Colored Magazine in America." *The Crisis* 5, no. 1 (November 1912): 33–35.

———. "Criteria of Negro Art." 1926. In *Within the Circle: An Anthology of African American Literary Criticism from the Harlem Renaissance to the Present*, edited by Angelyn Mitchell, 60–68. Duke University Press, 1994.

———. *The Souls of Black Folk*. 1903. Penguin Classics, 1996.

———. "Strivings of the Negro People." *Atlantic Monthly* 80, no. 478 (August 1897): 204–16. Reprinted as "Of Our Spiritual Strivings," in *The Souls of Black Folk*, 3–12. Penguin, 1996.

———. "Two Novels." *The Crisis* 35, no. 6 (June 1928): 202.

Du Bois, W. E. B., and Alain Locke. "The Younger Literary Movement." *The Crisis* 27, no. 4, 161–63.

duCille, Ann. "Blues Notes on Black Sexuality: Sex and the Texts of Jessie Fauset and Nella Larsen." *Journal of the History of Sexuality* 3, no. 3 (January 1993): 418–44.

———. *The Coupling Convention: Sex, Text, and Tradition in Black Women's Fiction*. Oxford University Press, 1993.

———. "Of Race, Gender, and the Novel; or, Where in the World Is Toni Morrison?" *Novel: A Forum on Fiction* 50, no. 3 (November 2017): 375–87.

Duck, Leigh Anne. "'Go There tuh *Know* There': Zora Neale Hurston and the Chronotype of the Folk." *American Literary History* 13, no. 2 (2001): 265–94.

Dugdale, John. "Roots of the Problem: The Controversial History of Alex Haley's Book." *The Guardian*, February 9, 2017. https://www.theguardian.com/books/booksblog/2017/feb/09/alex-haley-roots-reputation-authenticity.

Dunbar, Eve. "Loving Gorillas: Segregation Literature, Animality, and Black Liberation." *American Literature* 92, no. 1 (2020): 123–49.

Early, Sarah J. W. "The Organized Efforts of the Colored Women of the South to Improve Their Condition." In *World's Congress of Representative Women*, vol. 1, edited by May Wright Sewall, 719–24. Rand McNally, 1894. https://catalog.hathitrust.org/Record/004399612.

E.C. "Book of the Week." Review of *Maud Martha*, by Gwendolyn Brooks. *Jet*, December 24, 1953, 50.

"Editor's Note." *Forum* 83, no. 4 (April 1930): 41.

"Editorial and Publishers' Announcements." *Colored American Magazine* (May 1900): 60–64.

Edwards, Erica R. *Charisma and the Fictions of Black Leadership*. University of Minnesota Press, 2012.

———. *The Other Side of Terror: Black Women and the Culture of US Empire*. New York University Press, 2021.

Elliot, R. S. "The Story of Our Magazine." *Colored American Magazine* (May 1901): 43–77.

Ellis, Kate, and Stephen Smith, eds. *Say It Plain, Say It Loud: A Century of Great African American Speeches*. American RadioWorks, American Public Media. 2023. https://americanradioworks.publicradio.org/features/blackspeech/lhansberry.html.

Ellison, Ralph. "The Art of Fiction: An Interview." Interview by Alfred Chester and Vilma Howard. 1955. In *The Collected Essays of Ralph Ellison*, edited by John Callahan, 210–24. Modern Library, 2003.

———. Introduction to *Shadow and Act*. 1964. In *The Collected Essays of Ralph Ellison*, edited by John Callahan, 49–60. Modern Library, 2003.

———. *Invisible Man*. 1952. Vintage Books, 1980.

———. "On Initiation Rites and Power: A Lecture at West Point." 1969. In *The Collected Essays of Ralph Ellison*, edited by John Callahan, 524–45. Modern Library, 2003.

———. "The World and the Jug." 1963–64. In *The Collected Essays of Ralph Ellison*, edited by John Callahan, 155–88. Modern Library, 2003.

Engle, Paul. "Chicago Can Take Pride in New, Young Voice in Poetry." Review of *A Street in Bronzeville*, by Gwendolyn Brooks. *Chicago Daily Tribune*, August 16, 1945, E11.

English, Daylanne K. *Each Hour Redeem: Time and Justice in African American Literature*. University of Minnesota Press, 2013.

Erkkila, Betsy. *The Wicked Sisters: Women Poets, Literary History, and Discord*. Oxford University Press, 1992.

Estes, Steve. *I Am a Man! Race, Manhood, and the Civil Rights Movement*. University of North Carolina Press, 2005.

Ewing, Eve L. "On 'What I Mean When I Say I'm Sharpening My Oyster Knife.'" Poetry Society of America. Accessed July 10, 2022. https://poetrysociety.org/features/in-their-own-words/eve-l-ewing-on-what-i-mean-when-i-say-im-sharpening-my-oyster-knife#.

Fabre, Michael. *From Harlem to Paris: Black American Writers in France, 1840–1980*. University of Illinois Press, 1991.

———. "Margaret Walker's Richard Wright: A Wrong Righted or Wright Wronged?" *Mississippi Quarterly* 42, no. 4 (Fall 1989): 429–50.

Fanon, Frantz. *Wretched of the Earth*. 1961. Grove Press, 2004.

Fauset, Jessie Redmon. "Impressions of the Second Pan-African Congress." *The Crisis* 23, no. 1 (November 1921): 12–18.

———. "Jessie Fauset." Interview by Marion L Starkey. *The Southern Workman* (May 1932): 217–20.

———. "The New Books." *The Crisis* 27, no. 4 (February 1924): 174–77.

Favor, J. Martin. *Authentic Blackness: The Folk in the New Negro Renaissance*. Duke University Press, 1999.

Ferguson, Roderick A. *Aberrations in Black: Toward a Queer of Color Critique*. University of Minnesota Press, 2003.

Ferguson, Sally Ann H. "Dorothy West." In *Afro-American Writers, 1940–1955*, edited by Trudier Harris-Lopez. Dictionary of Literary Biography, vol. 76. Gale, 1988. https://link.gale.com/apps/doc/H1200000576/LitRC?u=viva_jmu&sid=summon&xid=79e57460.

Filene, Benjamin. *Romancing the Folk: Public Memory and American Roots Music*. University of North Carolina Press, 2000.

Forbes, Curdella. "X Press Publications: Pop Culture, 'Pop Lit' and Caribbean Literary Criticism: An Essay of Provocation." *Anthurium: A Caribbean Studies Journal* 4, no. 1 (2006): article 2.

Ford, Nick Aaron. "Blueprint for Negro Authors." *Phylon* 11, no. 4 (4th Quarter, 1950): 374–77.

Ford, Thomas F., and Lillian C. Ford. "The Kind of Books Los Angeles Reads." *Los Angeles Times*, April 30, 1922, pt. 3, pp. 29, 31.

Foreman, P. Gabrielle, Sarah Patterson, and Jim Casey. "Introduction to the Colored Conventions Movement." Colored Conventions Project. 2015. https://coloredconventions.org/introduction-movement/.

Frazier, Franklin E. *The Negro Family in the United States.* University of Chicago Press, 1939.

Frazier, Valerie. "Domestic Epic Warfare in *Maud Martha.*" *African American Review* 39, no. 1–2 (2005): 133–41.

Fuller, Edmund. "Validity Lacking." Review of *The Narrows,* by Ann Petry. *San Diego Union,* September 20, 1953, sec. E, p. 2.

Gabbin, Joanne V. "Blooming in the Whirlwind: The Early Poetry of Gwendolyn Brooks." In *The Furious Flowering of African American Poetry,* edited by Joanne V. Gabbin, 252–73. University Press of Virginia, 1999.

Gage, F. D. [Frances Dana]. "Sojourner Truth." *The Independent* (New York), April 23, 1863, p. 1.

Gaines, Kevin. "Black Americans' Racial Uplift Ideology as 'Civilizing Mission': Pauline E. Hopkins on Race and Imperialism." In *Cultures of United States Imperialism,* edited by Amy E. Kaplan and Donald E. Pease, 433–55. Duke University Press, 1993.

———. *Uplifting the Race: Black Leadership, Politics, and Culture in the Twentieth Century.* University of North Carolina Press, 1996.

Garvey, Amy Jacques. "On Langston Hughes: I Am a Negro—and Beautiful." 1926. In *Double-Take: A Revisionist Harlem Renaissance Anthology,* edited by Venetria K. Patton and Maureen Honey, 45–46. Rutgers University Press, 2021.

Garza, Alicia. "A Herstory of the #BlackLivesMatter Movement." *The Feminist Wire,* October 7, 2014. https://thefeministwire.com/2014/10/blacklivesmatter-2/.

Gates, Henry Louis, Jr. "In Her Own Write." Foreword to *Short Fiction by Black Women, 1900–1920,* edited by Elizabeth Ammons, xiii–xxviii. Oxford University Press, 1991.

———. *The Signifying Monkey: A Theory of African-American Literary Criticism.* Oxford University Press, 1989.

———. "Writing 'Race' and the Difference It Makes." *Critical Inquiry* 12, no. 1 (Autumn 1985): 1–20.

Gaylard, Rob. "Welcome to the World of Our Humanity: (African) Humanism, Ubuntu and Black South African Writing." *Journal of Literary Studies* 20, no. 3–4 (2004): 265–82.

Gibson, Donald B., ed. *Five Black Writers: Essays on Wright, Ellison, Baldwin, Hughes, and LeRoi Jones.* New York University Press, 1970.

Gibson, Richard. "A No to Nothing." *The Kenyon Review* 13, no. 2 (Spring 1951): 252–55.

Giddings, Paula. *When and Where I Enter: The Impact of Black Women on Race and Sex in America.* 1984. Amistad, 2006.

Gillman, Susan. "Pauline Hopkins and the Occult: African-American Revisions of Nineteenth-Century Sciences." *American Literary History* 8 (Spring 1996): 57–82.

Gilroy, Paul. *The Black Atlantic: Modernity and Double Consciousness.* Harvard University Press, 1993.

———. Introduction to *Eight Men,* by Richard Wright, xi–xxi. Harper Perennial, 1996.

Gilyard, Keith. *John Oliver Killens: A Life of Black Literary Activism.* University of Georgia Press, 2010.

Givens, Archie, Jr. Epilogue to *Of One Blood: Or, The Hidden Self,* by Pauline Hopkins, 195–96. Washington Square Press, 2004.

Gloster, Hugh M. "Race and the Negro Writer." *Phylon* 11, no. 4 (4th Quarter, 1950): 369–71.

Goldsby, Jacqueline. "A Salon for the Masses: Black Reading Circles during the Chicago Renaissance," James Madison University, Dept. of English, February 29, 2016.

―――. "'Something Is Said in the Silences': Gwendolyn Brooks's Years at Harper's." *American Literary History* 33, no. 2 (2021): 244–70.

―――. *A Spectacular Secret: Lynching in American Life and Literature*. University of Chicago Press, 2006.

Goldsmith, Meredith. "Jessie Fauset's Not-So-New Negro Womanhood: The Harlem Renaissance, the Long Nineteenth Century, and Legacies of Feminine Representation." *Legacy: A Journal of American Women Writers* 32, no. 2 (2015): 258–80.

Goldstein, Philip. "Richard Wright's *Native Son*: From Naturalist Protest to Modernist Liberation and Beyond." In *New Directions in American Reception Study*, edited by Philip Goldstein and James L. Machor, 119–37. Oxford University Press, 2007.

Googasian, Victoria. "Zora Neale Hurston and the Limits of the Will to Humanize." *Journal of Modern Literature* 44, no. 4 (2021): 19–36.

Govan, Christine Noble. "Negro Community." Review of *The Narrows*, by Ann Petry. *Chattanooga Times*, September 13, 1953, 20.

Govan, Sandra Y. "Black Women as Cultural Conservators: Biographers and Builders of Our Cultural Heritage." *Langston Hughes Review* 7, no. 2 (Fall 1988): 1–14.

Graff, Gerald. *Beyond the Culture Wars: How Teaching the Conflicts Can Revitalize American Education*. Norton, 1992.

Graham, Maryemma. *The House Where My Soul Lives: The Life of Margaret Walker*. Oxford University Press, 2022.

―――. Preface to *Fields Watered with Blood: Critical Essays on Margaret Walker*, edited by Maryemma Graham, xi–xiv. University of Georgia Press, 2014.

Greenfield-Sanders, Timothy. *Toni Morrison: The Pieces I Am*. Magnolia Home Entertainment, 2019.

Grier, Barbara (Gene Damon). "Lesbiana." *The Ladder* 14, no. 5–6 (February–March 1970): 31–35.

Griffin, Farah Jasmine. "Hunting Communists and Negroes in Ann Petry's *The Narrows*." In *Revising the Blueprint: Ann Petry and the Literary Left*, edited by Alex Lubin, 137–49. University Press of Mississippi, 2007.

―――. "On Women, Teaching and *Native Son*." In *Approaches to Teaching Wright's "Native Son,"* edited by James A. Miller, 75–80. Modern Language Association of America, 1997.

Guttman, Sondra. "What Bigger Killed For: Re-Reading Violence Against Women in *Native Son*." *Texas Studies in Literature and Language* 43, no. 2 (2001): 169–93.

Hagen, Julia. "Relational Principles in the Care of Suicidal Inpatients: Experiences of Therapists and Mental Health Nurses." *Issues in Mental Health Nursing* 38, no. 2 (2017): 99–106.

Hale, Grace Elizabeth. *Making Whiteness: The Culture of Segregation in the South, 1890–1940*. Pantheon Books, 1998.

Hall, Stuart. "The Question of Cultural Identity." In *Modernity and Its Futures: Understanding Modern Societies, Book IV*, edited by Stuart Hall, David Held Hall, and Anthony McGrew, 274–316. Polity Press, 1992.

Hansberry, Lorraine. "Dramatist Against Odds." Interview by Nan Robertson. *New York Times*, March 8, 1959, X3.

―――. "Interview with Lorraine Hansberry." Interview by Studs Terkel. 1959. In *Conversations with Lorraine Hansberry*, edited by Mollie Godfrey, 73–91. University Press of Mississippi, 2021.

―――. "The Legacy of W. E. B. Du Bois." *Freedomways* 5, no. 1 (Winter 1965): 19–20.

―――. Letter to Editor [from L.N.]. *The Ladder* 1, no. 11 (August 1957): 26–30.

———. "Miss Hansberry on 'Backlash.'" *Village Voice*, July 23, 1964, 10, 16.

———. *The Movement: Documentary of a Struggle for Equality*. Simon and Schuster, 1964.

———. "The Protest, Part I." Interview by Reverend William Hamilton. 1959. In *Conversations with Lorraine Hansberry*, edited by Mollie Godfrey, 59–62. University Press of Mississippi, 2021.

———. *To Be Young Gifted and Black: Lorraine Hansberry in Her Own Words*. Adapted by Robert Nemiroff. 1969. Vintage Books, 1995.

———. "Unaired Interview with Lorraine Hansberry." Interview by Mike Wallace. 1959. In *Conversations with Lorraine Hansberry*, edited by Mollie Godfrey, 63–72. University Press of Mississippi, 2021.

———. "Willie Loman, Walter Younger, and He Who Must Live." *Village Voice*, August 12, 1959, 7–8.

———. "Women Voice Demands in Capital Sojourn." *Freedom* 1, no. 10 (October 1951): 6.

Hansberry, Lorraine, and Lloyd Richards. "Interview with Lorraine Hansberry and Lloyd Richards." Interview by Frank Perry. 1961. In *Conversations with Lorraine Hansberry*, edited by Mollie Godfrey, 155–61. University Press of Mississippi, 2021.

Hardison, Ayesha K. *Writing through Jane Crow: Race and Gender Politics in African American Literature*. University of Virginia Press, 2014.

Harper, Frances E. W. "The Great Problem to Be Solved." 1875. In *A Brighter Coming Day: A Frances Ellen Watkins Harper Reader*, edited by Frances Smith Foster, 219–22. Feminist Press, 1990.

———. "We Are All Bound Up Together." 1866. In *A Brighter Coming Day: A Frances Ellen Watkins Harper Reader*, edited by Frances Smith Foster, 217–19. Feminist Press, 1990.

———. "Woman's Political Future." 1893. In *With Pen and Voice: A Critical Anthology of Nineteenth-Century African-American Women*, edited by Shirley Wilson Logan, 43–46. Southern Illinois University Press, 1995.

Harris, Marla. "Not Black and/or White: Reading Racial Difference in Heliodorus's *Ethiopica* and Pauline Hopkins's *Of One Blood*." *African American Review* 35, no. 3 (Fall 2001): 375–90.

Harris, Trudier. *Exorcising Blackness: Historical and Literary Lynching and Burning Rituals*. Indiana University Press, 1984.

———. "Native Sons and Foreign Daughters." In *New Essays on "Native Son,"* edited by Kenneth Kinnamon, 63–84. Cambridge University Press, 1990.

Hartman, Saidiya. *Scenes of Subjection: Terror, Slavery, and Self-Making in Nineteenth-Century America*. Oxford University Press, 1997.

Harvard Committee. *General Education in a Free Society: Report of the Harvard Committee*. Harvard University Press, 1945.

Hathaway, Rosemary. "'Almost Folklore': The Legend That Killed Nella Larsen's Literary Career." *Journal of American Folklore* 130, no. 517 (Summer 2017): 255–75.

Haviland, Beverly. "Passing from Paranoia to Plagiarism: The Abject Authorship of Nella Larsen." *Modern Fiction Studies* 43, no. 2 (1997): 295–318.

Hemenway, Robert E. *Zora Neale Hurston: A Literary Biography*. University of Illinois Press, 1977.

Henry, Alvin J. *Black Queer Flesh: Rejecting Subjectivity in the African American Novel*. University of Minnesota Press, 2021.

Hentoff, Nat. "The Town Hall Mugging." *Village Voice*, July 9, 1964, 4–6.

Hewes, Henry. "A Plant Grows in Chicago." Review of *A Raisin in the Sun*, by Lorraine Hansberry. *Saturday Review*, April 4, 1959, 28.

Hibben, Sheila "Vibrant Book Full of Nature and Salt." Review of *Their Eyes Were Watching God*, by Zora Neale Hurston. *New York Herald Tribune Weekly Book Review,* September 26, 1937, 2.

Hicks, Heather J. "Rethinking Realism in Ann Petry's *The Street.*" *MELUS* 27, no. 4 (Winter 2002): 89–105.

Higashida, Cheryl. "Aunt Sue's Children: Re-Viewing the Gender(ed) Politics of Richard Wright's Radicalism." *American Literature* 75, no. 2 (2003): 395–425.

———. *Black Internationalist Feminism: Women Writers of the Black Left, 1945–1995.* University of Illinois Press, 2011.

Higginbotham, Evelyn Brooks. *Righteous Discontent: The Women's Movement in the Black Baptist Church, 1880–1920.* Harvard University Press, 1993.

Hill, Mozell C., and M. Carl Holman. Preface to "The Negro in Literature: The Current Scene," edited by Mozell C. Hill and M. Carl Holman. Special issue, *Phylon* 11, no. 4 (4th Quarter, 1950): 296.

Hill Collins, Patricia. *Black Feminist Thought: Knowledge, Consciousness, and the Politics of Empowerment.* 1st ed. Routledge, 1990.

———. *Black Feminist Thought: Knowledge, Consciousness, and the Politics of Empowerment.* 2nd ed. 2000. Routledge, 2009.

Hoeller, Hildegard. "Race, Modernism, and Plagiarism: The Case of Nella Larsen's 'Sanctuary.'" *African American Review* 40, no. 3 (2006): 421–37.

Hoffman, Frederick L. *The Race Traits and Tendencies of the American Negro.* Macmillan, 1896.

Holladay, Hilary. *Ann Petry.* Twayne Publishers, 1996.

hooks, bell. "Choosing the Margin as a Space of Radical Openness." 1989. In *Women, Knowledge, and Reality: Explorations in Feminist Philosophy,* 2nd ed., edited by Ann Garry and Marilyn Pearsall, 48–55. Routledge, 2015.

———. Interview in *Black Is . . . Black Ain't.* Directed by Marlon Riggs. California Newsreel, 1994.

Hopkins, Pauline. "The Dark Races of the Twentieth Century." 1905. In *Daughter of the Revolution: The Major Nonfiction Works of Pauline E. Hopkins,* edited by Ira Dworkin, 305–31. Rutgers University Press, 2007.

———. "Echoes from the Annual Convention of Northeastern Federation of Colored Women's Clubs." *Colored American Magazine* (October 1903): 709–13.

———. "Famous Men of the Negro Race. V: Edwin Garrison Walker." *Colored American Magazine* (March 1901): 358–66.

———. "Famous Women of the Negro Race. VIII: Educators (Concluded)." *Colored American Magazine* (July 1902): 206–13.

———. "Famous Women of the Negro Race. IX: Club Life among Colored Women." *Colored American Magazine* (August 1902): 273–77.

———. "Famous Women of the Negro Race. X: Artists." *Colored American Magazine* (September 1902): 362–67.

———. "How a New York Newspaper Man Entertained a Number of Colored Ladies and Gentlemen at Dinner in the Revere House, Boston, and How the Colored American League Was Started." *Colored American Magazine* (March 1904): 151–60.

———. *The Magazine Novels of Pauline Hopkins.* Edited by Henry Louis Gates Jr. Oxford University Press, 1988.

———. *Of One Blood: Or, The Hidden Self.* 1902–3. Washington Square Press, 2004.

———. *One Blood.* 1902–3. The X Press, 1996.

———. Preface to *Contending Forces: A Romance Illustrative of Negro Life North and South*, edited by Henry Louis Gates Jr., 13–16. 1900. Oxford University Press, 1988.

———. *A Primer of Facts Pertaining to the Early Greatness of the African Race and the Possibility of Restoration by Its Descendants—with Epilogue*. 1905. In *Daughter of the Revolution: The Major Nonfiction Works of Pauline E. Hopkins*, edited by Ira Dworkin, 333–52. Rutgers University Press, 2007.

———. "Talma Gordon." *Colored American Magazine* (October 1900): 271–90.

Howe, Irving. "Black Boys and Native Sons." In *A World More Attractive: A View of Modern Literature and Politics*, 98–122. Horizon Press, 1963.

Huggins, Nathan Irvin. *Harlem Renaissance*, updated ed. Oxford University Press, 2007.

Hughes, Langston. *The Big Sea: An Autobiography*. 1940. Hill and Wang, 1993.

———. "The Negro Artist and the Racial Mountain." 1926. In *Within the Circle: An Anthology of African American Literary Criticism from the Harlem Renaissance to the Present*, edited by Angelyn Mitchell, 55–59. Duke University Press, 1994.

———. "Some Practical Observations: A Colloquy." *Phylon* 11, no. 4 (4th Quarter, 1950): 307–11.

Hull, Akasha (Gloria T.). "Black Women Poets from Wheatley to Walker." *Negro American Literature Forum* 9, no. 3 (1975): 91–96.

———. *Color, Sex, and Poetry: Three Women Writers of the Harlem Renaissance*. Indiana University Press, 1987.

Hull, Akasha (Gloria T.) and Barbara Smith. "The Politics of Black Women's Studies." 1982. Introduction to *But Some of Us Are Brave: Black Women's Studies*, edited by Akasha (Gloria T.) Hull and Barbara Smith, xvii–xxxii. Feminist Press, 2015.

Hurston, Zora Neale. "Characteristics of Negro Expression." 1934. In *Within the Circle: An Anthology of African American Literary Criticism from the Harlem Renaissance to the Present*, edited by Angelyn Mitchell, 79–94. Duke University Press, 1994.

———. "Court Order Can't Make Races Mix." 1955. In *Folklore, Memoirs, and Other Writings*, edited by Cheryl Wall, 956–58. Library of America, 1995.

———. *Dust Tracks on a Road: An Autobiography*. 1942. In *Folklore, Memoirs, and Other Writings*, edited by Cheryl Wall, 557–808. Library of America, 1995.

———. "How It Feels to Be Colored Me." 1928. In *Folklore, Memoirs, and Other Writings*, edited by Cheryl Wall, 826–29. Library of America, 1995.

———. *Mules and Men*. 1935. In *Folklore, Memoirs, and Other Writings*, edited by Cheryl Wall, 1–267. Library of America, 1995.

———. *Tell My Horse*. 1938. In *Folklore, Memoirs, and Other Writings*, edited by Cheryl Wall, 269–555. Library of America, 1995.

———. *Their Eyes Were Watching God*. 1937. Harper Collins, 1998.

———. "What White Publishers Won't Print." 1950. In *Folklore, Memoirs, and Other Writings*, edited by Cheryl Wall, 950–55. Library of America, 1995.

Hutchinson, George B. *The Harlem Renaissance in Black and White*. Belknap Press, 1997.

———. *In Search of Nella Larsen: A Biography of the Color Line*. Belknap Press, 2006.

H.W.R. "A Story of the Revolt of a Negro School Teacher." *Boston Evening Transcript*, June 20, 1928, pt. 3, p. 2.

"In the Editor's Sanctum." *Colored American Magazine* (May 1904): 382–83.

Inge, Thomas M., Maurice Duke, and Jackson R. Bryer. *Black American Writers: Biographical Essays.* Vol. 2. St. Martin's Press, 1978.

Ireland, Philippa Ruth. "Material Factors Affecting the Publication of Black British Fiction." PhD diss., Open University, 2011.

Jackson, Blyden. "An Essay in Criticism." *Phylon* 11, no. 4 (4th Quarter, 1950): 338–43.

———. "A Poet's First Novel." Review of *Maud Martha,* by Gwendolyn Brooks. *Phylon* 14, no. 4 (4th Quarter, 1953): 436.

Jackson, Lawrence P. *The Indignant Generation: A Narrative History of African American Writers and Critics, 1934–1960.* Princeton University Press, 2010.

Jackson, Zakiyyah Iman. "Animal: New Directions in the Theorization of Race and Posthumanism." *Feminist Studies* 39, no. 3 (2013): 669–85.

———. *Becoming Human: Matter and Meaning in an Antiblack World.* New York University Press, 2020.

Jacobs, Karen. "From 'Spy-Glass' to 'Horizon': Tracking the Anthropological Gaze in Zora Neale Hurston." *Novel: A Forum on Fiction* 30, no. 3 (1997): 329–60.

JanMohamed, Abdul R. *The Death-Bound-Subject: Richard Wright's Archaeology of Death.* Duke University Press, 2005.

Japtok, Martin. "Pauline Hopkins's *Of One Blood,* Africa, and the 'Darwinist Trap.'" *African American Review* 36, no. 3 (Fall 2002): 403–15.

Jarrett, Gene Andrew. *Deans and Truants: Race and Realism in African American Literature.* University of Pennsylvania Press, 2007.

———. *Representing the Race: A New Political History of African American Literature.* New York University Press, 2011.

Jenkins, Candice M. "Decoding Essentialism: Cultural Authenticity and the Black Bourgeoisie in Nella Larsen's *Passing.*" *MELUS* 30, no. 3 (Fall 2005): 129–54.

———. *Private Lives, Proper Relations: Regulating Black Intimacy.* University of Minnesota Press, 2007.

Johnson, Abby Arthur. "Literary Midwife: Jessie Redmon Fauset and the Harlem Renaissance." *Phylon* 39, no. 2 (June 1978): 143–53.

Johnson, Barbara. "The Re(a)d and the Black." In *Richard Wright's "Native Son,"* edited by Harold Bloom, 115–23. Chelsea, 1988.

———. *A World of Difference.* 1987. Johns Hopkins University Press, 1989.

Johnson, Charles C. "The Debut of the Younger School of Negro Writers." *Opportunity* 2, no. 17 (May 1924): 143–44.

Johnson, James Weldon. *The Autobiography of an Ex-Colored Man.* 1912. Penguin, 1990.

———. "The Dilemma of the Negro Author." 1928. In *Writings,* 744–52. Library of America, 2004.

———. Preface to revised edition. 1931. In *The Book of American Negro Poetry,* 3–8. Harcourt, Brace & World, 1958.

Jones, Sharon Lynette. "Black Excesses and Deprivations in Literature and Photography of the 1930s." In *African American Literature in Transition 1930–1940,* edited by Eve Dunbar and Ayesha K. Hardison, 33–58. Cambridge University Press, 2022.

Joyce, James. *A Portrait of the Artist as a Young Man.* 1916. Lerner Publishing Group, 2015.

Joyce, Joyce A. *Black Studies as Human Studies: Critical Essays and Interviews.* State University of New York Press, 2005.

Kadlec, David. "Zora Neale Hurston and the Federal Folk." *Modernism/Modernity* 7, no. 3 (September 2000): 471–85.

Kaplan, Carla. "The Erotics of Talk: 'That Oldest Human Longing' in *Their Eyes Were Watching God*." *American Literature* 67, no. 1 (March 1995): 115–42.

———, ed. *Zora Neale Hurston: A Life in Letters*. Anchor Books, 2003.

Kaplan, E. Ann. *Motherhood and Representation: The Mother in Popular Culture and Melodrama*. Routledge, 1992.

Kassanoff, Jennie A. "'Fate Has Linked Us Together': Blood, Gender, and the Politics of Representation in Pauline Hopkins's *Of One Blood*." In *The Unruly Voice: Rediscovering Pauline Elizabeth Hopkins*, edited by John Cullen Gruesser, 158–81. University of Illinois Press, 1996.

Kaye-Smith, Sheila. *All the Books of My Life*. Harper & Brothers, 1956.

———. "Mrs. Adis." In *Joanna Godden Married and Other Stories*, 190–204. Harper & Brothers, 1926. Reprinted from *Century Magazine* 103, no. 3 (January 1922): 321–26 and from *John O' London's Weekly*, March 26, 1921, 761+.

Kendi, Ibram X. *The Black Campus Movement: Black Students and the Racial Reconstitution of Higher Education, 1965–1972*. Palgrave Macmillan, 2012.

Kent, George E. "Aesthetic Values in the Poetry of Gwendolyn Brooks." In *A Life Distilled: Gwendolyn Brooks, Her Poetry and Fiction*, edited by Maria K. Mootry and Gary Smith, 30–46. University of Illinois Press, 1989.

———. *A Life of Gwendolyn Brooks*. University Press of Kentucky, 1990.

Killens, John Oliver. "The Black Writer vis-à-vis His Country." In *The Black Aesthetic*, edited by Addison Gayle Jr., 357–73. Doubleday, 1971.

Kim, Daniel Y. "Invisible Desires: Homoerotic Racism and Its Homophobic Critique in Ralph Ellison's *Invisible Man*." *Novel: A Forum on Fiction* 30, no. 3 (1997): 309–28.

Kimmage, Michael. *The Conservative Turn: Lionel Trilling, Whittaker Chambers, and the Lessons of Anti-Communism*. Harvard University Press, 2009.

King, Charles. *Gods of the Upper Air: How a Circle of Renegade Anthropologists Reinvented Race, Sex, and Gender in the Twentieth Century*. Doubleday, 2019.

King, Martin Luther, Jr. "A Letter from Birmingham Jail." *Ebony* (August 1963): 23–32.

Knickmeyer, W. L. "Notable Studies of Negro Life." Review of *Their Eyes Were Watching God*, by Zora Neale Hurston. *St. Louis Post-Dispatch*, September 19, 1937, 4H.

Kogan, Herman. "Two Chicagoans Charm, Shock." Review of *Maud Martha*, by Gwendolyn Brooks. *Chicago Sun-Times*, October 4, 1953, 6.

Kotin, Joshua. "Funding the Black Arts Repertory Theatre/School." *American Literary History* 34, no. 4 (Winter 2022): 1358–88.

Kramer, Lloyd S. *Nationalism in Europe and America: Politics, Cultures, and Identities since 1775*. University of North Carolina Press, 2011.

Lamothe, Daphne. *Inventing the New Negro: Narrative, Culture, and Ethnography*. University of Pennsylvania Press, 2008.

———. "Vodou Imagery, African-American Tradition and Cultural Transformation in Zora Neale Hurston's *Their Eyes Were Watching God*." *Callaloo* 22, no. 1 (1999): 157–75.

Larsen, Nella. "The Author's Explanation." *The Forum* 83, no. 4 (April 1930): xli.

———. *Passing*. 1929. In *"Quicksand" and "Passing,"* edited by Deborah E. McDowell, 143–242. Rutgers University Press, 1989.

———. *Quicksand*. 1928. In *"Quicksand" and "Passing,"* edited by Deborah E. McDowell, 1–135. Rutgers University Press, 1989.

———. "Sanctuary." In *The Sleeper Wakes: Harlem Renaissance Stories by Women*, edited by Marcy Knopf, 250–55. Rutgers University Press, 1993. Reprinted from *Forum* 83 (January 1930): 15–18.

Larson, Kelli A. "Surviving the Taint of Plagiarism: Nella Larsen's 'Sanctuary' and Sheila Kaye-Smith's 'Mrs. Adis.'" *Journal of Modern Literature* 30, no. 4 (Summer 2007): 82–104.

Lattin, Vernon E. "Ann Petry and the American Dream." *Black American Literature Forum* 12, no. 2 (Summer 1978): 69–72.

Lee, Ulysses. "Criticism at Mid-Century." *Phylon* 11, no. 4 (4th Quarter, 1950): 328–37.

Leshinsky, Amy. "The Power of Mentorship: The Impact of Alice Childress on Hansberry's *A Raisin in the Sun*." In *Critical Insights: A Raisin in the Sun*, edited by Peter J. Bailey, 129–44. Salem Press, 2023.

Levenson, Michael. *Genealogy of Modernism: A Study of English Literary Doctrine 1908–1922*. Cambridge University Press, 1984.

Leverty, Sally. "Beauty, Freshness, Poetry Make Novel Noteworthy." Review of *Their Eyes Were Watching God*, by Zora Neale Hurston. *Richmond Times-Dispatch*, September 26, 1937, 16.

Levy, Valerie. "'That Florida Flavor': Nature and Culture in Zora Neale Hurston's Work for the Federal Writers' Project." In *Such News of the Land: US Women Nature Writers*, edited by Thomas S. Edwards and Elizabeth A. Dewolfe, 85–94. University Press of New England, 2001.

Lewis, Herbert S. Introduction to *Anthropology and Modern Life*, by Franz Boas, xvii–xxi. 1928. Routledge, 2021.

Lewis, Leslie W. "Naming the Problem Embedded in the Problem That Led to the Question 'Who Shall Teach African American Literature?'; or, Are We Ready to Discard the Concept of Authenticity Altogether?" In *White Scholars / African American Texts*, edited by Lisa A. Long, 52–67. Rutgers University Press, 2005.

Lewis, Theophilus. "*The Narrows*." Review of *The Narrows*, by Ann Petry. *America*, October 3, 1953, 22.

Li, Stephanie. *Playing in the White: Black Writers, White Subjects*. Oxford University Press, 2015.

Lillvis, Kristen. *Posthuman Blackness and the Black Female Imagination*. University of Georgia Press, 2017.

Lincoln, Abraham. "A House Divided: Speech Delivered at Springfield, Illinois, at the Close of the Republican State Convention, June 16, 1858." In *Abraham Lincoln: His Speeches and Writings*, edited by Roy P. Basler, 372–81. World Publishing Company, 1946.

Lipari, Lisbeth. "The Rhetoric of Intersectionality: Lorraine Hansberry's 1957 Letters to the *Ladder*." In *Queering Public Address: Sexualities in American Historical Discourse*, edited by Charles E. Morris III, 220–48. University of South Carolina Press, 2007.

Lipsitz, George. "The Racialization of Space and the Spatialization of Race Theorizing the Hidden Architecture of Landscape." *Landscape Journal* 26, no. 1 (2007): 10–23.

Llorens, David. "Writers Converge at Fisk University." *Negro Digest* 15, no. 8 (1966): 54–68.

Locke, Alain. "Art or Propaganda?" 1928. In *Voices from the Harlem Renaissance*, edited by Nathan Irvin Huggins, 312–13. Oxford University Press, 1995.

———. "A Critical Retrospect of the Literature of the Negro for 1947." *Phylon* 9, no. 1 (1st Quarter, 1948): 3–12.

———. "Fire: A Negro Magazine." Review of *Fire!!: A Quarterly Devoted to Younger Negro Artists*, edited by Wallace Thurman. *The Survey* (August 15–September 15, 1927): 563.

———. Foreword to *The New Negro: Voices of the Harlem Renaissance*, edited by Alain Locke, xxv–xxvii. 1925. Atheneum, 1992.

———. "Negro Youth Speaks." 1925. In *The New Negro: Voices of the Harlem Renaissance*, edited by Alain Locke, 47–53. Atheneum, 1992.

———. "The New Negro." 1925. In *The New Negro: Voices of the Harlem Renaissance*, edited by Alain Locke, 3–16. Atheneum, 1992.

———. Review of *Their Eyes Were Watching God*. 1938. In *Zora Neale Hurston: Critical Perspectives Past and Present*, edited by Henry Louis Gates Jr. and Kwame Anthony Appiah, 18. Amistad, 1993.

———. "The Saving Grace of Realism: Retrospective Review of the Negro Literature of 1933." *Opportunity* 12 (January 1934): 8–11, 30.

———. "Self-Criticism: The Third Dimension in Culture." *Phylon* 11, no. 4 (4th Quarter, 1950): 391–94.

Lockhart Jack, "Zora Hurston Pens Novel of Own Race." Review of *Their Eyes Were Watching God*, by Zora Neale Hurston. *Memphis Commercial Appeal*, October 3, 1937, sec. 4, p. 9.

Lorde, Audre. "An Interview with Audre Lorde." Interview by Adrienne Rich. 1979. In *Conversations with Audre Lorde*, edited by Joan Wylie Hall, 45–70. University Press of Mississippi, 2004.

———. "Poetry Is Not a Luxury." 1977. In *Sister Outsider: Essays and Speeches*, 36–39. Crossing Press, 2012.

———. "The Uses of Anger: Women Responding to Racism." 1981. In *Sister Outsider: Essays and Speeches*, 124–33. Crossing Press, 2012.

Lordi, Emily. "Souls Intact: The Soul Performances of Audre Lorde, Aretha Franklin, and Nina Simone." *Women & Performance: A Journal of Feminist Theory* 26, no. 1 (2016): 55–71.

Love Has No Labels. "Fight for Freedom." Ad Council, June 17, 2020. YouTube video, 1:00, https://www.youtube.com/watch?v=Y8_598SQAts.

Lowney, John. *Jazz Internationalism: Literary Afro-Modernism and the Cultural Politics of Black Music*. University of Illinois Press, 2017.

Lubin, Alex. Introduction to *Revising the Blueprint: Ann Petry and the Literary Left*, edited by Alex Lubin, 3–14. University Press of Mississippi, 2007.

M.P. "Evil Results of Crowding." Review of *The Street*, by Ann Petry. *Worcester Sunday Telegram*, February 10, 1946, 4.

MacDonald, Tara. "'red-headed animal': Race, Sexuality and Dickens's Uriah Heep." *Critical Survey* 17, no. 2 (2005): 48–62.

MacKenzie, John M. *Museums and Empire: Natural History, Human Cultures and Colonial Identities*. Manchester University Press, 2009.

Madhubuti, Haki. "Gwendolyn Brooks: Beyond the Wordmaker—The Making of an African Poet." 1972. In *On Gwendolyn Brooks: Reliant Contemplation*, edited by Stephen Caldwell Wright, 81–96. University of Michigan Press, 2001.

Manne, Kate. "Humanism: A Critique." *Social Theory and Practice* 42, no. 2 (April 2016): 389–415.

Mannes, Marya. "Sour Bird, Sweet Raisin." Review of *A Raisin in the Sun*, by Lorraine Hansberry. *The Reporter*, April 16, 1959, 34–35.

Maroto, Inés Casas. "'So This Was a Marriage!': Intersections of Natural Imagery and the Semiotics of Space in Zora Neale Hurston's *Their Eyes Were Watching God.*" *Journal of English Studies* 11 (2013): 69–82.

Marshall, Paule. "The Art and Politics of Paule Marshall: An Interview." Interview by James C. Hall and Heather Hathaway. 2001. In *Conversations with Paule Marshall,* edited by James C. Hall and Heather Hathaway, 157–88. University Press of Mississippi, 2010.

———. "From the Poets in the Kitchen." In *Reena and Other Stories,* 1–12. Feminist Press, 1983.

———. "Gwendolyn Brooks—An Appreciation." In *Gwendolyn Brooks and Working Writers,* edited by Jacqueline Imani Bryant, 53. Third World Press, 2007.

———. "Interview with Paule Marshall." Interview by Sandi Russell. 1988. In *Conversations with Paule Marshall,* edited by James C. Hall and Heather Hathaway, 77–83. University Press of Mississippi, 2010.

———. "*PW* Interviews Paule Marshall." Interview by Sally Lodge. 1984. In *Conversations with Paule Marshall,* edited by James C. Hall and Heather Hathaway, 72–76. University Press of Mississippi, 2010.

———. "A Talk with Mary Helen Washington." Interview by Mary Helen Washington. 1981. In *Conversations with Paule Marshall,* edited by James C. Hall and Heather Hathaway, 54–58. University Press of Mississippi, 2010.

Martin, Gertrude. "Book Reviews." Review of *Maud Martha,* by Gwendolyn Brooks. *Chicago Defender,* October 15, 1953, 11.

Matthews, T. S. "What Gods! What Gongs!" Review of *Quicksand,* by Nella Larsen, and *Home to Harlem,* by Claude McKay. *New Republic* 55 (30 May 1928): 50–51.

Matthews, Victoria Earle. "The Value of Race Literature: An Address." 1895. *The Massachusetts Review* 27, no. 2 (Summer 1986): 169–91.

McCarthy, Jesse. "The Blues in Print: Wright's 'Blueprint for Negro Writing' Reconsidered." In *Richard Wright in Context,* edited by Michael Nowlin, 205–14. Cambridge University Press, 2021.

McCray, Judith, dir. *For My People: The Life and Writing of Margaret Walker.* California Newsreel, 1998.

McDougald, Elise Johnson. "The Task of Negro Womanhood." 1925. In *The New Negro: Voices of the Harlem Renaissance,* edited by Alain Locke, 369–82. Atheneum, 1992.

McDowell, Deborah E. *"The Changing Same": Black Women's Literature, Criticism, and Theory.* Indiana University Press, 1995.

———. Introduction to *Of One Blood: Or, The Hidden Self,* by Pauline Hopkins, v–xx. Washington Square Press, 2004.

———. Introduction to *"Quicksand" and "Passing,"* by Nella Larsen, edited by Deborah McDowell, ix–xxxvii. Rutgers University Press, 1989.

———. "The Neglected Dimension of Jessie Redmon Fauset." In *Conjuring: Black Women, Fiction, and Literary Tradition,* edited by Marjorie Pryse and Hortense J. Spillers, 86–104. Indiana University Press, 1985.

McHenry, Elizabeth. *Forgotten Readers: Recovering the Lost History of African American Literary Societies.* Duke University Press, 2002.

McKay, Claude. *A Long Way from Home.* Lee Furman, 1937.

McKay, Nellie Y. Introduction to *The Narrows,* by Ann Petry, vii–xx. Mariner, 1999.

McKittrick, Katherine. *Demonic Grounds: Black Women and the Cartographies of Struggle.* University of Minnesota Press, 2006.

Melamed, Jodi. *Represent and Destroy: Rationalizing Violence in the New Racial Capitalism.* University of Minnesota Press, 2011.

Menke, Pamela Glenn. "'Black Cat Bone and Snake Wisdom': New Orleanian Hoodoo, Haitian Voodoo, and Rereading Hurston's *Their Eyes Were Watching God.*" In *Songs of The New South: Writing Contemporary Louisiana,* edited by Suzanne Disheroon Green and Lisa Abney, 123–39. Greenwood Press, 2001.

"Miss Kaye-Smith, a Novelist, Dead." *New York Times,* January 16, 1956, 21.

Mitchell, Koritha. *From Slave Cabins to the White House: Homemade Citizenship in African American Culture.* University of Illinois Press, 2020.

———. *Living with Lynching: African American Lynching Plays, Performance, and Citizenship, 1890–1930.* University of Illinois Press, 2011.

Monteith, Sharon. Review of *The Norton Anthology of African American Literature,* by Henry Louis Gates Jr. and Nellie Y. McKay. *Critical Survey* 9, no. 2 (1997): 148–51.

Moody-Turner, Shirley. *Black Folklore and the Politics of Racial Representation.* University Press of Mississippi, 2013.

Mootry, Maria K. "'Down the Whirlwind of Good Rage': An Introduction to Gwendolyn Brooks." In *A Life Distilled: Gwendolyn Brooks, Her Poetry and Fiction,* edited by Maria K. Mootry and Gary Smith, 1–17. University of Illinois Press, 1987.

Morgan, Joan. "Why We Get Off: Moving Towards a Black Feminist Politics of Pleasure." *The Black Scholar* 45, no. 4 (2015): 36–46.

Morgan, Stacy I. *Rethinking Social Realism: African American Art and Literature, 1930–1953.* University of Georgia Press, 2004.

Morris, Wright. "The Complexity of Evil." Review of *The Narrows,* by Ann Petry. *New York Times Book Review,* August 16, 1953, 4.

Morrison, Toni. *Playing in the Dark: Whiteness and the Literary Imagination.* 1992. Vintage Books, 2004.

Morsink, Johannes. *Inherent Human Rights: Philosophical Roots of the Universal Declaration.* University of Pennsylvania Press, 2009.

Moss, Alfred A., Jr. *The American Negro Academy: Voice of the Talented Tenth.* Louisiana State University Press, 1981.

Moten, Fred. "Black Op." *PMLA* 123, no. 5 (2008): 1743–47.

Moynihan, Daniel P. "The Negro Family: The Case for National Action." Office of Policy Planning and Research, US Department of Labor, March 1965. https://www.dol.gov/general/aboutdol/history/webid-moynihan.

Moynihan, Sinéad. *Passing into the Present: Contemporary American Fiction of Racial and Gender Passing.* Manchester University Press, 2010.

Mullen, Bill. *Popular Fronts: Chicago and African-American Cultural Politics, 1935–46.* University of Illinois Press, 1999.

———. "Popular Fronts: *Negro Story* Magazine and the African American Literary Response to World War II." *African American Review* 50, no. 4 (Winter 2017): 938–48.

Muñoz, José Esteban. *Disidentifications: Queers of Color and the Performance of Politics.* Vol. 2. University of Minnesota Press, 1999.

Murray, Pauli. "Inquietude." *Challenge* 1, no. 1 (March 1934): 43.

———. "Song." *Challenge* 1, no. 3 (May 1935): 15.

———. "Why Negro Girls Stay Single." *Negro Digest* 5, no. 9 (July 1947): 4–8.

Musser, Amber Jamilla. *Sensational Flesh: Race, Power, and Masochism.* New York University Press, 2014.

Myrdal, Gunnar. *An American Dilemma: The Negro Problem and Modern Democracy.* Vol. 1. 1944. Routledge, 2017.

Nash, Jennifer C. *Black Feminism Reimagined: After Intersectionality.* Duke University Press, 2018.

Neal, Larry. "The Black Writer's Role, II: Ellison's Zoot Suit." 1970. In *Visions of a Liberated Future: Black Arts Movement Writings,* by Larry Neal, 30–56. Thunder's Mouth Press, 1989.

Newfield, Jack. "Mugging the White Liberal." *Village Voice,* June 25, 1964, 5, 15.

Nishikawa, Kinohi. "From Poet to Publisher: Reading Gwendolyn Brooks by Design." In *The Contemporary Small Press: Making Publishing Visible,* edited by Georgina Colby, Kaja Marczewska, and Leigh Wilson, 47–71. Palgrave Macmillan, 2020.

Nobile, Philip. "Uncovering Roots." *Village Voice,* February 23, 1993, 31–38.

North, Michael. *The Dialect of Modernism: Race, Language, and Twentieth-Century Literature.* Oxford University Press, 1994.

North, Sterling. "*Wasteland*'s Realism Leans Too Far Backward in Racial Self-Analysis." Review of *The Street,* by Ann Petry. *Washington Post,* February 17, 1946, 4S.

Nott, J. C., and George R. Gliddon. *Types of Mankind: Or, Ethnological Researches, Based Upon the Ancient Monuments, Paintings, Sculptures, and Crania of Races, and Upon Their Natural, Geographical, Philological and Biblical History.* Lippincott, Grambo, 1854.

Nowviskie, Bethany. "Capacity through Care." In *Debates in the Digital Humanities 2019,* edited by Matthew K. Gold and Lauren F. Klein, 424–26. University of Minnesota Press, 2019.

O'Connor, Clare. "Lost in Citation: Afterlives of the 1968 Memphis Sanitation Strike." *International Journal of Communication* 16 (2022): 4684–700.

Olson, Liesl. *Chicago Renaissance: Literature and Art in the Midwest Metropolis.* Yale University Press, 2017.

Otten, Thomas J. "Pauline Hopkins and the Hidden Self of Race." *ELH* 59, no. 1 (Spring 1992): 227–56.

Ottley, Roi. "Handkerchief Head, Female." *Chicago Defender,* September 10, 1955, 8.

———. "What's Wrong with Negro Women." *Negro Digest* 9, no. 2 (December 1950): 71–75.

Palmer-Mehta, Valerie. "'We Are All Bound Up Together': Frances Harper and Feminist Theory." In *Black Women's Intellectual Traditions,* edited by Kristin Waters and Carol B. Conaway, 192–215. Brandeis University Press, 2022.

Park, Robert E., and Ernest W. Burgess. *Introduction to the Science of Sociology.* University of Chicago Press, 1921.

Parry, Tyler D. "The Politics of Plagiarism: Roots, Margaret Walker, and Alex Haley." In *Reconsidering Roots: Race, Politics, and Memory,* edited by Erica L. Ball and Kellie Carter Jackson, 43–52. University of Georgia Press, 2017.

Parten, Bennett. "'The Science of Human Rights': American Abolitionism and the Language of Human Rights." *Slavery & Abolition* 44, no. 2 (2023): 377–93.

Patterson, Orlando. *Slavery and Social Death: A Comparative Study.* Harvard University Press, 1982.

Patterson, Tiffany Ruby. *Zora Neale Hurston and a History of Southern Life.* Temple University Press, 2005.

Perry, Imani. *Looking for Lorraine: The Radiant and Radical Life of Lorraine Hansberry.* Beacon Press, 2018.

———. *More Beautiful and More Terrible: The Embrace and Transcendence of Racial Inequality in the United States.* New York University Press, 2011.

Petry, Ann. "Ann Petry." In *Contemporary Authors Autobiography Series,* vol. 6, 253–69. Gale Research Company, 1988.

———. "Ann Petry." Interview by John O'Brien. *Interviews with Black Writers,* edited by John O'Brien, 153–63. Liveright, 1973.

———. "Ann Petry Startled by Controversy." Interview. *Roanoke Times,* August 16, 1953, 20.

———. "Ann Petry Talks about First Novel." Interview by James Ivy. *The Crisis* 53, no. 2 (February 1946): 48–49.

———. "The Common Ground." 1965. In *Horn Book Reflections on Children's Books and Reading; Selected from Eighteen Years of the Horn Book Magazine, 1949–1966,* edited by Elinor Whitney Field, 67–72. Horn Book, 1969.

———. "First Novel." Interview. *Ebony* 1, no. 6 (April 1946): 35–39.

———. "A *MELUS* Interview: Ann Petry—The New England Connection." Interview by Mark K. Wilson. *MELUS: Multi-Ethnic Literature of the United States* 15, no. 2 (1988): 71–84.

———. *The Narrows.* 1953. Mariner, 1999.

———. "The Novel as Social Criticism." In *The Writer's Book,* edited by Helen R. Hull, 32–39. Harper, 1950.

———. *The Street.* 1946. Mariner, 1991.

———. "What's Wrong with Negro Men?" *Negro Digest* 5 (March 1947): 4–7.

Petry, Elisabeth. *At Home Inside: A Daughter's Tribute to Ann Petry.* University Press of Mississippi, 2009.

Plant, Deborah G. "The Benedict-Hurston Connection." *CLA Journal* 46, no. 4 (June 2003): 435–56.

Platt, Tony. "E. Franklin Frazier and Daniel Patrick Moynihan: Setting the Record Straight." *Crime, Law and Social Change* 11, no. 3 (1987): 265–77.

Poston, Carol H. "Childbirth in Literature." *Feminist Studies* 4, no. 2 (June 1978): 18–31.

Pratt, Lloyd. *The Strangers Book: The Human of African American Literature.* University of Pennsylvania Press, 2015.

Puig de la Bellacasa, Maria. *Matters of Care: Speculative Ethics in More than Human Worlds.* University of Minnesota Press, 2017.

Quashie, Kevin. *Black Aliveness, or a Poetics of Being.* Duke University Press, 2021.

Rabinowitz, Paula. "Pulping Ann Petry: The Case of *Country Place*: Ann Petry and the Literary Left." In *Revising the Blueprint: Ann Petry and the Literary Left,* edited by Alex Lubin, 49–71. University of Mississippi Press, 2007.

"Race, Gender, and Generations: A Roundtable Discussion." *Women's Review of Books* 34, no. 2 (March/April 2017): 3–10.

Ragan, Marjorie. "Melodrama of the Racial Angle." Review of *The Narrows,* by Ann Petry. *News and Observer* (Raleigh, NC), September 13, 1953, sec. 4, p. 5.

Randall, Dudley. "Black Publisher, Black Writer, an Answer." *Negro Digest* 24, no. 5 (March 1975): 32–37.

Raynaud, Claudine. "Changing Texts: Censorship, 'Reality,' and Fiction in *Native Son*." In *Richard Wright: New Readings in the 21st Century*, edited by Alice Mikal Craven, 171–92. Palgrave Macmillan, 2011.

Reagon, Bernice Johnson. "Coalition Politics: Turning the Century." In *Home Girls: A Black Feminist Anthology*, edited by Barbara Smith, 343–55. 1983. Rutgers University Press, 2000.

Redding, J. Saunders. "The Negro Writer—Shadow and Substance." *Phylon* 11, no. 4 (4th Quarter, 1950): 371–73.

Reddy, Chandan. *Freedom with Violence: Race, Sexuality, and the US State*. Duke University Press, 2011.

Reid-Pharr, Robert F. *Archives of Flesh: African America, Spain, and Post-Humanist Critique*. New York University Press, 2016.

———. *Once You Go Black: Choice, Desire, and the Black American Intellectual*. New York University Press, 2007.

Resnikoff, Ned. "Historic Fast Food Strike Draws Lessons from MLK's Last Campaign." MSNBC, April 4, 2013. https://www.msnbc.com/all-in/historic-fast-food-strike-draws-lessons-msna55814.

Retman, Sonnet. *Real Folks: Race and Genre in the Great Depression*. Duke University Press, 2011.

Review of *Maud Martha*, by Gwendolyn Brooks. *Bulletin from Virginia Kirkus' Bookshop Service* 11, no. 14 (July 1953): 458.

Rich, Charlotte J. *Transcending the New Woman: Multiethnic Narratives of the Progressive Era*. University of Missouri Press, 2009.

Robinson, Marius. "Women's Rights Convention: Sojourner Truth." *Anti-Slavery Bugle*, June 21, 1851, 160.

Rubin, Rachel, and James Smethurst. "Ann Petry's 'New Mirror.'" In *Revising the Blueprint: Ann Petry and the Literary Left*, edited by Alex Lubin, 15–34. University of Mississippi Press, 2007.

Ruffin, Josephine St. Pierre. "Address of Josephine St. P. Ruffin, President of Conference." *The Woman's Era* 2, no. 5 (August 1895): 13–15.

Rusert, Britt. "Delany's Comet: Fugitive Science and the Speculative Imaginary of Emancipation." *American Quarterly* 65, no. 4 (December 2013): 799–829.

Rushdy, Ashraf H. A. "The Neo-Slave Narrative." In *Cambridge Companion to the African American Novel*, edited by Maryemma Graham, 87–105. Cambridge University Press, 2004.

Samatar, Sofia. "Toward a Planetary History of Afrofuturism." *Research in African Literatures* 48, no. 4 (2017): 175–91.

Saunders, Catherine E. "Makers or Bearers of Meaning? Sex and the Struggle for Self-Definition in Ralph Ellison's *Invisible Man*." *Critical Matrix* 5, no. 1 (1989): 1–28.

Sawaya, Francesca. *Modern Women, Modern Work: Domesticity, Professionalism, and American Writing, 1890–1950*. University of Pennsylvania Press, 2004.

Schneider, John W. "Remaking the Renaissance Man: General Education and the Golden Age of the American University." *American Quarterly* 73, no. 1 (March 2021): 53–74.

Schrager, Cynthia D. "Pauline Hopkins and William James: The New Psychology and the Politics of Race." In *The Unruly Voice: Rediscovering Pauline Elizabeth Hopkins*, edited by John Cullen Gruesser, 182–209. University of Illinois Press, 1996.

Schuyler, George. "The Negro-Art Hokum." 1926. In *Within the Circle: An Anthology of African American Literary Criticism from the Harlem Renaissance to the Present*, edited by Angelyn Mitchell, 51–54. Duke University Press, 1994.

Scott, Darieck. *Extravagant Abjection: Blackness, Power, and Sexuality in the African American Literary Imagination.* New York University Press, 2010.

Scott, Eleanor M. "In the Narrows." Review of *The Narrows,* by Ann Petry. *Providence Sunday Journal,* August 16, 1953, sec. 6, p. 8.

Sehgal, Parul. "May's Book Club Pick: Two by Ann Petry, a Writer Who Believed in Art That Delivers a Message." Review of *"The Street," "The Narrows,"* edited by Farah Jasmine Griffin. *New York Times,* April 16, 2019. https://www.nytimes.com/2019/04/16/books/review-street-narrows-ann-petry.html.

Sharpe, Christina. *In the Wake: On Blackness and Being.* Duke University Press, 2016.

"Sheila Kaye-Smith's Sequel to *Joanna Godden.*" Review of *Joanna Godden Married,* by Sheila Kaye-Smith. *New York Times,* October 24, 1926.

Sherrard-Johnson, Cherene. "City Place/Country Place: Negotiating Class Geographies in Ann Petry's Writing." In *Black Harlem and the Jewish Lower East Side: Narratives Out of Time,* edited by Catherine Rottenberg, 65–85. State University of New York Press, 2013.

———. *Portraits of the New Negro Woman: Visual and Literary Culture in the Harlem Renaissance.* Rutgers University Press, 2007.

Shinn, Thelma J. "Women in the Novels of Ann Petry." *Critique: Studies in Contemporary Fiction* 16, no. 1 (1974): 110–20.

Shockley, Evie. *Renegade Poetics: Black Aesthetics and Formal Innovation in African American Poetry.* University of Iowa Press, 2011.

Smith, Barbara. "Barbara Smith." In *How We Get Free: Black Feminism and the Combahee River Collective,* edited by Keeanga-Yamahtta Taylor, 29–69. Haymarket Books, 2017.

———. "Black Women Writers" syllabus. 1973. In *But Some of Us Are Brave: Black Women's Studies,* edited by Akasha (Gloria T.) Hull, Patricia Bell-Scott, and Barbara Smith, 367–68. Feminist Press, 2015.

———. "Toward a Black Feminist Criticism." 1977. In *But Some of Us Are Brave: Black Women's Studies,* edited by Akasha (Gloria T.) Hull, Patricia Bell-Scott, and Barbara Smith, 157–75. Feminist Press, 2015.

Smith, C. Alphonso. "Dialect Writers." In *Cambridge History of American Literature,* vol. 2, edited by William Peterfield Trent et al., 347–66. G. P. Putnam's Sons, 1918.

Smith, William Gardner. "The Negro Writer: Pitfalls and Compensations." *Phylon* 11, no. 4 (4th Quarter, 1950): 297–303.

Sollors, Werner. Foreword to *Race and the Rhetoric of Resistance,* by Jeffrey B. Ferguson, ix–xiii. Rutgers University Press, 2021.

Soper, Kate. *Humanism and Anti-Humanism.* Open Court, 1986.

Spelman, Elizabeth V. *Fruits of Sorrow: Framing Our Attention to Suffering.* Beacon Press, 1997.

Spillers, Hortense. "Mama's Baby, Papa's Maybe: An American Grammar Book." *Diacritics* 17, no. 2 (Summer 1987): 65–81.

Steele, Catherine Knight. "Black Feminist Pleasure on TikTok: An Ode to Hurston's 'Characteristics of Negro Expression.'" *Women's Studies in Communication* 44, no. 4 (2021): 463–69.

Stevenson, Pascha A. "Of One Blood, of One Race: Pauline Hopkins's Engagement of Racialized Science." *CLA Journal* 45, no. 4 (June 2002): 422–43.

Stewart, Catherine A. *Long Past Slavery: Representing Race in the Federal Writers' Project.* University of North Carolina Press, 2016.

Strain, Tracy Heather, dir. *Lorraine Hansberry: Sighted Eyes/Feeling Heart.* PBS American Masters Series, 2018.

Sundquist, Eric J. *To Wake the Nations: Race in the Making of American Literature.* Harvard University Press, 1993.

Swinnerton, Frank. "Miss Kaye-Smith, Galsworthy Lead Popularity Parade." *Chicago Daily Tribune,* May 5, 1928, 16.

Sylvander, Carolyn W. "Ralph Ellison's *Invisible Man* and Female Stereotypes." *Negro American Literature Forum* 9, no. 3 (Fall 1975): 77–79.

Tate, Claudia. *Domestic Allegories of Political Desire: The Black Heroine's Text at the Turn of the Century.* Oxford University Press, 1992.

———. "Nella Larsen's *Passing*: A Problem of Interpretation." *Black American Literature Forum* 14, no. 4 (Winter 1980): 142–46.

Taylor, Charles. "The Politics of Recognition." In *Multiculturalism: Examining the Politics of Recognition,* edited by Amy Gutman, 25–73. Princeton University Press, 1994.

Taylor, Keeanga-Yamahtta. Introduction to *How We Get Free: Black Feminism and the Combahee River Collective,* edited by Keeanga-Yamahtta Taylor, 1–14. Haymarket Books, 2017.

———. "Until Black Women Are Free, None of Us Will Be Free." *New Yorker,* July 20, 2020. https://www.newyorker.com/news/our-columnists/until-black-women-are-free-none-of-us-will-be-free.

Thaggert, Miriam. *Riding Jane Crow: African American Women on the American Railroad.* University of Illinois Press, 2022.

Thompson, Era Bell. "Negro Publications and the Writer." *Phylon* 11, no. 4 (4th Quarter, 1950): 304–6.

Thornton, Hortense E. "Sexism as Quagmire: Nella Larsen's *Quicksand*." *CLA Journal* 16, no. 3 (March 1973): 285–301.

Thorsson, Courtney. *The Sisterhood: How a Network of Black Women Writers Changed American Culture.* Columbia University Press, 2023.

Thurman, Wallace. "Fire Burns: A Department of Comment." *Fire!! A Quarterly Devoted to the Younger Negro Artists* 1, no. 1 (1926): 47–48.

———. *Infants of the Spring.* 1932. Dover Publications, 2013.

———. "Negro Artists and the Negro." *New Republic* 52, no. 665 (31 August 1927): 37–39.

Tillman, N. P. "The Threshold of Maturity." *Phylon* 11, no. 4 (4th Quarter, 1950): 387–88.

Tompkins, Lucille "In the Florida Glades." Review of *Their Eyes Were Watching God,* by Zora Neale Hurston. *New York Times Book Review,* September 26, 1937, 29.

Toppins, Aggie. "Beyond the Bauhaus: I AM A MAN." AIGA Design Educators Community, August 18, 2020. https://educators.aiga.org/beyond-the-bauhaus-i-am-a-man/.

Tracy, Steven C. Introduction to *Writers of the Black Chicago Renaissance,* edited by Steven C. Tracy, 1–14. University of Illinois Press, 2012.

Trilling, Lionel. *The Liberal Imagination.* 1950. New York Review of Books, 2008.

Tronto, Joan. *Moral Boundaries: A Political Argument for an Ethic of Care.* Routledge, 2015.

VanderHaagen, Sara C. "'A Grand Sisterhood': Black American Women Speakers at the 1893 World's Congress of Representative Women." *Quarterly Journal of Speech* 107, no. 1 (2021): 1–25.

Von Eschen, Penny M. *Race Against Empire: Black Americans and Anticolonialism, 1937–1957.* Cornell University Press, 2019.

V.P.H. "New England Novel Fine Despite Central Theme Flaw." Review of *The Narrows*, by Ann Petry. *Omaha World-Herald Magazine*, September 6, 1953, sec. G, p. 20.

Wald, Alan M. *Exiles from a Future Time: The Forging of the Mid-Twentieth-Century Literary Left.* University of North Carolina Press, 2002.

Walker, Alice. "African-American Literature: Black Women Writers" syllabus. 1972. In *But Some of Us Are Brave: Black Women's Studies*, edited by Akasha (Gloria T.) Hull, Patricia Bell-Scott, and Barbara Smith, 376–78. Feminist Press, 2015.

———. "In Search of Our Mothers' Gardens: The Creativity of Black Women in the South." *Ms. Magazine* (May 1974): 64–70, 105.

———. *In Search of Our Mothers' Gardens: Womanist Prose*. 1983. Houghton Mifflin Harcourt, 2004.

———. "Looking for Zora." 1975. In *I Love Myself When I Am Laughing . . . And Then Again When I Am Looking Mean and Impressive*, edited by Alice Walker, 297–313. Feminist Press, 1979.

———. "On Refusing to Be Humbled by Second Place in a Contest You Did Not Design: A Tradition by Now." In *I Love Myself When I Am Laughing . . . And Then Again When I Am Looking Mean and Impressive*, edited by Alice Walker, 1–5. Feminist Press, 1979.

———. "Zora Neale Hurston—A Cautionary Tale and a Partisan View." Foreword to *Zora Neale Hurston: A Literary Biography*, by Robert E. Hemenway, xi–xvii. University of Illinois Press, 1977.

Walker, Margaret. "The Humanistic Tradition of Afro-American Literature." 1970. In *How I Wrote Jubilee and Other Essays on Life and Literature*, edited by Maryemma Graham, 121–33. Feminist Press, 1990.

———. "Humanities with a Black Focus." 1972. In *On Being Female, Black, and Free: Essays by Margaret Walker, 1932–1992*, edited by Maryemma Graham, 98–107. University of Tennessee Press, 1997.

———. "New Poets." *Phylon* 11, no. 4 (4th Quarter, 1950): 345–54.

———. "On Being Female, Black, and Free." 1980. In *On Being Female, Black, and Free: Essays by Margaret Walker, 1932–1992*, edited by Maryemma Graham, 3–11. University of Tennessee Press, 1997.

———. "Phillis Wheatley and Black Women Writers, 1773–1973." In *On Being Female, Black, and Free: Essays by Margaret Walker, 1932–1992*, edited by Maryemma Graham, 35–40. University of Tennessee Press, 1997.

———. "Reflections on Black Women Writers." In *On Being Female, Black, and Free: Essays by Margaret Walker, 1932–1992*, edited by Maryemma Graham, 41–53. University of Tennessee Press, 1997.

———. *Richard Wright, Daemonic Genius: A Portrait of the Man, a Critical Look at His Work.* Warner Books, 1988.

Wall, Cheryl A. "Jessie Fauset and the Historiography of the Harlem Renaissance." In *Crossing Borders: Essays on Literature, Culture, and Society in Honor of Amritjit Singh*, edited by Tapan Basu and Tasneem Shahnaaz, 149–63. Fairleigh Dickinson University Press, 2017.

———. "*Mules and Men* and Women: Zora Neale Hurston's Strategies of Narration and Visions of Female Empowerment." *Black American Literature Forum* 23, no. 4 (Winter 1989): 661–80.

———. "Passing for What? Aspects of Identity in Nella Larsen's Novels." *Black American Literature Forum* 20, no. 1–2 (Spring–Summer 1986): 97–111.

———. *Women of the Harlem Renaissance*. Indiana University Press, 1995.

Wallinger, Hanna. *Pauline E. Hopkins: A Literary Biography.* University of Georgia Press, 2005.

Walther, Malin LaVon. "Re-Wrighting *Native Son*: Gwendolyn Brooks's Domestic Aesthetic in *Maud Martha*." *Tulsa Studies in Women's Literature* 13, no. 1 (1994): 143–45.

Warren, Kenneth W. "Back to Black: African American Literary Criticism in the Present Moment." *American Literary History* 34, no. 1 (Spring 2022): 369–79.

———. *So Black and Blue: Ralph Ellison and the Occasion of Criticism.* University of Chicago Press, 2003.

———. *What Was African American Literature?* Harvard University Press, 2011.

Washington, Booker T. "Democracy and Education." 1896. In *African-American Social and Political Thought, 1850–1920*, edited by Howard Brotz, 362–71. Routledge, 1991.

———. *Up from Slavery: An Autobiography.* Doubleday, 1901.

Washington, Mary Helen. "Alice Childress, Lorraine Hansberry, and Claudia Jones: Black Women Write the Popular Front." In *Left of the Color Line: Race, Radicalism, and Twentieth-Century Literature of the United States*, edited by Bill Mullen and James Smethurst, 183–204. University of North Carolina Press, 2003.

———. Book Review of *Black Women Novelists: The Development of a Tradition, 1892–1976* by Barbara Christian. *Signs* 8, no. 1 (Autumn 1982): 177–82.

———. *Invented Lives: Narratives of Black Women, 1860–1960.* Anchor, 1987.

———. *The Other Blacklist: The African American Literary and Cultural Left of the 1950s.* Columbia University Press, 2014.

———. "'Taming All That Anger Down': Rage and Silence in Gwendolyn Brooks's *Maud Martha*." *The Massachusetts Review* 24, no. 2 (Summer 1983): 453–66.

———. "Uplifting the Women and the Race: The Forerunners—Harper and Hopkins." In *Invented Lives: Narratives of Black Women, 1860–1960*, edited by Mary Helen Washington, 73–86. Anchor Books, 1987.

———. "Zora Neale Hurston: A Woman Half in Shadow." Introduction to *I Love Myself When I Am Laughing . . . And Then Again When I Am Looking Mean and Impressive*, edited by Alice Walker, 7–25. Feminist Press, 1979.

Watson, Reginald. "The Tragic Mulatto Image in Charles Chesnutt's *The House Behind the Cedars* and Nella Larsen's *Passing*." *CLA Journal* 46, no. 1 (September 2002): 48–71.

Wechsler, James A. "Sound Barrier." *New York Post*, June 22, 1964, 26.

Weheliye, Alexander G. "'Feenin': Posthuman Voices in Contemporary Black Popular Music." *Social Text* 20, no. 2 (Summer 2002): 21–47.

———. *Habeas Viscus: Racializing Assemblages, Biopolitics, and Black Feminist Theories of the Human.* Duke University Press, 2014.

Wells-Barnett, Ida B. "Booker T. Washington and His Critics." *World Today* 6 (April 1904): 518–21.

———. *A Red Record.* 1898. In *Women's Political and Social Thought: An Anthology*, edited by Hilda Smith and Berenice Carroll, 271–81. Indiana University Press, 2000.

———. "A Woman Lynched." *New York Times*, 20 August 1886, 3.

Wesseling, Elisabeth, Andrea Mei-Ying Wu, and Claudia Nelson. Introduction to *The Routledge Companion to Children's Literature and Culture*, edited by Elisabeth Wesseling, Andrea Mei-Ying Wu, and Claudia Nelson, 1–5. Routledge, 2023.

West, Dorothy. "Alive and Well and Living on the Island of Martha's Vineyard: An Interview with Dorothy West, October 29, 1988." Interview by Katrine Dalsgård. *The Langston Hughes Review* 12, no. 2 (Fall 1993): 28–44.

———. "Conversations with Dorothy West." Interview by Deborah E. McDowell. *The Harlem Renaissance Re-Examined,* edited by Victor A. Kramer, 265–82. AMS Press, 1987.

———. "Dear Reader." *Challenge* 1, no. 4 (January 1936): 38.

West, M. Genevieve. "Subversions of Boasian Anthropology in Zora Neale Hurston's Great Migration Fiction and Ethnography." In *African American Literature in Transition 1930–1940,* edited by Eve Dunbar and Ayesha K. Hardison, 154–76. Cambridge University Press, 2022.

Wilderson, Frank B., III. *Red, White & Black: Cinema and the Structure of U.S. Antagonisms.* Duke University Press, 2010.

Williams, Linda. *Playing the Race Card: Melodramas of Black and White from Uncle Tom to O. J. Simpson.* Princeton University Press, 2001.

Williams, Sherley Anne. "Papa Dick and Sister-Woman: Reflections on Women in the Fiction of Richard Wright." In *American Novelists Revisited: Essays in Feminist Criticism,* edited by Fritz Fleischmann, 394–415. G. K. Hall, 1982.

Winslow, Henry F. "Soft Meditations." Review of *Maud Martha,* by Gwendolyn Brooks. *The Crisis* 61, no. 2 (February 1954): 114.

Wolfe, Cary. *What Is Posthumanism?* University of Minnesota Press, 2009.

Wright, Richard. "Between Laughter and Tears." Review of *Their Eyes Were Watching God,* by Zora Neale Hurston. *New Masses* 25, no. 2 (October 1937): 22, 25.

———. "Blueprint for Negro Writing." 1937. In *Within the Circle: An Anthology of African American Literary Criticism from the Harlem Renaissance to the Present,* edited by Angelyn Mitchell, 97–106. Duke University Press, 1994.

———. "How 'Bigger' Was Born." 1940. In *Native Son,* by Richard Wright, 431–62. Harper Perennial, 2005.

———. "I Tried to Be a Communist." 1944. In *The God That Failed,* edited by Richard Crossman, 116–64. Bantam, 1952.

———. Introduction to *Black Metropolis: A Study of Negro Life in a Northern City,* by St. Clair Drake and Horace R. Cayton, xvii–xxxiv. 1945. Harper & Row, 1962.

———. *Native Son.* 1940. Perennial Classics, 1998.

———. *12 Million Black Voices.* 1941. Basic Books, 2008.

Wurst, Gayle. "Ben Franklin in Harlem: The Drama of Deferral in Ann Petry's *The Street.*" In *Deferring a Dream: Literary Sub-Versions of the American Columbiad,* edited by Ernst Rudin, 1–23. Birkhäuser, 1994.

Wynter, Sylvia. "Unsettling the Coloniality of Being/Power/Truth/Freedom." *CR: The New Centennial Review* 3, no. 3 (2003): 257–337.

Yoon, Irene. "The Art of Stealing: Plagiarism and the Modernist Bounds of Authenticity." BA thesis, University of Chicago, 2006.

INDEX

Abbie Crunch (fictional character), 127, 132, 133, 134–38
adaptation and appropriation, 60, 60n26, 60n28, 65, 178. *See also* imitation; Signifyin(g)
Africa World Press, 28n3
African American literary movements, male-centered, 20–21, 22, 171
Afropessimism, 12
agency, 5, 10, 97–98, 105, 120–21, 129, 136–37
aliveness, aesthetics of, 12
Allen, Amy, 106–7
Allison & Busby, 28n3
"Am I Not a Woman and a Sister?" engraving, 15, 16 fig. 1
American Dilemma, The (Myrdal), 147
"American Family Brown" (Brooks), 157, 158
American Museum of Unnatural History, The, 101–2, 109
Amsterdam News, 115
anger and rage, Black women's, 153, 162
animal/human binary, 102–4, 105, 108–10
Anne Grey (fictional character), 77, 78, 81

Annie Allen (Brooks), 142, 156–58
Annie Poole (fictional character), 62, 63, 79–80, 81, 82
anthropology and anthropologists, 88–92, 99–100
Association of Artists for Freedom forum, 26–27, 172–73, 178, 179–81, 179n41
Aswell, Edward, 155
"Atlanta Exposition Address" (Washington), 36–37
Aubrey Livingston (fictional character), 33, 47, 48, 49
Audrey Denney (fictional character), 78–79, 82
authenticity: disruption of, 82–83; Fauset on, 69; gendered aspects of, 73–74; Hurston and, 83; imitation and, 69–70; Johnson and, 69n68; Larsen's fictions and, 58; *Passing* and, 77–78; *Quicksand* and, 56–57; recognition politics and, 70–71, 72; in "Sanctuary," 81. *See also* imitation; particularity; primitivism
Autobiography of an Ex-Colored Man, The (Johnson), 64, 68, 69n68

Baldwin, James, 112, 114, 115n25, 118–19, 122, 171

"Ballad of Pearl May Lee" (Brooks), 156, 159

Bambara, Toni Cade, 4, 173

Baraka, Amiri (LeRoi Jones), 173, 175–76, 179

Barnes, Albert C., 59

Barrett, Lindon, 135

Berry, Michael, 134

Big Sea, The (Hughes), 75

Bigger Thomas (fictional character), 113, 118–19, 120, 122, 129, 159, 162. See also *Native Son* (Wright); Wright, Richard

"Birth" (Nin), 164n128

Black Aesthetic, The (Gayle), 142, 176n19

Black Arts Movement, 21n102, 143–44, 149, 173

Black Boy (Wright), 111n2

"Black Boys and Native Sons" (Howe), 114–15

Black Chicago Renaissance, 26, 142–43, 145, 146, 149–52. See also Brooks, Gwendolyn

Black Classic Press, 28n3

Black distinctiveness, 68, 69

Black female sexuality, 73, 88, 93, 95–99. See also pleasure

Black female voices, silencing, 49–51

Black feminism: care and, 115–16; coalitions and, 7, 140, 179, 180; critiques of, 8; Hansberry and, 177; humanism of, 3–4, 7–8, 9–10, 178, 181–82; intersectionality and, 6. See also gender; *and specific theorists*

Black folk art and folklore, 67–69, 87–90, 89n20, 91n35

Black histories, hidden, 44, 51–53

Black humanistic vision, 1–2, 11–13, 44–45, 145–46, 178, 181–82. See also Brooks, Gwendolyn; Hansberry, Lorraine; Hopkins, Pauline; Hurston, Zora Neale; Larsen, Nella; Petry, Ann

Black Lives Matter movement, 3, 181

Black male writers: Black Chicago Renaissance and, 114; female peers of, 74–75; gender and, 20–22; Hurston and, 75–76; masculinity and, 113, 114, 119, 134, 136, 150; protest fiction and, 115. See also *specific writers*

Black Metropolis (Drake), 112

Black optimism, 12

Black periodicals, 20, 20nn95–96, 70–71. See also *specific titles*

Black publishers, 28, 28n3, 169, 170. See also *specific publishers*

"Black Revolution and the White Backlash, The" forum, 26–27, 172–73, 178, 179–81, 179n41

Black studies, 2–3, 6, 12

Black Studies as Human Studies (Joyce), 3n12

Black Woman, The (Bambara), 173

Black Woman's Era, 32

Black women's club movement, 18, 38–39

Black women's studies, 6

Black World, 76

Black writing groups, 150–52

blood brotherhood, 43–44

"Blueprint for Negro Writing" (Wright), 14, 112, 113–14, 155

Boas, Franz, 88–92, 93–94, 95–96, 101, 102–3, 109

Bock, Frederick, 169

Bogle-L'Ouverture Publications, 28n3

Bone, Robert, 75, 111

Bonner, Marita, 73–74

Book of American Negro Poetry, The (Johnson), 20n99, 68

Boone House, 151

Boston Evening Transcript, 56

Bourne, George, 15, 16 fig. 1

Boyd, Marion, 55

Boyd, Melba Joyce, 144, 151

Braithwaite, William Stanley, 68

brave humanism, 4–6, 24, 27, 178, 181–82

Breman, Paul, 151

Br'er Rabbit stories, 103

British Society for the Abolition of the Slave Trade, 14

Broadside Press, 28n3, 143n13, 169, 170

Brooks, Gwendolyn: career of, 144–45, 168–70; Hansberry compared to, 178; humanism in relation to, 153–54; "I AM A MAN" iconography in relation to, 16; on *Maud Martha*, 158–59, 167, 168; *New Negro Poets* and, 141–42, 147; relations with Wright, 156; role in Black Chicago Renaissance, 151; role in marketing, 154–56; significance of, 4, 5, 26, 146, 170; on universality, 141–42; vulnerability and, 152–54; Wright and, 158. *See also* Brooks, Gwendolyn, works of

Brooks, Gwendolyn, works of: *Annie Allen,* 142, 156; "Ballad of Pearl May Lee," 156, 159, 166; *Bronzeville Boys and Girls,* 158; "Gay Chaps at the Bar," 167; *In the Mecca,* 169; "Poets Who Are Negroes," 146–47; "The Rise of Maud Martha," 167–68; *A Street in Bronzeville,* 142, 154–56; "Why Negro Women Leave Home," 116; *The World of Gwendolyn Brooks,* 168, 169. See also *Maud Martha* (Brooks)

brotherhood, blood, 43–44

brotherhood, human, 31, 33, 38–40, 40n54, 44–47, 48–54

Brown Girl, Brownstones (Marshall), 161n111, 173

Brown v. Board, 86, 87

Browne, Simone, 163

Browning, Alice, 20n95, 151

Burgess, Ernest, 117, 119

Burr, Zofia, 170

Burroughs, Margaret, 151

But Some of Us Are Brave (Hull), 6, 9, 179, 181–82

cakewalk dance, 65

Callahan, Cynthia, 137–38

Cambridge History of American Literature, 59

Candace (fictional character), 50–51

Cane (Toomer), 54

Carby, Hazel, 23, 32

care networks: Black feminist, 115–16; Hansberry and, 178; intraracial, 136; Lutie and, 130; in *The Narrows,* 132, 137, 139; nature of, 121; in *The Street,* 126, 128–29

Century, The, 55, 55n2

Césaire, Aimé, 12

Challenge, 20, 113, 114

"Changing Same, The" (McDowell), 23

"Characteristics of Negro Expression" (Hurston), 83

Charles, John, 152

Charlie Vance (fictional character), 33, 42–43, 53

Chesnutt, Charles, 38–39

Chicago Public Library Hall Branch, 143, 151

childbirth writing, 164n128, 164n132

children's literature, 139, 168, 169

Choi, Yoon Young, 134, 136

Christian, Barbara, 13–14, 143, 160

citizenship, 24, 30, 31

civil rights movement, 15, 18, 164n132

Clansman, The (Dixon), 45

Clare Kendry (fictional character), 61, 77–78, 79, 81–83

Clark, Keith, 124

Clark, Suzanne, 91

Clayton, Horace R., Jr., 112

Coal (Lorde), 170–71

coalition-building, 7, 140, 179–80

Colbert, Soyica Diggs, 23, 177

Cold War and unlabeled universalism, 142–43, 145, 147–50

Colored American Magazine, 20, 32, 45–46, 47, 50, 53–54, 54n127

Combahee River Collective (CRC), 6, 7, 179

"Common Ground, The" (Petry), 139

Communist Party of the United States of America (CPUSA), 92, 110, 112

Congress of Colored Women, 39

Contending Forces (Hopkins), 28, 38, 39, 46n90, 50

Cooper, Anna Julia, 3, 20n96, 20n99, 38–39, 51, 89n20

Cooper, Brittney, 3–4, 22, 27, 181

Coupling Convention, The (duCille), 23

"Courts and the Negro, The" (Chesnutt), 38–39

Crenshaw, Kimberlé, 6, 17

Crisis, The, 20, 54, 69, 70, 71, 148

"Criteria of Negro Art" (Du Bois), 68

Cruse, Harold, 173, 174, 175

Cullen, Countee, 55–56

cultural relativism, 89–90

Daniels, Melissa, 51

Danner, Margaret, 151
"Dark Races of the Twentieth Century, The" (Hopkins), 39–40
Davie, Sharon, 95, 105, 108
Davis, Allison, 70–71
Davis, Jane, 122
Death of a Salesman (Miller), 178
Declaration of Independence, US, 10, 35
Dee, Ruby, 180n48
Delany, Martin, 33
Denning, Michael, 92
Dianthe Lusk (fictional character), 33, 43, 47, 48–50, 51–53
difference and sameness binary framework, 22, 31, 34, 46
"Dilemma of the Negro Author, The" (Johnson), 68
distinctiveness, Black, 68, 69
Dixon, Thomas, 45
Doll's House, A (Ibsen), 60n26
Drake, Kimberly, 127, 128
Drake, St. Clair, 112, 116, 117, 134
Dred Scott v. Sandford, 35
Drinking Gourd, The (Hansberry), 176
Du Bois, Shirley Graham, 20, 20n96
Du Bois, W. E. B.: Bonner compared to, 74; Cooper and, 20n99; "Criteria of Negro Art," 68; on double consciousness, 40; on Helga Crane, 69; on *Home to Harlem*, 69; Petry in relation to, 120; on recognition, 57; on social equality, 18–19; *The Souls of Black Folk*, 20, 54, 67–68, 100; "Strivings of the Negro People," 47, 54
duCille, Ann, 14, 23, 61, 73
Duck, Leigh Anne, 87, 95
Dunbar, Eve, 163
Dunbar, Paul Laurence, 59
DuSable Museum of African American History and Art, 151
Dust Tracks on a Road (Hurston), 101

Early, Sarah J. W., 32
Eatonville community, 106
Ebony, 20, 20n96, 162
Edwards, Erica, 152–53

Eliot, T. S., 59
Ellison, Ralph, 112, 114–15, 119, 130–32, 171
Eminent Victorians (Strachey), 161n113
empathy and identification, 132, 162
Engle, Paul, 142
English, Daylanne, 19, 34
Enlightenment man, 6–7, 10–11, 12, 13, 95, 97. See also humanism, Western
Estes, Steve, 14
ethic of care, 128–29, 137
ethic of justice, 129, 137
eugenics, 45, 102
Ewing, Eve L., 93
exclusionary humanism. See humanism, Western

familial language, 44–45
Fanon, Frantz, 12
Fauset, Jessie, 20, 20n95, 52–53, 54, 60n26, 69, 70, 74–75
Federal Writers' Project, 92
female deference, 48
FIRE!!, 71
Fisk University Black Writers Conference, 169, 173
folk art and folklore, Black, 67–69, 87–90, 89n20, 91n35, 92
Fortune, 172
Forum, The, 55, 55n2, 65
Fourteenth Amendment, 35
Franklin, Benjamin, 124, 125
Frazier, E. Franklin, 117
Freedom, 150, 175, 175n16
Freedomways, 20, 20n96, 150, 175

Gabbin, Joanne, 166
Gage, Frances, 16
Gaines, Kevin, 48
Garvey, Amy Jacques, 72n85
Garza, Alicia, 3
Gates, Henry Louis, Jr., 28n1, 65, 67, 103, 130
"Gay Chaps at the Bar" (Brooks), 161n109, 167
Gaylard, Rob, 10

gender: authenticity and, 73–74; Black pathology in relation to, 117–18; hierarchies, 48; "I AM A MAN" iconography in relation to, 15–16, 17 fig. 2; male-centered literary movements, 20–21, 22; male-female identification, 132; masculinity, 113, 114, 119, 134, 136, 150; *Native Son* in relation to, 121–22; primitivism in relation to, 76; protest fiction in relation to, 115; writing groups and, 150–51. *See also* Black female sexuality; Black feminism

General Federation of Women's Clubs (GFWC), 45–46

Giddings, Paula, 32

Gillman, Susan, 29–30, 43

Gilroy, Paul, 122

Giovanni, Nikki, 3

Givens Foundation for African American Literature, 29

Googasian, Victoria, 105, 108

Govan, Sandra, 19

Great American Novel (Williams), 60n28

Griffin, Farah Jasmine, 122

Hale, Grace Elizabeth, 20n99

Haley, Alex, 2

Hall, Stuart, 10

Hampton Folklore Society, 89n20, 91n35

Hansberry, Lorraine: at Association of Artists for Freedom forum, 172, 173, 178, 179; Black feminists and, 177; "I AM A MAN" iconography in relation to, 16; letter to *The Ladder*, 176–77, 182; *A Raisin in the Sun*, 174–76, 178; significance of, 4, 5, 26–27, 178, 181–82; on white liberals, 179–80

Hardison, Ayesha, 21, 123, 127, 128, 130, 135, 137

Harlem Renaissance writers: gendered aspects of, 73–75; goals of, 57, 67, 82; recognition politics and, 57, 72; universality in relation to, 58, 69; white audiences and, 70; *Women of the Harlem Renaissance*, 23. *See also* authenticity; *and specific writers*

Harlem Writers Guild, 143–44, 150

Harper, Frances E. W., 28, 32, 33

Harper & Brothers, 154–58, 169

Harriet Tubman (Petry), 139–40

Harris, Trudier, 122

Harsh, Vivian, 151

Hartman, Saidiya, 19, 30, 31, 97

Hathaway, Rosemary, 66

Haviland, Beverly, 60n26, 79

Helga Crane (fictional character), 56, 61, 69, 76–77, 78, 79, 82

Hemenway, Robert, 87

Henry, Alvin, 97

Hentoff, Nat, 180

Heritage Press, 151

hidden Black histories, 44, 51–53

hidden self, the, 40–48, 40n56, 51

Higashida, Cheryl, 122

Hill Collins, Patricia, 7–8, 24n113

Hoeller, Hildegard, 60, 60n28, 67

Hoffman, Frederick L., 33

Home Girls (Smith), 7

Home to Harlem (McKay), 69

hooks, bell, 181

Hopkins, Pauline: *Colored American Magazine* and, 20, 20n95, 45–46, 53–54; *Contending Forces*, 9n39, 28, 38–39, 50; "The Dark Races of the Twentieth Century," 40; Hansberry compared to, 177–78; human family vision of, 44–47; "I AM A MAN" iconography in relation to, 16; *The Magazine Novels of Pauline Hopkins*, 28n1; NACW and, 32; *A Primer of Facts Pertaining to the Early Greatness of the African Race*, 33–34; relations with Booker T. Washington, 50; significance of, 4, 5, 24; "Talma Gordon," 44. *See also Of One Blood* (Hopkins)

"How 'Bigger' Was Born" (Wright), 113

"How It Feels to Be Colored Me" (Hurston), 98

Howe, Irving, 114–15, 119

Hughes, Langston, 57, 61, 72, 75–76, 86, 114, 141

Hull, Akasha (Gloria T.), 6

human brotherhood, 31, 35, 38–40, 40n54, 44–47, 48–54. *See also* humanity, shared; universality

human rights and the rights of man, 6–7, 10–11. *See also* Enlightenment man; humanism, Western human/animal binary, 102–4

humanism, brave, 178, 181–82. *See also* Brooks, Gwendolyn; Hansberry, Lorraine; Hopkins, Pauline; Hurston, Zora Neale; Larsen, Nella; Petry, Ann

humanism, Western: animal/human binary in relation to, 103, 105; Black women's literature in relation to, 13–14; characteristics of, 10; Enlightenment man, 6–7, 10–11, 12, 13, 95, 97; human rights and the right of man, 6–7, 10–11; reimagining of, 4–6, 181; Renaissance Man in, 147, 153; sovereignty in, 163–64; as universal, 30–31. *See also* universality

"Humanistic Tradition of Afro-American Literature, The" (Walker), 1

humanity, shared, 11, 40, 53, 94, 101. *See also* brotherhood, human; universality

Hurston, Zora Neale: animal/human binary in relation to, 103, 105; authenticity and, 83–84; background of, 88–89; Boas and, 88, 91; and dialect, 86; fieldwork of, 90n29; folk art and, 87–88; folklore work of, 89, 91; Hansberry compared to, 178; "I AM A MAN" iconography in relation to, 16; male writers and, 75–76; and nature, 88, 91, 95, 102–3; and pleasure, 88, 93, 95–96, 97–98, 99; power relations and, 103–5, 110; primitivism and, 87–88; recognition politics and, 87; significance of, 4, 5, 25, 87–88, 99, 102, 110; spy-glass of anthropology in relation to, 99–100; Alice Walker and, 85–86, 87. *See also* Hurston, Zora Neale, works of

Hurston, Zora Neale, works of: "Characteristics of Negro Expression," 83; *Dust Tracks on a Road*, 101; "How It Feels to Be Colored Me," 98; *Mules and Men*, 89, 91, 99–100, 103–5; *Tell My Horse*, 89, 91, 95; "What White Publishers Won't Print," 101–2. See also *Their Eyes Were Watching God* (Hurston)

"I AM A MAN" iconography, 15–16
I AM A (WO)MAN photograph, 17 fig. 2
Ibsen, Henrik, 60n26
imitation, 25, 56, 57, 59–60, 67, 69–70, 73–74, 76
"In Search of Our Mothers' Gardens" (Walker), 2n9, 151
In the Mecca (Brooks), 169

incest, 43–44

Incidents in the Life of a Slave Girl (Jacobs), 60n28

individual uplift, 125, 128, 129–30

inside and outside perspectives, 88, 96–97, 98–99

interracial marriage, 133

intersectionality, 6

Invisible Man (Ellison), 130–31, 132, 134–35

Iola Leroy (Harper), 28

Irene Redfield (fictional character), 61, 77–79, 82

Jackman, Harold, 55–56
Jackson, Esther Cooper, 20, 20n96
Jackson, Lawrence, 142–43, 149
Jackson, Zakiyyah, 11, 13
Jacobs, Harriet, 60n28
Jacobs, Karen, 99–100
James, William, 40n56
Jane Crow era, 4–5, 18–20, 116
Janie Crawford (fictional character), 94–95, 96–97, 100–101, 105–6, 107–8, 109
JanMohamed, Abdul, 122
Jarrett, Gene Andrew, 20
Jenkins, Candice, 21, 115, 123, 125–26, 150, 152
Jim Hammer (fictional character), 61, 62, 63–64, 79–81, 82
Jim Titus (fictional character), 33, 42–43, 80–81
Joanna Godden Married (Kaye-Smith), 55n2
Joe Starks (fictional character), 95–96, 105–6
John O'London's Weekly, 55n2
Johnson, Barbara, 109–10
Johnson, Charles S., 74–75
Johnson, Elise, 58
Johnson, James Weldon, 64, 68–69, 69n68, 71
Jones, LeRoi. *See* Baraka, Amiri (LeRoi Jones)
Joyce, James, 161
Joyce, Joyce A., 3n12
Jubine (fictional character), 133–34

"Kabnis" (Toomer), 64

Kaplan, Carla, 109
Kaye-Smith, Sheila, 55, 61–64, 65n47
Killens, John Oliver, 142, 144, 172, 176n19, 181
King, Martin Luther, Jr., 179
Knight, Catherine, 98

Ladder, The, 177, 182
Ladies' Home Journal, 60n28
Larsen, Nella: "Adrian and Evadne," 60n27; Hansberry compared to, 178; "I AM A MAN" iconography in relation to, 16; *Passing*, 61, 77–78, 79, 82; *Quicksand*, 56–57, 61, 69, 77, 79, 82; on "Sanctuary" scandal, 65; significance of, 4, 5, 24–25, 83. See also "Sanctuary" (Larsen)
Larson, Kelli, 60, 60n28, 80
Lattin, Vernon, 124
Lawrence, Elizabeth, 154–58
"Letter from Birmingham Jail, A" (King), 179
Levenson, Michael, 59
Levy, Builder, 17 fig. 2
liberal humanism. *See* humanism, Western
Lige Moss (fictional character), 93–94
Ligon, Glenn, 15
Lillvis, Kristen, 11, 13
Lipari, Lisbeth, 177
Lipsitz, George, 126, 127
Livingston, Derek Charles, 15
Locke, Alain: on Black artists, 85; on Fauset, 70; *The New Negro*, 58, 59, 68, 73, 74; racial awakening of, 61; *The Survey Graphic*, 54, 55; on *Their Eyes Were Watching God*, 86; treatment of Fauset, 74–75
Lomax, Alan, 89
Lorde, Audre, 13, 150, 153–54, 170–71
Lordi, Emily, 21
Lubin, Alex, 133
Lutie Johnson (fictional character), 120, 122, 123–27, 129–30, 138
lynching, 14–15, 64, 66, 80

Madhubuti, Haki, 142
Magazine Novels of Pauline Hopkins, The (Hopkins), 28n1

Mamie Powther (fictional character), 127, 128, 132–33, 134, 135, 137, 138
"Man Was Lynched Yesterday, A" flag, 14–15
Manne, Kate, 53
Marshall, Paule, 161, 161n111, 173, 178–79
Martin Luther King Memorial March for Union Justice and to End Racism, 17 fig. 2
masculinity, 113, 114, 119, 134, 136, 150. See also gender
Matthews, T. S., 56, 69
Matthews, Victoria Earle, 39
Maud Martha (Brooks): childbirth in, 164–65; Christian on, 161; Lawrence on, 158–59; mouse scene in, 163; *Native Son* compared to, 162; sequel to, 168; significance of, 146, 159–60; *The Street* compared to, 161; universality and, 156; vulnerability in relation to, 163–64; worldview of, 162–63, 166–67. See also Brooks, Gwendolyn; Brooks, Gwendolyn, works of
McDougald, Elise Johnson, 58
McDowell, Deborah, 23, 30, 60n26
McKay, Claude, 69
McKay, Nellie, 135, 136
McKittrick, Katherine, 21
Melamed, Jodi, 147–48
"Melanctha" (Stein), 59, 60
Miller, Arthur, 178
Min (fictional character), 127, 128
Minus, Marian, 113–14
Mira (fictional character), 33, 43, 47, 51–52
Mitchell, Koritha, 21, 22, 53, 94, 153
modernism, white, 59–60
monogenesis, 34
Moody-Turner, Shirley, 91n35
Morgan, Joan, 97–98
Morgan, Stacy, 110, 143
Morison, Emily, 154
Morrison, Toni, 8–9
Moseley, Mathilda, 104, 105
Moten, Fred, 12
Moynihan, Daniel P., 117
"Mrs. Adis" (Kaye-Smith), 57–58, 61–64, 66, 79

Mules and Men (Hurston), 89, 91, 99–100, 103–4, 105
Mullen, Bill, 143
Muñoz, José Esteban, 123
Murray, Pauli, 4, 114, 116
Myrdal, Gunnar, 147

NACW. *See* National Association of Colored Women (NACW)
Nanny (fictional character), 95, 96, 109
Narrows, The (Petry), 120–21, 127, 131–39. *See also* Petry, Ann; Petry, Ann, works of
Nation, The, 71, 72
National Association of Colored Women (NACW), 32, 45–46
National Association for the Advancement of Colored People (NAACP), 14–15, 54
National Association of Colored Women's Clubs (NACWC), 31, 48
National Conference of Artists (NCA), 151
National Conference of Colored Women of America, 32
national family and the human family, 35, 44–45
National Guardian, 179n41, 180n48
Native Son (Wright): agency in, 120; Bigger Thomas in, 113, 118–19, 120, 122, 129, 159, 162; Gates on, 130; gendered aspects of, 121–22; marketing of, 155; *Maud Martha* compared to, 158, 162; *The Narrows* compared to, 133; *The Street* compared to, 111–12, 122–23, 124. *See also* Wright, Richard
naturalism, 123, 125, 140
nature, 88, 90, 91, 95, 102–3
nature/nurture debate, 91, 93–96
Negro Digest, 20, 116
"Negro Family, The" (Moynihan), 117
Negro Family in Chicago, The (Frazier), 117
Negro Family in the United States, The (Frazier), 117
Negro Story, 20, 151
Negro World, The, 72n85
"Negro-Art Hokum, The" (Schuyler), 70–71, 72
Nemiroff, Robert, 175–76

neoclassical tradition, 59, 61
networks of care. *See* care networks
New Beacon Books, 28n3
New Challenge, 20, 114. See also *Challenge*
New Masses, 86
New Negro, The (Locke), 58, 59, 68, 73, 74. *See also* Locke, Alain
New Negro Movement, 54, 75
New Negro Poets (Hughes), 141–42, 147, 164n132
New Republic, 56
New York Post, 172–73
New York Times, 175, 176
New York Times Book Review, 85
Nin, Anaïs, 164n128
Nishikawa, Kinohi, 154–55
"Novel as Social Criticism, The" (Petry), 115, 119–20, 136–37
novels, political value of, 35, 38–40
Nowviskie, Bethany, 128–29
nuclear families, 137–38

Of One Blood (Hopkins): Black womanhood and, 48–51; critics on, 29–30; female deference in, 48; female voices in, 49–51; humanism in, 39–40; language of blood in, 34; monogenesis in, 34; national family in, 35, 44–45; passing in, 52; *Plessy v. Ferguson* in relation to, 34; plot of, 32–33; racial uplift in, 50; reprintings of, 28–29; sameness and difference binary in, 31, 34; significance of, 31, 48, 50; universalism and, 30–31. *See also* Hopkins, Pauline
Olson, Liesl, 145
"On Being Young—a Woman—and Colored" (Bonner), 73–74
Opportunity, 74, 88–89
Ottley, Roi, 86, 116, 117

pain, 2, 25, 84, 88, 93, 95–96, 97–98, 178
Pan-African Congress, 52–53
Park, Robert E., 117, 119
particularity, 40, 47, 50, 52, 56, 57, 58, 81, 83. *See also* authenticity; universality
Passing (Larsen), 61, 77, 79, 82. *See also* Larsen, Nella

passing, racial, 52, 79–80
pathology, and Black people, 110, 115, 117–20, 122, 152–54, 163–64
People's Voice, 115
Perry, Imani, 19
Peter Bullock (fictional character), 133, 134
Peter Crouch (fictional character), 63
Petry, Ann: children's literature of, 139–40; Hansberry compared to, 178; "I AM A MAN" iconography in relation to, 16; on Lutie, 125; naturalism and, 123, 140; in protest fiction debate, 119; relations with Wright, 115; significance of, 4, 5, 25–26, 110, 115–16, 140; on *The Street*, 122–23. *See also* Petry, Ann, works of
Petry, Ann, works of: "The Common Ground," 139; *Harriet Tubman*, 139–40; *The Narrows*, 120–21, 127, 131–39; "The Novel as Social Criticism," 115, 119–20; "What's Wrong with Negro Men?," 116. *See also Street, The* (Petry)
Phillis Wheatley Poetry Festival, 2, 151
Phylon, 146–47, 148–50
play of imagination, 95–96, 109
pleasure, 88, 93, 95–96, 97–98, 99. *See also* Black female sexuality
Plessy v. Ferguson, 4, 31, 32–40, 47–48
"Poetry Is Not a Luxury" (Lorde), 13
Poetry Magazine, 169
"Poets Who Are Negroes" (Brooks), 146–47
polygenesis, 33
Popular Front, 92
Portrait of the Artist as a Young Man, A (Joyce), 161
posthumanism, 11–13
power relations, 103, 105–7, 110
Primer of Facts Pertaining to the Early Greatness of the African Race, A (Hopkins), 33–34
primitivism: and aesthetic double standard, 59–60; assimilationism and, 61; authenticity in relation to, 74; Black folk art and, 92; gendered aspects of, 76; Hansberry and, 178; Hughes on, 72; Hurston and, 86; modernists and, 59; neoclassicism and, 67; pleasure and, 98–99; *Quicksand* and *Passing* in relation to, 77, 78, 79; recognition politics and, 71;

stereotypes and, 92; Wall on, 99. *See also* authenticity
Principia of Ethnology (Delany), 33
Private Lives, Proper Relations (Jenkins), 21
property and propriety, 126, 127, 129
protest fiction debate, 25–26, 114–18, 121
Puig de la Bellacasa, Maria, 121

Quashie, Kevin, 12, 13
Quicksand (Larsen), 56–57, 61, 69, 77, 79, 82. *See also* Larsen, Nella

Race Traits and Tendencies (Hoffman), 33
racial authenticity. *See* authenticity
racial uplift, 31, 48–49, 50, 61
rage and anger, 153, 162
Raisin in the Sun, A (Hansberry), 174–76, 178. *See also* Hansberry, Lorraine
Randall, Dudley, 170
Reagon, Bernice Johnson, 7
Reason, Patrick Henry, 16 fig. 1
recognition politics, 25, 57, 70–72
Reconstructing Womanhood (Carby), 23
Red Record, A (Wells-Barnett), 50
Reid-Pharr, Robert, 13
repetition and revision tradition, 65, 67, 83. *See also* Signifyin(g)
respectability politics, 74, 76–77, 123, 125, 127, 135–36, 152
Retman, Sonnet, 92–93
Reuel Briggs (fictional character), 32–33, 40, 41–42, 48, 49, 52
Richards, I. A., 147
rights of man and human rights, 6–7, 10–11
"Rise of Maud Martha, The" (Brooks), 167–68
Robertson, Nan, 175, 176
Robeson, Paul, 133, 150, 175
Roots (Haley), 2
Ruffin, Josephine St. Pierre, 32

Sam Watson (fictional character), 93–94
sameness and difference binary framework, 22, 31, 34, 46

"Sanctuary" (Larsen): authenticity in relation to, 81; Larson and Hoeller on, 60; "Mrs. Adis" compared to, 61–64; origin of, 65; passing in, 79–80; plagiarism scandal, 55–56, 67; primitivism and neoclassicism in, 61; repetition and revision in, 65; significance of, 25, 57–58; Signifyin(g) in, 66. *See also* Larsen, Nella

Sappho Clark (fictional character), 50

satiric subversions, 65

Saturday Review, 174

Saunders, Catherine, 131

Schuyler, George, 70–71, 72

segregation: hidden self and, 48; Hopkins and, 38, 45, 50, 51; Jane Crow era in relation to, 18–20, 22, 23, 30; Lipsitz on, 126; *Plessy v. Ferguson* and, 47

sexual freedom, 82

sexuality, Black female, 73, 88, 93, 95–99

Sharpe, Christina, 12

Sherrard-Johnson, Cherene, 123

Shockley, Evie, 160

Signifyin(g), 65, 66, 130

"Signifying Monkey" stories, 103

Silberman, Charles E., 172, 180

Slavery Illustrated in Its Effects upon Woman (Bourne), 15, 16 fig. 1

"Sleeper Wakes, The" (Fauset), 60n26

Smith, Barbara, 6, 7, 9

Smith, William Gardner, 149–50

sociology, influence of, 110, 112–13, 115–18, 120, 124, 139

Sojourners for Truth and Justice (STJ), 175n16

Soper, Kate, 10

Souls of Black Folk, The (Du Bois), 54, 67–68, 100

South Side Writers Group, 151

sovereignty, 163–64

Spillers, Hortense, 97

Stark, Inez Cunningham, 158

Stein, Gertrude, 59, 60

Stowe, Harriet Beecher, 118–19

Strachey, Lytton, 161n113

Street, The (Petry): agency in, 120; care in, 128; individual uplift in, 125, 128, 129–30; *The Narrows* compared to, 127; *Native Son* compared to, 111–12, 122–23, 124; respectability in, 123; significance of, 121; value systems in, 127. *See also* Petry, Ann; Petry, Ann, works of

Street in Bronzeville, A (Brooks), 142, 154–56

"Strivings of the Negro People" (Du Bois), 47, 54

Student Nonviolent Coordinating Committee, 175

Survey Graphic, The, 54, 55, 75, 114

Susskind, David, 172, 181

Sylvander, Carolyn, 131

"Talma Gordon" (Hopkins), 44

Taney, Roger Brook, 35

"Task of Negro Womanhood, The" (McDougald), 58

Tate, Claudia, 44, 144, 169

Tea Cake (fictional character), 95, 96, 106, 109

Tell My Horse (Hurston), 89, 91, 95

Their Eyes Were Watching God (Hurston): humanism in relation to, 30–31, 97; inside and outside perspective in, 88, 96–97, 98–99, 100–101; nature in, 88, 102–3, 104; nature/nurture debate in, 93–94; pleasure in, 88, 94–95, 97–98, 99; power relations in, 105–7; reception of, 85–86; significance of, 25, 88; *The Souls of Black Folk* juxtaposed to, 100. *See also* Hurston, Zora Neale; Hurston, Zora Neale, works of

There Is Confusion (Fauset), 54, 74

Third World Press, 28n3

This Bridge Called My Back (Moraga), 179

Thompson, Era Bell, 20, 20n96

Thorsson, Courtney, 8

Thurman, Wallace, 71–72, 88, 114

Tompkins, Lucille, 85

Toomer, Jean, 54, 64

Trilling, Lionel, 147

Tronto, Joan, 121

Truth, Sojourner, 15–16

12 Million Black Voices (Wright), 162

Universal Declaration of Human Rights, United Nations, 11

universality: Black art and, 57, 82–83, 93; and Black Chicago Renaissance, 142–43;

Black visions of, 145–46; Brooks and, 144, 145; Brooks on, 141–42; disruption of, 57–58; Hansberry and, 174–75; *Maud Martha* and, 156; modernity and, 59; Petry on, 119–20; Renaissance Man in relation to, 147, 153; universal humanity, 30–31; unlabeled, 142–43, 145, 147–50; uplift novels and, 30. *See also* humanism, Western; particularity

Up from Slavery (Washington), 37

uplift, individual, 125, 128, 129–30

uplift, racial, 31, 48–49, 50, 61

uplift novels, 30

"Value of Race Literature, The" (Matthews), 39

Village Voice, 178, 180

Voice from the South, A (Cooper), 38–39

Von Eschen, Penny, 143, 147

voodoo, 91

vulnerability, 152–54, 163–64, 166

Walker, Alice, 2n9, 9, 86–87, 151

Walker, Margaret, 1–2, 3n12, 76, 113, 114, 115, 151

Wall, Cheryl: on female artists, 75; on Hurston, 84, 104; on Larsen, 72–73, 79; on *Mules and Men*, 105; on *Passing*, 78; on primitivism, 99; on stasis and claustrophobia, 73; *Women of the Harlem Renaissance*, 23

Wallace, Mike, 176

Wallinger, Hanna, 31, 41

Warren, Kenneth, 22

Washington, Booker T., 20, 31, 36, 37–38, 48–49, 50, 53–54

Washington, Mary Helen, 23, 128, 144, 147, 159

Washington Square Press, 29

Wechsler, James, 172–73, 179

Weheliye, Alexander, 12

Wells-Barnett, Ida B., 19, 48, 50

West, Dorothy, 20n95, 76, 76n108, 113–14, 115

Western humanism. *See* humanism, Western

"What White Publishers Won't Print" (Hurston), 101–2

"What's Wrong with Negro Men?" (Petry), 116

"What's Wrong with Negro Women" (Ottley), 116, 117

Wheatley, Phillis, 2, 151

white literary establishment: at Association of Artists for Freedom forum, 172–73, 179–80; as gatekeepers, 69, 70; Hurston on, 101–2; imitation and, 59; modernists and, 59–60; pathology and, 110, 152; *Phylon* special issue in relation to, 148–50; primitivism and, 92, 110; refusal of, 15, 22–23, 26, 65, 150; on *Their Eyes Were Watching God*, 85–86. *See also* humanism, Western; universality

"Why Men Leave Home" (Drake), 116, 117, 134

"Why Negro Girls Stay Single" (Murray), 116

"Why Negro Women Leave Home" (Brooks), 116

"Why Women Always Take Advantage of Men" (Hurston), 104

Williams, Linda, 138

Williams, William Carlos, 60n28

Wolfe, Cary, 11

Woman's Era Club, 32

"Woman's Political Future" (Harper), 32

Women of the Harlem Renaissance (Wall), 23

Works Progress Administration (WPA), 92

World of Gwendolyn Brooks, The (Brooks), 168, 169

World's Congress of Representative Women (WCRW), 32

Wright, Richard: Baldwin and, 171; *Black Boy*, 111n2; "Blueprint for Negro Writing," 14, 112, 113, 155; Brooks and, 158; Brooks compared to, 162; Ellison and, 112, 130–31; "How 'Bigger' Was Born," 113; influence of sociology on, 118; *New Challenge* and, 20, 113–14; relations with Brooks, 156; on *A Street in Bronzeville*, 155; on *Their Eyes Were Watching God*, 86; *12 Million Black Voices*, 162. *See also Native Son* (Wright)

Writing through Jane Crow (Hardison), 21

Wynter, Sylvia, 12

X Press, 28, 28n3

www.ingramcontent.com/pod-product-compliance
Lightning Source LLC
Chambersburg PA
CBHW020652230426
43665CB00008B/400